The
Paraprofessional's
Handbook for
Effective Support in
Inclusive
Classrooms

Second Edition

The Paraprofessional's Handbook for Effective Support in Inclusive Classrooms

by

Julie Causton, Ph.D.
Inclusive Schooling

and

Kate MacLeod, Ph.D.
University of Maine at Farmington
Inclusive Schooling

PAUL·H·
BROOKES
PUBLISHING Co.®

Baltimore • London • Sydney

Paul H. Brookes Publishing Co.
Post Office Box 10624
Baltimore, Maryland 21285-0624
USA

www.brookespublishing.com

Typeset by Paul H. Brookes Publishing Co., Inc., Towson, Maryland.
Manufactured in the United States of America by Sheridan Books, Inc.

Library of Congress Cataloging-in-Publication Data

Names: Causton, Julie, author. | MacLeod, Kate, 1985- author.
Title: The paraprofessional's handbook for effective support in inclusive classrooms / by Julie Causton, Ph.D. Inclusive Schooling and Kate MacLeod, Ph.D., University of Maine at Farmington, Inclusive Schooling.
Description: Second edition. | Baltimore : Paul H. Brookes Publishing Co., [2020] | Includes bibliographical references and index.
Identifiers: LCCN 2020032674 (print) | LCCN 2020032675 (ebook) | ISBN 9781681254517 (paperback) | ISBN 9781681254524 (epub) | ISBN 9781681254531 (pdf)
Subjects: LCSH: Inclusive education--Handbooks, manuals, etc. | Children with disabilities--Education--Handbooks, manuals, etc. | Children with disabilities--Services for--Handbooks, manuals, etc. | Teachers' assistants--Handbooks, manuals, etc.
Classification: LCC LC1200 .C38 2021 (print) | LCC LC1200 (ebook) | DDC 371.9/046--dc23
LC record available at https://lccn.loc.gov/2020032674
LC ebook record available at https://lccn.loc.gov/2020032675

British Library Cataloguing in Publication data are available from the British Library.

2024   2023   2022
10   9   8   7   6   5   4   3

Contents

About the Forms and Online Materials

Purchasers of *The Paraprofessional's Handbook for Effective Support in Inclusive Classrooms, Second Edition* are granted permission to download, print, and photocopy the blank forms and resource materials in the text for educational purposes. These forms may not be reproduced to generate revenue for any program or individual. Photocopies may only be made from an original book. *Unauthorized use beyond this privilege may be prosecutable under federal law.* You will see the copyright protection notice at the bottom of each photocopiable page.

The Paraprofessional's Handbook for Effective Support in Inclusive Classrooms, Second Edition also offers online companion materials to supplement and expand the knowledge and strategies provided in this text. All purchasers of the book may access, download, and print the online materials.

To access the materials that come with this book,

1. Go to the Brookes Publishing Download Hub: http://downloads.brookespublishing.com

2. Register to create an account or log in with an existing account.

3. Filter or search for the book title *The Paraprofessional's Handbook for Effective Support in Inclusive Classrooms, Second Edition.*

About the *Facilitator's Guide to The Paraprofessional's Handbook for Effective Support in Inclusive Classrooms, Second Edition*

Planning and conducting professional development training sessions can be a complicated, time-consuming process. That's why authors Julie Causton and Kate MacLeod created a *Facilitator's Guide* as a helpful companion to this book. User-friendly and comprehensive, this guide is your one-stop resource for effectively planning and delivering six 1-hour live or virtual training sessions on *The Paraprofessional's Handbook for Effective Support in Inclusive Classrooms, Second Edition.*

Designed to work with groups of all sizes, each training session outlined in the guide aligns with one or more chapters from the book and will deepen paraprofessionals' understanding of key topics in inclusive education. You'll use the guide to lead meaningful discussions with staff, communicate immediately useful information on scheduling and preparation, and enhance on-the-job knowledge and skills of the paraprofessionals you work with and/or supervise.

The digital *Facilitator's Guide* includes everything you need to conduct sessions:

- A manual, complete with checklists, key terms to know, talking points, activities, discussions, and frequently asked questions

- Presentation slides for each session

- Video clips from the authors introducing each session

- Email templates to communicate with attendees

- An editable certificate of completion

To learn more about *The Paraprofessional's Handbook: Facilitator's Read-Along Guide, Second Edition,* visit https://brookespublishing.com/causton-para-facilitators-guide

About
the Authors

Julie Causton, Ph.D.

Julie Causton is founder and chief executive officer of Inclusive Schooling. She is a former professor in the Inclusive and Special Education Program in the Department of Teaching and Leadership at Syracuse University. She has spent the past 20 years studying and creating best practices for inclusive education, with a specific focus on supporting students whose behavior challenges the educational system. As a former special education teacher herself, Dr. Causton knows firsthand how belonging leads to better outcomes for students. She works with administrators, teachers, paraprofessionals, and families across the country to help them create inclusive experiences. Dr. Causton is the author of seven books about inclusive education and she has published articles in more than 30 educational research and practitioner journals. She lives in Manlius, New York, with her wife, two adorable teenagers, dog, and three cats.

Kate MacLeod, Ph.D.

Kate MacLeod is an assistant professor of special education at the University of Maine at Farmington and founder and consultant at Inclusive Schooling. Her teaching, research, writing, and consulting are guided by a passion for inclusive education and social justice. She is a former high school special education teacher in New York City and now works with administrators, educators, and families around the country to create more inclusive practices for all students. Dr. MacLeod's research and writing are focused on understanding the culture of inclusive schools, inclusive school reform, and best teaching practices for supporting students with diverse and complex support needs. She is the author of two books about inclusive education, and she has published articles in educational research and practitioner journals. Kate lives in Maine with her husband, two dogs, a cat, and a flock of chickens.

Foreword

My first introductions and connections as a teacher were built with paraprofessionals. Their experience and patience were guiding lights and their compassion was a shoulder to lean on in my journey toward understanding inclusion for our students. I cannot imagine my life without the paraprofessionals with whom I've crossed paths and many I still call close friends.

I also learned early in my career how frustrating it can be to be a paraprofessional. The role of these incredible individuals has long been taken for granted and undervalued. Their perspectives are not always invited to the table, and they are often on the receiving end of frustration when advocacy efforts for students who need the most support go awry. Many have shouted their praises, yet so often, paraprofessionals continue to not be included in professional development and ignored when engaging in problem-solving efforts.

Students, parents, teachers, and administrators all know that, despite the challenges, success for students can sometimes be the direct result of the profound impact of a supportive paraprofessional—one who knows when to support and when to step back. One who coaches and facilitates relationships and senses tension within seconds. One who seeks connection through strengths and interests and responds to unique needs without shame. Our paraprofessionals are the translators for many, and the complexity of their critical role could not be captured better than by Julie and Kate in this practical, accessible, and invaluable resource.

This book will be an anchor to those navigating the paraprofessional world for the first time, as well as those who come from a lifetime of experience working to advocate for students with disabilities. As we continue to become more inclusive in our classrooms, schools, and communities, the ways we support students and teachers are changing. When paradigm shifts occur, paraprofessionals are sometimes left to catch up without guidance. Instead, this book leads the way and can be universally understood by any stakeholder who is invested in, and committed to, making education better for all students.

I am proud to introduce this book to the world in the hope that, in whatever role you hold, you read these words through the lens of a paraprofessional, whose role needs to be celebrated and valued. If we hold up our paraprofessionals, they will hold up our students, our classrooms, and our teachers, and they may even help all of us to better understand how to support the critical and everchanging role of a paraprofessional.

Shelley Moore, M.Ed.
Inclusion Advocate and Researcher
Outside Pin Consulting
British Columbia, Canada

Preface

· ·

We are willing and ready to connect with other kids, and adults must quietly step into the background, camouflaging their help as a tiger who may hide in full view. It's the needed disguise of the adult who smooths the way for friendship, then stands back in the shadows, observing the complicated dance of steps taking you to the feeling of confidence.

—Jamie Burke, a student with autism, who now attends Syracuse University
(Tashie, Shapiro-Barnard, & Rossetti, 2006, p. 185)

What Would Felicia Do?

A few years ago, we were working in a New York public middle school to support a district's inclusive reform efforts. We were in a general education sixth-grade English and Language Arts (ELA) 90-minute block when we first met Felicia, a paraprofessional assigned to support two students in the class. On this particular day, we watched as she moved around the classroom helping students settle in to class, asked them about special events in their lives, checked off student homework, offered kind words, set up partnerships for reading groups, stepped back when students were successful, encouraged a conversation between a student who did not speak and her peers, ran to get an adhesive bandage for a student from the nurse, wrote directions on the board as the ELA teacher gave instructions, read a chapter aloud to a small group of students, provided visual cues (very subtly) to kids, and made copies for the next class. Felicia managed to do all of this with lightning speed and effortless grace . . . and all that in a 90-minute ELA block!

When we spoke with Felicia and the teachers she supported later that day in a debrief group, what we came to admire most about her was not her efficiency, her versatility, or even her energy, but her ability to do what Jamie Burke calls for in the opening quote. It was Felicia's ability to seamlessly support all students in unobtrusive ways. She has the ability to "camouflage her help" to smooth the way and to stick up for students while simultaneously standing back to allow them to succeed. She not only created an opportunity for communication between students but also stepped away from them as soon as they began interacting in order to allow for natural interactions. She provided academic support to the two students she was assigned but supported the whole classroom so it was not evident to others whom she was there to support. Felicia's support was powerful because she allowed students to be themselves, to interact naturally with others, and to connect socially and academically. At times, she provided invisible supports, and at other times she was visible—supporting the entire class. But it was her light touch, her ability to support and then float, that impressed us the most.

On Inclusion

Not a day goes by when we don't think about inclusion. When we think of the amazing students we have had the privilege of teaching, we are reminded of what *teachers* they were to us. They have taught us that everyone has a right to belong, to have friends, to have engaging curricula, and to have powerful instruction. Everyone has a right to be treated with dignity and with gentle, respectful support, and to experience that learning is intimately connected with feeling like you're a part of the classroom. Every student deserves to receive support in a warm and welcoming place. The more this happens, the more we have created the environment for substantial learning. It isn't, therefore, just about creating a sense of belonging for belonging's sake; that sense of connection and welcome paves the way for academic and social growth. This book is designed as a guide for paraprofessionals and other team members as they work to include students with disabilities in gentle and respectful ways.

How This Book Is Organized

The first three chapters provide the context for the rest of the book. Chapter 1 focuses on the role of the paraprofessional, Chapter 2 provides background about inclusive education, and Chapter 3 provides basic information about special education. These first chapters provide the foundation necessary to more effectively interpret the rest of the book's framework for situating professional roles within schools and classrooms. Chapter 4 is about collaboration within the special education environment, with the students, the students' families, and all of the paraprofessional's colleagues. Chapter 5 is designed to help paraprofessionals rethink students. In this chapter, we ask paraprofessionals to look at students through the lens of strengths and abilities—to reconsider some of the negative descriptors—for the sake of being able to reach and support all students more effectively. Chapters 6–9 are strategy-specific chapters that focus on providing academic, social, and behavioral supports, and learning how to effectively build student independence and resilience. These strategy-specific chapters provide ideas and tools that are immediately applicable in schools. The last chapter focuses on self-care and problem solving. The job of supporting students in our school systems who pose the greatest challenges and require the most complex problem solving is not an easy one. Chapter 10 is meant to give helpful ideas for how paraprofessionals can care for themselves in order to provide the best possible support for students.

In this book, we have provided many opportunities for self-reflection, activities to help apply learning in unique contexts, quick learning checks to help readers retain information, and reproducible templates and tools to support the reader's work in schools. We have also included many digital resources and tools, commonly asked questions and answers, and short to-do lists. We hope these opportunities, tools, and resources will help the you, the reader, to feel engaged, supported, and empowered to implement the ideas and strategies discussed throughout.

Who Will Find This Book Useful?

As more and more schools move toward inclusive education, paraprofessionals are one of the most critical factors for success because they are on the front lines, making daily decisions that support or deny access to curricula and peers. We value paraprofessionals deeply because they play a key role in the facilitation of learning for students and the successful functioning of an inclusive education team. This means that paraprofessionals also require and deserve appropriate training and support in order to support student success and collaborate with a professional team effectively. Although this book will primarily serve paraprofessionals who want to learn more about supporting students in inclusive classrooms, we believe this book should be read by the special educators, general educators, administrators, and parents who are all part of the team of caregivers supporting students in inclusive school communities.

Special Educators

Special educators support students in inclusive classrooms. This book identifies approaches, strategies, and suggestions for supporting all students in inclusive classrooms. Special educators also often oversee the work of paraprofessionals. This book can be used for paraprofessionals and special educators to read and discuss together in an in-service or book club format.

General Educators

General educators are an important part of the classroom team. Learning more about paraprofessionals and support strategies allows general educators to offer a seamless and thoughtful integration of services. This book can be used for paraprofessionals and general and special educators to read and discuss together in an in-service or book club format.

Administrators

This book is an invaluable resource for principals who oversee paraprofessionals and seek to build effective schoolwide inclusive practices.

Parents of Students With Disabilities

Parents can benefit from this book by understanding the best practices for paraprofessional support in inclusive classrooms. This book can also be a resource to secure the appropriate training and support for the paraprofessional working with their children.

Professional Development Personnel

This book offers new approaches for supporting students with disabilities. Paraprofessionals are often most in need of professional development (PD) even though they work closely with the most complex and challenging students in our schools. To provide the essential knowledge, support, and resources, we recommend using this book as part of in-service paraprofessional PD.

Acknowledgments

Our book is about meaningful, respectful, and thoughtful support that allows individuals to reach their full potential and become the best version of themselves. We see support as necessary for every person to be a valued learner and member in any community.

I would like to acknowledge all of the supports in my own life and career that have made this work possible.

First, to my coauthor Kate—who makes every project somehow more than twice as fun—you are an excellent friend and beautiful light in my world.

To my family, Ella, Sam, and Ellen. Thank you for making my life so joyful. Your commitment to making the world a better place inspires me daily.

To Kathy and Deb, your morning phone calls and consistent support buoy me daily.

—Julie

The support and love of many people have provided me with the opportunity to write this book and to create a joyful life committed to education and inclusion.

To Julie, my coauthor, marble-jar friend, mentor, and all around super-human—thank you for making life, work, and the world better, more just, and more fun.

To my parents—thank you for supporting me and for showing me how to live with integrity, empathy, and deep commitment to family and community.

To Danny, my heart—your love, integrity, and humor are guiding lights for me. Thank you for keeping me afloat this spring and always. I can't wait to raise a child with you.

—Kate

To Ella, Sam, and Ellen
—Julie

To Danny and bb mac
—Kate

The Paraprofessional

· ·

I was told I got the job, and I knew I would be supporting a student named Helena. But before school started, I hadn't met her and I wasn't really sure what I would be doing day in and day out. I thought it might be a good idea to have some information or training about what the job of paraprofessional really entailed.

—*Maria (paraprofessional)*

I cannot do all the good that the world needs. But the world needs all the good that I can do.

—Jana Stanfield

Like Maria, some paraprofessionals are hired each year with limited training or knowledge about how to support students with disabilities. Alternatively, other paraprofessionals enter the field with teaching degrees or the equivalent in experience. This book is meant to support any person in this role with any amount of knowledge or training and to provide essential knowledge and guidance about the following topics:

1. What it means to be a paraprofessional
2. Basic information about inclusive education
3. Information about special education
4. How to work within a team
5. How to think about the students you support
6. How to provide academic supports
7. Strategies to provide social supports
8. How to provide behavioral supports
9. How to build student independence
10. How to take care of yourself while doing this incredibly important work

Throughout this book, we will provide you with numerous resources and strategies to support your work, and we encourage you to actively engage in the following tasks, which will be indicated by a corresponding icon:

REFLECTIONS

ACTIVITIES

QUICK QUIZ

TO-DO LIST

DEFINITIONS

FAQs

LEGAL INFORMATION

STRATEGIES

- Reflection
- Activities
- Quick Quiz learning tests
- To-Do lists

To further your understanding of the concepts discussed throughout this book, you will also see important information indicated by the following icons:

- Definitions
- FAQs (Frequently Asked Questions)
- Legal information
- Strategies

This book was designed to better prepare and guide you through the incredible daily work of supporting students with disabilities in authentic and positive ways. To begin, let's walk together into a kindergarten classroom and meet a student named Helena.

Helena arrives in her kindergarten classroom. Helena's friend Sam greets her. Both students talk excitedly for a little bit about their weekend as they proceed to the folder bucket. Maria, Helena's paraprofessional, helps remove Helena's take-home folder from her backpack and then puts the folder into the bucket. Maria then helps Helena remove her jacket, boots, and mittens. Sam races ahead to his table, and Helena follows close behind, driving her motorized wheelchair to her table. Maria follows and sits down next to them.

Helena is a creative, bright little girl who is supported by a paraprofessional. Because Helena has cerebral palsy, she needs someone to assist her with several tasks throughout the school day. Maria helps to position Helena on the floor for circle time, helps her use her computer to answer questions in class, writes down her ideas for stories and assignments, and facilitates social interactions with the other children in her class. The nature of Helena's physical disability requires regular and ongoing adult support from Maria to ensure meaningful access and authentic inclusion in her kindergarten class.

This chapter will familiarize you with the job of an inspired paraprofessional. We will first provide a definition of the title *paraprofessional* and then briefly outline the history of paraprofessionals in the classroom. The rest of this chapter discusses other foundational information for effective paraprofessional supports, including the many roles of paraprofessionals, the powerful benefits of paraprofessionals, the different types of settings in which paraprofessionals work, the most common tasks for paraprofessionals, and some commonly asked questions.

What Does Paraprofessional Mean?

Before we provide the formal definition of paraprofessional, we think it is pertinent to share that the prefix *para* means *next to* or *alongside*. *Paraeducator* therefore means someone who works *alongside* educators. This alongside position is a respected and critical role in many professions. For example, in restaurants, sous-chefs help to prepare dishes by washing, cutting, and chopping food for chefs to put together in their final masterpieces. In medicine, physician assistants support doctors in providing medical care to patients. In law, paralegals perform essential tasks, such as filing briefs and drafting documents, to support the work of lawyers. In education, you, the paraprofessional, support the work of teachers to effectively educate students.

In classrooms, paraprofessionals are analogous to each of these professions in certain ways, working with direction from both general and special educators. Although their role is not to plan or design classroom instruction, paraprofessionals make important contributions to classroom instruction when they can effectively implement important tasks—tasks for which paraprofessionals are specifically trained. Paraprofessionals are often gateways to information and creative ideas about how students with disabilities might access and respond to supports across environments. In short, paraprofessionals are critical partners who help keep classrooms running efficiently and effectively (Causton-Theoharis, Giangreco, Doyle, & Vadasy, 2007).

How the Law Defines *Paraprofessional*

The job title *paraprofessional* is described in Section 14B of the Individuals with Disabilities Education Improvement Act (IDEA) of 2004 (PL 108-446; IDEA 2004):

Paraprofessionals . . . who are appropriately trained and supervised, in accordance with State law, regulations, or written policy . . . are to be used to assist in the provision of special education and related services . . . to children with disabilities. (20 U.S.C. § 1412)

LEGAL INFORMATION

In other words, paraprofessionals are hired to support special education services for children with disabilities. You should be trained and supervised by experienced general and special educators; your training should begin before you start to work in the schools, and it should continue throughout your career. Many school systems use this book as part of your training.

The No Child Left Behind (NCLB) Act of 2001 (PL 107-110) defines *paraprofessional* as someone who

is employed in a preschool, elementary school, or secondary school under the supervision of a certified or licensed teacher, including individuals employed in language instruction, educational programs, special education, or migrant education (20 U.S.C. § 119).

According to NCLB, all paraprofessionals should have:

A. completed at least 2 years of study at an institution of higher education;

B. obtained an associate (or higher) degree; and

C. met a rigorous standard of quality and can demonstrate through a formal academic assessment

   a. knowledge of, and the ability to assist in instruction, reading, writing, and mathematics; or

   b. knowledge of, and the ability to assist in instructing reading readiness, writing readiness, and mathematics readiness, as appropriate. (20 U.S.C. § 6319 [c])

Now that we have listed the legal definition of *paraprofessional* and the legal qualifications for doing the job, let's discuss what this means in practical terms. What might your title be? What might your students want from you? What will you actually be doing?

My Title Is *Teaching Assistant.* Is That the Same Thing?

You might not be called a *paraprofessional*; instead, you might be called a *teaching assistant* or some other term. Just as the job has evolved, the title *paraprofessional* has changed over time and still varies from district to district. The terms *aide, assistant, paraeducator, education technician, one-to-one, teacher aide, program assistant, clerical assistant, instructional assistant,* and *teaching assistant* are commonly used to describe the role of paraprofessionals. Although this title varies, many times, the job responsibilities are similar but distinguishable by the number of students that the person supports or the tasks they are assigned. A *one-to-one assistant* tends to support a single student, a *teaching assistant* usually supports more students, a *clerical assistant* tends to do more work with the materials for instruction, and a *program assistant* typically supports an entire classroom.

What Does a Paraprofessional Do?

Paraprofessionals engage in many different daily responsibilities. Those job tasks vary from school to school. Generally, if you work in a school, the types of responsibilities you can expect fall under the categories of *instructional tasks, behavioral support tasks, clerical tasks, supervision tasks, planning or preparation,* and *personal care tasks* (Giangreco, Broer, & Edelman, 2002). Table 1.1 describes each type of task and provides an example. These are examples of tasks that you could be assigned, but you may be assigned additional tasks not included here.

Table 1.1.   Typical responsibilities of paraprofessionals

Type of task	Examples of tasks
Instructional tasks	Reviewing vocabulary with a student Reteaching a math method Prereading a book with a student Running a center at center time Helping a small group during a science lab
Behavioral support tasks	Providing positive reinforcement Addressing sensory needs Following a behavior plan Helping a student calm down
Clerical tasks	Making copies Creating modifications planned by educators Enlarging materials (increasing font size)
Supervision tasks	Supervising students on the playground, on the bus, or in the cafeteria
Planning or preparation tasks	Making a math or vocabulary game Creating a communication board Preparing or labeling materials
Personal care tasks	Helping students dress after physical education Providing support while students put on or take off outdoor clothing Assisting students in brushing hair or teeth Helping students use the restroom

REFLECTIONS

Take a moment to consider the tasks and roles you currently do on a daily basis. Do they align with the roles and tasks in Table 1.1? If not, what roles and tasks in the figure might you want to incorporate into your daily work? Take a moment and write them down. Might those additional roles and tasks require collaboration with colleagues? Teamwork is critical to student and professional success, so in Chapter 4 we will discuss how you can approach and collaborate with your general and special educators to discuss and clarify your roles and tasks.

Job tasks also depend on the type of support you are assigned to give. You may provide one-to-one instruction and small-group instruction. You might be responsible for student observation and data collection with regard to academic support or behavioral support. You may also supervise students on the playground, at lunch, or on the bus, helping to support student behavior control, or take on more clerical tasks to support teaching and learning, such as typing, recording grades, and photocopying (French, 1998).

Another Type of Job Description: What Your Students Want You to Know

Legal definitions, job titles, and practical job descriptions are incredibly useful. But we think one of the most important job descriptions comes directly from your students.

Listen to me. Learn from me. Watch me. Hear me. Ask me questions. Support my belonging. Be there, but give me space. Expect that I will learn. Facilitate friendships. Let me fail sometimes. Encourage independence. Love me. Always speak kindly. Ask, "What do you need?" Be safe. Handle me with care. Be respectful. Be gentle. Be trustworthy. Remember, I am a person first. If I am loud, be quiet. Encourage interdependence. If I am sad, wipe my tears. Help me connect to others. Assume friendship is possible. Celebrate my diversity. Allow us to create together, laugh together, and have fun together. Assume competence always. Attribute the best possible motive consistent with the facts. Spark curiosity. Do not control. When I am happy, step back. Allow choice. Relax. Be a learner yourself. Ask, "How can I best help you?" Share positive stories with my parents or caregivers. Set me up to be successful. When I have difficulties, kindly redirect me to get me on track. Breathe. Speak softly. Encourage softly. Redirect softly. Follow my lead. Lead by loving. Watch me thrive. Include me always.

The History of Paraprofessionals

The history of inclusive education has had a large impact on the employment of paraprofessionals (Chopra & Giangreco, 2019). It has only been since the passage of the Education for All Handicapped Children Act of 1975 (PL 94-142) that students with disabilities have had a legally protected right to attend public school. Before this time, students with disabilities were educated mainly in the home, in segregated settings, or in institutions. It was believed that students with disabilities could not learn as much as students without disabilities and that they did not need certified teachers to support them; therefore, before 1975, students with disabilities were typically supported by people in paraprofessional roles (Brown, Farrington, Knight, Ross, & Ziegler, 1999).

BEFORE 1975

In the 1970s and 1980s, however, a strong parent-driven movement began, advocating to educate children with disabilities in general education settings alongside peers, friends, and neighbors without disabilities. At this time, the Regular Education Initiative began (Will, 1986), and parents began to learn about the idea of *mainstreaming* or what we now call *inclusion*. The role of

1970's - 80's

1990'S

2000-Present

paraprofessionals accordingly shifted as students with disabilities began participating in general education classrooms. At this time, paraprofessionals began to provide greater academic and behavioral support.

By the 1990s, a wider array of students with more significant disabilities was included in classrooms across all grade levels in school, and there was a large boom in the hiring of paraprofessionals. From 2000 to the present, inclusive education and high expectations for students with disabilities has become a greater legal mandate. Two precedent setting court cases, *Endrew F. v. Douglas County School District* (2017) and *L.H. v. Hamilton County* (2018), have recently interpreted IDEA to 1) clearly prefer the inclusion of students with disabilities in general education classrooms, and 2) provide students with access to high expectations through appropriate supports and services.

Therefore, the use of paraprofessionals to support students in inclusive settings has increased steadily (U.S. Department of Education, 2020). As students with many more significant disabilities are being included in general education settings, paraprofessionals are more critical than ever.

From Caregiver to Learning Facilitator

Paraprofessionals in the United States number about 1,380,300, and that number is increasing (U.S. Department of Labor, 2019). This increase is attributable to many factors. The number has increased primarily because many more students with more significant disabilities and complex support needs (e.g., autism spectrum disorder [ASD] and cognitive disabilities) are included in general education classrooms. In addition, there has been a slow increase in the number of students who are being identified as having disabilities. Many educators view the support of a paraprofessional as key for an inclusive classroom. In other words, students are included in general education settings *because* they are accompanied by paraprofessionals.

Moreover, the role of paraprofessionals has become much more complex as it has moved from caregiver to facilitator of learning. In the past, students with disabilities were educated separately in rooms for only children with disabilities, and the supports they received were more related to personal care and keeping students occupied. Educational goals for students with significant disabilities were essentially limited to life skills and job-related tasks. For example, common activities for such students—regardless of age—were to learn to cook, practice dressing, or use appropriate table manners. As a result, the role of paraprofessionals was mainly caregiving.

Now, educators in the field have learned that students with disabilities are just as capable of learning as their general education counterparts, and federal laws mandate that educators hold all students to high expectations to make progress on general education content and curriculum. Consequently, the goals many students now have in their individualized education programs (IEPs) closely resemble those of their same-age peers. Paraprofessionals are now responsible for helping to educate students using materials appropriate to their grade levels and for helping to facilitate complex social networks and friendships. Because of these new roles, paraprofessionals have become integral members of teaching teams with increasingly challenging new responsibilities.

The Role of Paraprofessionals Today

Currently, paraprofessionals have varied responsibilities. Your role is likely determined by the classroom context and the unique needs of the students you support. The role of a paraprofessional in a kindergarten classroom is quite different from a paraprofessional who works in a high school classroom. In general, however, these responsibilities include supporting students socially, academically, physically, and behaviorally.

Social Support

Social support includes helping students make and maintain friendships with other students. For example, a paraprofessional might assist a student in communicating with a peer, in selecting a partner for group work, or in finding a friend to play with at recess time.

Academic Support

Academic support involves helping students as they attend to academic content and learn new material. For example, you might be responsible for helping a student prepare for a test, outline a chapter, or put together an insect collection. Any academic task that students do in school may require paraprofessional support, and it is all based on the needs of the individual student.

Physical Support

Some children also require physical support. For example, a child using a wheelchair may need help when eating, dressing, or transferring from a seated to a standing position. Because of the nature of their physical disability, some students require more physical support than others.

Behavioral Support

Another common responsibility involves providing behavioral supports. An example of this type of support is giving a child a fidget toy or other sensory item so that the student can pay attention during a read-aloud story or lecture. You may also provide positive reinforcement at key times or help a student take movement breaks throughout the day so that they are better able to stay on task during seated instructional time.

QUICK QUIZ

What roles did paraprofessionals have historically? Compare those roles to today.

The student's IEP will be a framework for the amount and type of support you provide. The team of teachers you work with should also help you identify your roles within the classroom and school day. Generally speaking, your role will be to reinforce and reteach skills, help support behavior regulation, and, possibly, provide personal care or mobility support. Because each student is unique, your job will differ according to the needs of the students you support.

Classroom Settings

Providing social, physical, academic, and behavioral supports to students will be the core of your daily work. But where you provide these supports will vary depending on your district and school, your role, and the students you support. You may work for the majority of the day in a single setting, or you may find yourself working across settings.

Inclusive Classrooms

Inclusive classrooms are generally places in which students with and without disabilities are educated together. Other terms you might hear are *general education classroom, co-taught classroom, third-grade classroom, regular classroom,* or *typical classroom*. A more outdated term for an inclusive classroom is a *mainstreamed classroom*. More information about inclusion can be found in Chapter 2.

Non-Inclusive Classrooms

Although this book focuses on supporting students in inclusive classrooms, you might find yourself in different types of classrooms. The following descriptions describe other types of settings that are not considered inclusive.

Resource Rooms

A resource room is a place in which students are generally supposed to spend a short amount of time working on a specific skill or subject before returning to the general education classroom. The instruction in these classrooms is typically delivered in a small group with one educator teaching a small group of students or with one teacher working directly with one student.

Self-Contained Classrooms

A self-contained classroom is designed for the instruction of only students with disabilities. The purpose of this kind of classroom was initially to group students who had similar learning needs. However, these types of classrooms are very controversial because students in self-contained classrooms interact on a very limited basis—if at all—with students who do not have disabilities.

Self-Contained or Alternative School

A self-contained or alternative school is a place where students with similar learning, behavior, or social needs are provided instruction for the duration of the school day. These schools are often highly controversial because students in self-contained or alternative schools spend their entire day without contact with peers who do not have disabilities.

Community-Based Classrooms

Some paraprofessionals work in community-based classrooms. If you work in a community-based classroom you are likely to work in a high school setting. The idea behind community-based instruction is that some students require instruction to prepare them for life in the community, so the curriculum typically includes working on career and independent living skills. Therefore, some students receive their instruction in the community. Some types of community-based locations include job sites, recreational facilities, grocery stores, or other settings within the community.

Benefits of Paraprofessionals

Paraprofessionals offer crucial support that is helpful to both teachers and students. They can expand learning opportunities by giving students repeated practice with skills or concepts. They also provide students with more individualized instruction and even facilitate positive interactions with peers throughout the day. The presence of a paraprofessional allows teachers to have more planning time and the ability to support more students individually. Students with disabilities can be more carefully monitored, supported, and generally involved in instruction to a greater extent when a paraprofessional is present in the classroom.

Paraprofessionals also come to this work with richly varied backgrounds, skills, and talents. Some paraprofessionals have business backgrounds and some are multilingual. Other paraprofessionals are artists and musicians, athletes, or coach sports teams. Many paraprofessionals also serve as licensed specialists in a different field, and still others may have earned their license(s) in a different country. Other paraprofessionals are retired teachers, whereas some are currently in school to earn a teaching certificate. Over the years we have met thousands of paraprofessionals with incredible talents and experiences that can benefit the students and teachers they support. We want you to recognize and celebrate all of the unique knowledge, background, and experience you bring to this work. Having this understanding of your unique strengths can then determine how your various skills, talents, and experiences can serve students and teachers best in the classroom.

> We want you to recognize and celebrate all of the unique knowledge, background, and experience you bring to this work.

REFLECTIONS

How would you describe your role as a paraprofessional?

What unique skills/talents and background do you bring to this work?

How can these skills, talents, and backgrounds support students and teachers?

Commonly Asked Questions About the Role of Paraprofessionals

FAQs

Q. To whom do I report?

A. Typically, a paraprofessional reports to the special education teacher to whom they are assigned. After that, a building principal or director of special education would be next in the chain of command. However, you will also work closely with general education teachers and related services providers (e.g., occupational therapists, physical therapists, speech and language teachers), and they may provide guidance as well.

Q. How can I obtain a copy of my job description?

A. You can typically find this online. If not, request a copy of your job description by talking to someone in human resources or by asking the director of special education. Most districts will provide you a written job description if you do not already have one.

Q. Am I allowed to lead a small-group discussion?

A. Yes, you can lead a small-group discussion or review material with students under the direction of a certified teacher. You are not typically allowed to introduce new material, but you can reinforce material taught previously by a certified teacher.

Q.   Can I teach an entire class by myself?

A.   A paraprofessional generally does not teach an entire class new material, but you could be responsible for reading a book aloud to the class or supporting the work of the entire class under the direction and supervision of a certified teacher.

Q.   Who is ultimately responsible for the education of the student I am supporting?

A.   The special education teacher and general education teacher assigned to the student are responsible. The term *case manager* or *service coordinator* is sometimes used to refer to the special education teacher assigned to the student.

Q.   Should I work from written plans?

A.   Yes, you should work from written plans. If you don't have written plans, you can request them from the special education teacher with whom you are working. It is important to note that the plans provided will not account for every minute of the day; instead, they typically consist of a schedule and tasks for periods of the day.

Conclusion

Understanding your roles and responsibilities is essential in order to do your job effectively. This chapter discussed the importance of the job of a paraprofessional, surveyed the history of paraprofessionals, discussed the roles and responsibilities of paraprofessionals today, and provided answers to some commonly asked questions. Because paraprofessionals most often support students who receive special education services in a variety of inclusive settings, the next chapter is designed to give you background about inclusive education.

TO-DO LIST

To Do

After reading this chapter . . .

- Complete the reflection activities in the chapter.
- Review the list of common paraprofessional tasks (Table 1.1). Highlight those tasks that you commonly engage in. In a different color, highlight the ones that you would like to learn more about.
- Write down all of your specific questions about this chapter. Share your questions with your team.
- Celebrate (e.g., take a walk, get a cup of coffee, dance in your living room) the fact that you've begun this book and are committing to new learning about your important work.

2

Inclusive Education

In the not-so-distant past, students with disabilities were educated separately from students without disabilities. Luckily, today, most students are taught in diverse and inclusive settings. These types of settings allow for maximum academic and social growth if students are supported properly.

This chapter identifies the concepts necessary to understanding inclusive education, such as belonging, the history of inclusive education, major legal concepts, the definition of inclusive education, indicators of inclusive education, IEPs, and commonly asked questions.

The woods would be very silent if no birds sang there except those that sang best.

—Henry van Dyke

Belonging

I have the power to help create an environment of acceptance and tolerance. I am a role model of acceptance and inclusivity every day. I am always thinking how would I like to be supported if I had academic challenges. I try to be supportive and also respectful of each student. —Amy (paraprofessional)

One central reason that students are being included in general education is that every child, with or without disabilities, has the right to belong. They have the right to feel like they belong in a school and in a classroom and the right not to be separated because of differences. All human beings desire friendships, relationships, and intellectual challenge. Students with disabilities are no different.

REFLECTIONS

Think of a time you felt like you belonged: How did you feel? How did you act or behave?

Think of a time you felt excluded: How did you feel? How did you act or behave?

How does belonging affect your ability to focus, learn, or participate?

How does belonging affect a student's ability to focus, learn, or participate?

Think for a moment about yourself. You probably have been in a situation where you felt like you really, truly belonged. Maybe you felt that way when you were part of a team or a club, or in a work setting. Whatever the situation, think back to how you felt, and how you acted when you were in that group. The very comfort of belonging causes most people to feel safe and secure. It also means that people are more willing to take risks, to contribute, to share, and to learn in such environments. When you feel connected to a group of people, you are likely more talkative, more engaged, and more willing to be yourself. The same is true for children.

Now, on the contrary, think of a time when you felt you did not belong or were ostracized from a group. How did you behave? How did you feel? In those situations, many people respond by feeling sad or hurt, causing them to withdraw or shut themselves off from the group. Or, a person might respond by leaving the situation or getting angry. The same is true for children in school.

Inclusive education is a way of educating students so that they are not placed in separate settings but instead have access to and take part in the typical school experience because it is essential to feel connected to a group and the school community. Not only is this important for self-worth, it is also important for learning.

When working with a group of teachers and paraprofessionals, we asked the preceding questions. Their responses are shown in Table 2.1.

Examine the lists shown in the table. How do they relate to students in school? Have you seen students in school who feel sick, angry, withdrawn, or hurt? Have you seen students who behave in ways that let you know they do not feel that they belong? Conversely, have you noticed students who are engaged, acting like themselves, and freely taking learning risks (like raising their hand in class)? We regularly see students who feel connected, and we also routinely see students who do not. Helping students feel that they belong is one of the most important jobs of the paraprofessional in the school setting.

If the system of special education excludes students and puts them in separate rooms, hallways, or schools, the children in those programs will not behave as well or learn as well. School administrators and teachers all over the country are rethinking the practice of isolating students with disabilities (Bui, 2010; Ryndak et al., 2014). Isolating students in this way causes them to feel different from everyone else and not part of the larger school community. This type of segregation has real consequences for students' self-esteem and ability to learn (National Council on Disability, 2018). Inclusive education was built on the foundation that all people have the basic human right to belong.

Table 2.1.   Feelings associated with inclusion and exclusion

When I was included...	When I was excluded...
I felt loved.	I was angry.
I felt cared for.	I was withdrawn.
I took risks.	I was quiet.
I felt smart.	I was hurt.
I was myself.	I cried.
I laughed often.	I felt sick.
I was creative.	I did not participate.
I was open to learn.	I tried to leave the group.

REFLECTIONS

Think back to when you were in school. Where were students with disabilities educated?

Where did students with more significant support needs go?

What about students with behavioral challenges?

Did you have academic groups based on ability?

Were you in the low or high groups? What was that like for you?

You might have attended a school in which students with disabilities were educated down the hall, in a separate wing, or in a separate school altogether. You might have attended a school in which you sat beside other students with disabilities. Or, you might have had a situation where some students were included in typical classrooms and others were in special education rooms. Your own schooling experience might shape your personal thoughts about inclusive education.

The History of Inclusive Education

Before 1975, students with disabilities did not have the legal right to attend school. As a result, many students with more significant disabilities were educated in separate schools or in specialized institutions, or they were not educated at all. In 1975, Congress passed the Education for All Handicapped Children Act (PL 94-142), which has since been reauthorized most recently as IDEA 2004 (PL 108-446). This law, which guarantees all students with disabilities the right to a public education, has proved to be a major accomplishment for people with disabilities and their families. IDEA ensures that all students with disabilities have access to free appropriate public education (FAPE) in the least restrictive environment (LRE). Each of these terms is defined in the next section.

Free Appropriate Public Education

In order to understand what FAPE legally means for students with disabilities and their families, it is useful to consider each term separately.

LEGAL INFORMATION

Free

Free means that all students with disabilities have the right to attend school and that the supports, aids, services, and accommodations and modifications necessary to meet their unique educational needs will be free to them, paid for at the public expense.

Appropriate

Appropriate means that all students with disabilities must be provided the assistive technology, supports, aids, services, and accommodations and modifications that allow them to participate in both academic and nonacademic activities. These are all outlined in the student's IEP.

Public Education

Special education for students with disabilities is guaranteed in any public school setting.

DEFINITIONS

Least Restrictive Environment

The word *inclusion* does not appear in IDEA, but the law explicitly cites the term *least restrictive environment,* which is used to support the idea of inclusion. IDEA 2004 stipulates that all students with disabilities have the legal right to be placed in the LRE.

LRE means that, to the maximum extent appropriate, a school district must educate any student with a disability in the regular classroom with appropriate aids and supports—referred to as *supplementary aids and services*—along with the student's peers without disabilities, in the school they would attend if the student did not have a disability (IDEA, 2004).

Under LRE regulations, the general education classroom is the first place to be considered for placing a student with a disability before more restrictive options are considered. Figure 2.1 evidences the continuum of services that can be provided to a student who qualifies for special education.

One of the most significant changes in the 2004 update to IDEA concerns the requirement that students with disabilities receive access to the general curriculum. Specifically, the new amendments require that students with disabilities:

1. *Have access to* the general curriculum
2. *Be involved in* the general curriculum
3. *Progress in* the general curriculum

What Are Supplementary Aids and Services?

Legally, school systems must use a variety of supplementary aids and services to support a student with a disability in their LRE. Examples of supplementary aids and services are located in Figure 2.2. As you can see, these supports to students are in the areas of changing the environment, pacing, presentation of subject matter, materials, equipment, assignments, self-management, testing supports, social interaction support, and level of staff support. Paraprofessionals serve as a type of supplementary aid and service that may be assigned to one or more students in order to help them access the general education classroom.

> Under LRE regulations, the general education classroom is the first place to be considered for placing a student with a disability before more restrictive options are considered.

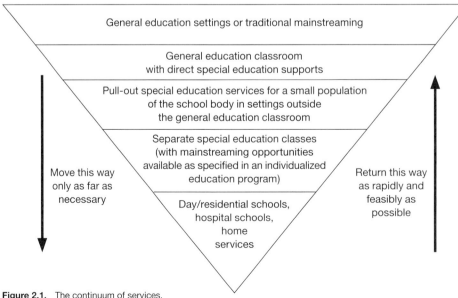

Figure 2.1.   The continuum of services.

Directions: When considering the need for personalized supports, aids, or services for a student, use this checklist to help identify which supports will be the least intrusive, individualized as necessary, and the most natural to the context of the classroom.

Environmental

_____ Preferential seating

_____ Planned seating arrangements   ___ *Bus*   ___ *Classroom*   ___ *Lunchroom*   ___ *Auditorium*   ___ *Other*

_____ Alter physical room arrangement. (Specify: _____)

_____ Use study carrels or quiet areas.

_____ Define area concretely (e.g., carpet squares, tape on floor, rug area).

_____ Reduce/minimize distractions.   ___ *Visual*   ___ *Spatial*   ___ *Auditory*   ___ *Movement*

_____ Teach positive rules for use of space.

Pacing of Instruction

_____ Extend time requirements.

_____ Allow breaks.

_____ Send additional copy of texts home for a summer preview of the next school year's content.

_____ Provide home set of materials for preview or review.

_____ Vary activity often.

_____ Omit assignments requiring copying in timed situations.

Presentation of Subject Matter

_____ Teach to the student's learning style/strength intelligences.   ___ *Verbal/Linguistic*   ___ *Logical/Mathematical*   ___ *Visual/Spatial*   ___ *Naturalist*   ___ *Bodily/Kinesthetic*   ___ *Musical*   ___ *Interpersonal*   ___ *Intrapersonal*

_____ Use active, experiential learning.

_____ Record class lectures and discussions to replay later.

_____ Provide prewritten notes, an outline, or an organizer (e.g., mind map).

_____ Present demonstrations and models.

_____ Highlight critical information or main ideas.

_____ Make and use vocabulary files or provide vocabulary lists.

_____ Use facilitated communication.

_____ Use paired reading/writing.

_____ Use diaries or learning logs.

_____ Preview and review major concepts in primary language.

_____ Use specialized curriculum.

_____ Use American Sign Language and/or total communication.

_____ Use manipulatives and real objects in mathematics.

_____ Pre-teach vocabulary.

_____ Reduce the language level of the reading assignment.

_____ Use visual organizers/sequences.

_____ Reduce seat time in class or activities.

_____ Reword/rephrase instructions and questions.

Materials

_____ Limit amount of material on page.

_____ Use study guides and advanced organizers.

_____ Provide note-taking assistance.

_____ Scan tests and class notes into computer.

_____ Use braille material.

_____ Provide assistive technology and software (e.g., IntelliTalk).

_____ Record texts and other class materials.

_____ Use supplementary materials.

_____ Copy class notes.

_____ Use large print.

_____ Use communication book or board.

Specialized Equipment or Procedure

_____ Wheelchair   _____ Walker   _____ Standing board   _____ Positioning

_____ Computer   _____ Computer software   _____ Electronic typewriter   _____ Video

_____ Modified keyboard   _____ Voice synthesizer   _____ Switches   _____ Suctioning

_____ Catheterization   _____ Braces   _____ Restroom equipment

_____ Customized mealtime utensils, plates, cups, and other materials

_____ Augmentative communication device

(continued)

Figure 2.2.   Supplementary aids and services.

From Villa, R. A., Thousand, J. S., & Nevin, A. I. (2013). *A guide to co-teaching: New Lessons and strategies to facilitate student learning* (3rd ed., pp. 198–201). Thousand Oaks, CA: Corwin Press, adapted by permission of SAGE Publications.

In *The Paraprofessional's Handbook for Effective Support in Inclusive Classrooms* by Julie Causton and Kate MacLeod.

Figure 2.2. *(continued)*

Assignment Modification

_____ Give directions in small, distinct steps (written/picture/verbal).
_____ Use pictures as supplement to oral directions.
_____ Raise difficulty level.
_____ Reduce paper-and-pencil tasks.
_____ Give extra cues or prompts.
_____ Adapt worksheets and packets.
_____ Use compensatory procedures by providing alternate assignments when demands of class conflict with student capabilities.

_____ Use written backup for oral directions.
_____ Lower difficulty level.
_____ Shorten assignments.
_____ Read to or record directions for the student(s).
_____ Allow student to record or type assignments.
_____ Ignore spelling errors/sloppy work.

Self-Management/Follow-Through

_____ Provide pictorial or written daily/weekly schedule(s).
_____ Check often for understanding/review.
_____ Teach study skills.
_____ Design/write/use long-term assignment timelines.

_____ Provide student calendars.
_____ Have student repeat directions.
_____ Use binders to organize material.
_____ Plan for generalization by teaching skill in several environments.

Testing Adaptations

_____ Provide oral instructions and/or read test questions.
_____ Read test to student.
_____ Ask questions that have applications in real settings.
_____ Administer test individually.   ___ *Use short answer.*   ___ *Use multiple choice.*   ___ *Shorten length.*   ___ *Extend time frame.*
      ___ *Use open-note/open-book tests.*

_____ Use pictorial instructions/questions.
_____ Preview language of test questions.
_____ Modify format to reduce visual complexity or confusion.

Social Interaction Support

_____ Use natural peer supports and multiple, rotating peers.
_____ Use cooperative learning group.
_____ Focus on social process rather than end product.
_____ Structure shared experiences in school and extracurricular activities.
_____ Structure opportunities for social interaction (e.g., Circle of Friends).
_____ Teach social communication skills.   ___ *Greetings*   ___ *Conversation*   ___ *Turn taking*   ___ *Sharing*   ___ *Negotiation*
      ___ *Other*

_____ Use peer advocacy.
_____ Institute peer tutoring.
_____ Teach friendship, sharing, and negotiation skills to classmates.

Level of Staff Support (Assess the need for staff support after considering previous categories)

_____ Consultation
_____ Daily in-class staff support
_____ One-to-one assistance
_____ Team teaching (parallel, supportive, complementary, or co-teaching)
_____ Specialized personnel support (if indicated, identify time needed)

_____ Stop-in support
_____ Total staff support (staff are in close proximity)

Support	Time Needed
_____ Instructional support assistant	_____
_____ Health care assistant	_____
_____ Behavior assistant	_____
_____ Signing assistant	_____
_____ Nursing	_____
_____ Occupational therapy	_____
_____ Physical therapy	_____
_____ Speech-language pathologist	_____
_____ Augmentative communication specialist	_____
_____ Transportation	_____
_____ Counseling	_____
_____ Adaptive physical education	_____
_____ Transition planning	_____
_____ Orientation/mobility	_____
_____ Career counseling	_____

REFLECTIONS

Take a look at this list of supplementary aids and services in Figure 2.2. Which of these do you already use? Circle them. Now, consider which might be useful for particular students you work with. Make a note of those.

Evaluating and Fading Supplemental Aids and Services

Providing students with supplemental aids and services gives them the opportunity for greater access to general education content, settings, and peers. However, it is also important that the entire team understands how to evaluate the aids and services, and then determine a timeline and plan for *whether* and *how* to fade supports so that the student can complete a skill or task more independently. For example, if a student, Caleb, is learning to eye-point in order to communicate, his team might use frequent verbal and gestural prompts to teach him how to eye-point using a particular communication application on a tablet (e.g., iPad). The team might then plan to fade the adult-only prompting by teaching Caleb's peers to use the same prompts, which will increase peer interaction and interdependence for Caleb. Then, the team would monitor Caleb's progress with eye-pointing and create a plan to fade his peers' use of verbal and gestural prompts too; the ultimate goal would be that Caleb uses eye-pointing to communicate without prompting supports from peers or adults.

QUICK QUIZ

Define these terms—look back if you need support.

FAPE:

LRE:

Continuum of services:

Supplementary aids and services:

Defining Inclusive Education

Although the term *inclusion* is not mentioned in IDEA, it is implied; people use LRE and a multitude of supplementary aids and services to support the idea and practice of inclusion. In order to better understand what inclusion means in a school setting, *inclusive education* has been defined by scholars.

Kunc (1992) defines *inclusive education* as:

the valuing of diversity within the human community. When inclusive education is fully embraced, we abandon the idea that children have to become "normal" in order to contribute to the world.... We begin to look beyond typical ways of becoming valued members of the community, and in doing so, begin to realize the achievable goal of providing all children with an authentic sense of belonging. (p. 20)

DEFINITIONS

Kunc has also provided educators with a way to describe inclusive education in practice outlined in Table 2.2. When these practices work together, true inclusive schooling can be realized for all students.

REFLECTIONS

After reviewing Kunc's definition and the practical aspects of inclusive education, consider how your school approaches inclusive education. Do Kunc's practical aspects match the practical aspects of your school? What inclusive practices would you like to see more of in your school?

Table 2.2. Kunc's practical aspects of inclusive education

Classroom model	A model in which students with and without disabilities are based in a regular structure and benefit from the shared ownership of general and special educators.
Student-centered approach, beginning with profiles	An approach that helps educators appreciate the strengths and challenges of learners with and without disabilities and the individualized accomplishments that can be attained.
Schedules	A schedule that accounts for the full range of needs in the class—where no student engages in "pull-out" or alternative activities to the extent that disruptions in the daily schedule and in peer relationships occur.
Curriculum	An engaging curriculum that is rich and accommodating for all students—and, when needed, is further individualized to meet the needs of a particular learner.
Teaming process	The process in which support staff work in flexible, coordinated ways to strengthen the collaborative relationships among special and regular educators, parents and educators, and educators and the community.
Classroom climate	A classroom environment that embraces diversity, fosters a sense of social responsibility, and supports positive peer relationships.

Source: Kunc, N. (1992). The need to belong. Rediscovering Maslow's hierarchy of needs. In R. A. Villa, J. S. Thousand, W. Stainback, & S. Stainback (Eds.), *Restructuring for caring and effective education: An administrative guide to creating heterogeneous schools* (pp. 25–39). Baltimore, MD: Paul H. Brookes Publishing Co.

Indicators of Inclusive Education

Some indicators of inclusive schooling environments include natural proportions, co-teaching, community building, universal design for learning (UDL), differentiation, access, heterogeneous grouping, engaging instruction, and digital tools.

Natural Proportions

In inclusive schools, staff work to create balanced and diverse classrooms in every way. One way to do that is to be sure that classrooms are not too overloaded with one type of need or disability. This is called *natural proportions*. In any one classroom, the number of students with disabilities should reflect the natural population of students with disabilities in the school (e.g., if 16% of the students in the school have labels, then no more than 16% of those students would be in any one classroom). In an inclusive classroom, half the class should not be made up of students with disabilities. Having a greater number of students with disabilities in one setting increases the density of need, making the class more like a special education setting.

Co-Teaching

Inclusive classrooms often have two teachers—one general and one special education teacher—with equitable responsibilities for teaching all of the students. Inclusive classrooms do not always have two teachers present. Sometimes, the general education teacher carries out adaptations that have been designed by a special education teacher. A paraprofessional can support the educator or the two co-teachers to provide additional support to the students who have disabilities while also supporting and working with all students in the classroom.

Community Building

In inclusive classrooms, teachers continually use community building to ensure that students feel connected to one another and to their teachers. A common theme in community building is that different people learn in different ways. Community building approaches vary, but, in an inclusive classroom, you might see the day start out with a morning meeting in which students share their feelings or important life events. You might also see organized community building in which students learn about each other in systematic ways. For example, the students might be doing a community-building exercise called "Homework in a Bag"; in this exercise, each student brings one item that represents him- or herself and shares the item with a small group of other students. Diversity and difference are embraced and celebrated as a way to help ensure that students feel connected to and part of a classroom community.

Universal Design for Learning (UDL)

UDL is a way of teaching that gives all students, especially those who experience learning differences, a way to flexibly engage with learning and show what they know. It is called *universal design for learning* because the lessons are designed with student differences in mind. An analogy for this kind of teaching and learning is to think about sidewalks with curb-cuts. When they were designed and the concrete was poured, they provided access for people who use wheelchairs, but they also benefit others. For example, if you have a stroller, a shopping cart, or are even wearing high heels, you may find a curb-cut to be quite handy. In classrooms, when we provide students with flexible ways to learn, we meet the needs of individual students as well as the entire class.

Differentiation

In an inclusive classroom, learners of various academic, social, and behavioral levels and needs share one learning environment. Differentiation of instruction is a strategy that inclusive educators use to respond to these diverse learning needs (Tomlinson, 2017). Therefore, teachers need to employ strategies like differentiation. *Differentiation* means:

At its most basic level, differentiating instruction means "shaking up" what goes on in the classroom so that students have multiple options for taking in information, making sense of ideas, and expressing what they learn. In other words, a differentiated classroom provides different avenues to acquiring content, to processing or making sense of ideas, and to developing products so that each student can learn effectively. (Tomlinson, 2017, p. 1)

Students might work on similar goals, but they do so in different ways and using different entry points. For example, all students might be working on math problems, with some using manipulatives, some drawing out their answers, some checking their problems using the calculator function of their tablets, and some using tablets or white boards.

Students Do Not Leave to Learn

In a truly inclusive classroom, you will not have a revolving door of children leaving for specialized instruction or related services. Therapies and services occur within the context of the general education classroom. For example, instead of going to a small room with a speech teacher, a student might work on their speech goals while participating in reading instruction. Paraprofessionals might be required to help make sure a student's goals are being met in the classroom.

Heterogeneous Groups

In inclusive classes, educators need to thoughtfully consider seating and grouping. Students with disabilities should be physically spread out in the classroom in an organic way. In other words, students with disabilities should not be clustered or grouped together. It may seem logical or even more convenient to seat students together if you are supporting a few students in the same classroom. However, it is critical that students are seen as individuals and surrounded by their typical peers and academic, social, and behavioral role models. When students are placed in ability groups, it can be stigmatizing to them and create significant social barriers.

Engaging Instruction

Inclusive classrooms do not entail many large-group lectures in which the teachers talk and the students passively sit and listen. Learning is exciting in inclusive classrooms. Teachers plan instruction with the range of learning styles in mind. In inclusive classrooms, students experience active learning; they often are up and out of their seats, with partner work and group work used frequently. The content is planned to meet the needs of students to move around, to work with others, and to see and experience their learning.

Digital Tools and Inclusion

Technology can be a powerful tool for facilitating effective inclusion for students with and without disabilities. Years ago, assistive technologies to support students with disabilities were often cumbersome, expensive, difficult to learn or use, and often isolating. But now, many digital tools can allow students to gain access to curriculum, learning, and peers—and they can do it right on the personal devices (e.g., laptops, tablets, smartphones) that they use in their daily school and home lives. For example, students can access videos and simulations on their devices to walk them through complex math or science concepts. Students can access a vast online library that personalizes any text to fit their unique needs (e.g., audio text, adapted reading levels, enlarged font) through the program BookShare. Students can enable voice dictation to write down their thoughts with ease and independence so you do not have to scribe for them. They can also create or animate videos to share their knowledge in new and creative ways.

Not only do digital tools provide greater individualized support and access, students can also use them to increase interaction and collaboration with peers and teachers. For example, students can collaborate with their peers via Google Classroom using shared documents or slides. Students can participate in online class discussions using platforms like Padlet, Flipgrid, and Socrative. They can also receive feedback from peers and teachers alike, even in real time via Google Docs, Google Chat, or videoconferencing platforms. It is very important that your students have access to 21st century digital tools in order to enhance learning and inclusion.

DIGITAL TOOLS

Educational Videos

PBS Learning Media: https://www.mainepublic.org/post/welcome-learning-space

Khan Academy: www.khanacademy.org

Teacher Tube: www.teachertube.com

Accessible Books

Bookshare: www.bookshare.org

Voice Dictation

Apple Voice Recognition

Windows Speech Recognition

Google Docs Voice Typing

SpeechNotes

Collaborative Online Tools

Google Classroom: www.classroom.google.com

Padlet: www.padlet.com

Flipgrid: www.flipgrid.com

Socrative: www.socrative.com

REFLECTIONS

Take a moment and write down the types of inclusive indicators that are present in your school or classrooms. Are there any indicators mentioned in this section that you would like to learn more about? Any particular ones that might be valuable for the students you work with? If so, take a moment to write down how you might bring this to the attention of your colleague(s). If you are not sure how to bring it up, we provide strategies in Chapter 4 to help you with communication and collaboration.

What Do I Need To Know About Individualized Education Programs?

Every student who receives special education services must have an IEP. A student who has an IEP has already been through testing and observation, and a team has determined that the student has a disability. An IEP is a legal plan written by a team of professionals that documents the learning priorities for the school year (Huefner, 2000). This team includes the parent, the student (when appropriate), the general education teacher, the special education teacher, a representative of the school district, and other professionals whose expertise is needed (e.g., psychologist, speech and language clinician, occupational or physical therapist). When writing this document, the team comes together annually to determine and document the student's unique needs and goals regarding their participation in the general school curriculum for the upcoming school year. According to the U.S. Department of Education (2004), every IEP must legally include the following information:

- *Present levels of performance.* How a student is performing across all subject areas must be consistently documented.
- *Measurable goals and objectives.* IEPs indicate the annual goals for a student across subject areas.
- *Special education and related services.* This includes the type, level, and amount of service that will be provided by special education and related service staff.
- *Modifications.* The student's necessary modifications or adaptations must be listed.
- *Participation in statewide tests.* The IEP indicates whether the student will participate in statewide tests and, if so, what modifications will be provided.
- *Locations of services to be provided.* This section of the IEP explains the amount of time and location at which students will receive services (e.g., therapy room, general education classroom).
- *Statement of transition services.* Each student who is at least 16 years of age must have a statement of preparation for adult life.

Paraprofessionals have the legal right to access the IEPs of the students they support. In some school systems, you may be asked to participate in a student's IEP meeting because you can provide important information relevant to the student's educational program. In other systems, paraprofessionals are not asked to participate. If you are asked to participate, you should meet first with the teacher to discuss your role in the meeting. Even if you do not attend the meeting, you should read the IEPs of the students you support (see Table 2.3). When reading an IEP, the best place to start is with two major sections: 1) the present level of performance and 2) the student's goals and objectives. When reading an IEP, create an "IEP at a glance" or a summary listing the goals and objectives and other important information. See Figure 2.3 for a copy of an IEP at a glance. You should understand that the information within the document is confidential and cannot be shared with anyone outside of the child's team. Sharing information about a student is not only disrespectful, it is also potentially illegal per IDEA 2004 (20 U.S.C. § 1412 [a][8]; § 1417 [c]).

Any student who has challenging behavior is also required to have a behavior intervention plan as part of their IEP. This plan includes a functional assessment of the student's behavior and a plan for addressing that student's behavior in positive ways. If a student whom you support has a behavior intervention plan, you are responsible for reading, knowing, understanding, and following the behavior plan as written.

Table 2.3. How to read an individualized education program

1. Find the present level of performance. Read it. Now ask yourself . . .	Do I have a clear picture of what this student does well?
	Do I have a clear picture of this student's skills?
	Do I know any strategies that work with this student?
	Do I know what to avoid when working with this student?
2. Find the annual goals. Read each goal. Now ask yourself . . .	Do I have a clear picture of what the student should be able to do by the end of the year?
3. Find the supplementary aids and services (aids, services, and supports to help the student be educated in the general education environment). Read it. Now ask yourself . . .	Do I understand the services and supports that this student needs in regular education environments?
	Do I know who is expected to provide the services or supports?
	If I am expected to provide a service or support, do I know what to do?
4. Find the section on specially designed instruction (direct teaching and services carried out by the special education staff). Read it. Now ask yourself . . .	What specially designed instruction does this student need?
	Where is the instruction provided?
	If I need to provide practice or support, do I understand what to do?
5. If the student has a behavior intervention plan, find it. Read it. Now ask yourself . . .	What are the strategies and techniques that will increase the likelihood that appropriate behaviors will occur?
	If problem behaviors begin to escalate, how can I redirect the student to more positive behaviors?
	If the student becomes aggressive, do I know the steps in the response plan to deescalate the situation?
6. Read the rest of the individualized education plan. Ask yourself . . .	Do I have any questions about this student, their needs, or their support that I should share with my teaching team?

⊙ IEP at a Glance ⊙

Student _____ Grade _____ Age _____

Date completed _____

Goal _____   Goal _____
Objectives: Objectives:

-
-
-
-
-
-
-
-
-

Goal _____   Goal _____
Objectives: Objectives:

-
-
-
-
-
-
-
-
-

Goal _____   Important
Objectives: student information:

-
-
-
-
-
-
-
-

Figure 2.3. Individualized education program (IEP) at a glance.

FAQs

Commonly Asked Questions About Inclusive Education

Q. **Is inclusive education really best for a student with disabilities?**

A. Research has consistently shown that the inclusive classroom is better educationally and socially for students with disabilities. Our challenge as educators is to figure out how to make the general education environment, curriculum, and instruction accessible to each student. We can do this by collaborating and designing differentiated supports that seamlessly integrate the curriculum with the student's strengths and needs.

Q. **I do not think my student is getting anything out of this class. What should I do?**

A. If you don't think a student is gaining anything from the class curriculum, it is the teacher's responsibility (with your support) to modify or adapt the content so that the student can benefit from the instruction. Sometimes, the goals of the lesson are not easy to see. In such cases, initiate a discussion with the teacher(s) about what the expected goals of the lesson are (e.g., the student might be working on social goals, fine motor goals, or simply gaining exposure to parts of the content).

Q. **Can an IEP be changed?**

A. Yes, an IEP can be changed and is changed at least every year. The document grows and shifts with the student. Much like we would not expect a student to wear the same size shoe all throughout their school career, the IEP changes and grows with the student. It is a dynamic document that should be revised when necessary.

Q. **When should I take a student out of the classroom?**

A. Every student has the right to an education in the general education classroom, and it is not your decision to remove a student because it is a legal placement decision. If a student is having behavioral issues, the team of teachers has the responsibility to identify and help the student manage the behavior within the context of the classroom. Provide an option for the student to identify when they might need a natural break and determine solutions to the challenge that allow the student to remain in class.

Q. **What could I do instead of removing a student?**

A. Remove yourself. Sometimes, switching adults or backing away is the best solution if you are having a difficult time with a student. Help students engage in a different way. Give the student a choice at that moment (e.g., a choice of materials, a choice of whom to work with). Chapter 8 presents many more ideas for fading support.

Q. **Will other students tease students with disabilities?**

A. If you see or hear teasing, you must deal with it or report it. Teasing is a form of bullying and should not be seen as an inevitable consequence of inclusion. In fact, inclusive environments are the best places to teach students that differences are merely diversity.

Q. What is RTI? And does it relate to inclusion?

A. Response to intervention (RTI) is a process educators use to support students who are struggling. The first tier is good instructional practices for all students in the general education setting, the second tier is more prescribed intervention or specific instructional practices, and the third tier is for even more focused instruction. When inclusive education is embraced, we realize that these interventions can take place right in the general education setting.

Q. Is inclusion really the law?

A. The law stipulates that *all* students must be placed in the LRE. The first consideration must be the general education setting, and schools must prove that they have attempted to teach all children in the general education setting with appropriate supplementary aids and services before even considering moving a student to more restrictive settings.

Conclusion

Thankfully, schools are becoming increasingly inclusive. Therefore, paraprofessionals working in inclusive settings need to understand the rationale for inclusive schooling, the history of inclusive schooling, major concepts in inclusive schooling, indicators of inclusion, and the concept of the IEP as a framework to fully support students in the LRE. The next chapter focuses on foundations for understanding special education and accompanying language that will help you in this work.

To Do

TO-DO LIST

After reading this chapter . . .

- Complete the reflections in the chapter.
- Read the IEPs for the students with whom you work. Follow the questions in Table 2.2.
- Create an IEP at a glance for each of the students you support. Work with your teacher to get access to the IEPs so that you can understand the needs of particular students.
- Write all of your specific questions about this chapter down. Share with an administrator or teacher and discuss.

3

Special Education

MORE THAN ONE WAY

I was in regular classes with a para for support. I became a cheerleader in high school. I was the first cheerleader in the state with Down syndrome. Since I've been out of high school, I was a fashion model in a Global Down syndrome Foundation Fashion Show. And I now go to the Bridge School where I am learning to be a public speaker. I have a lot of skills. I have a lot of dreams. What I want to say to you is... don't limit me! Don't limit me by thinking that I can't learn in your classroom. Don't limit me by thinking that I will always need someone to help me. Don't limit me by having low expectations for me. Include me, and all of your students, in your circle of learning. —Megan Bomgaars (2013; self-advocate, artist, and entrepreneur)

We begin with the question that many have asked when they began work in the field: What is special education? This chapter answers that question along with the following ones:

- Who receives special education?
- What does *disability* mean?
- Why should people be cautious of labels?
- What does all this terminology mean?
- What are the different categories of disabilities?

This chapter identifies the important concepts and ideas that are essential for anyone in the field of special and inclusive education to understand. Knowing this information empowers paraprofessionals with the knowledge they need in order to effectively work in the educational system of which they are now part.

What Is Special Education?

Simply put, *special education* is individualized instruction designed to meet

> Simply put, *special education* is individualized instruction designed to meet the unique needs of students with disabilities in order to give them access to general education.

A LEGAL DEFINITION OF SPECIAL EDUCATION

The legal definition under IDEA 2004 of *special education* is "specially designed instruction, at no cost to the child's parents, to meet the needs of a student with a disability" (20 U.S.C. § 1401 [25]). This definition recognizes that some students have challenges with learning, behaving, or physically accessing general education because of their disabilities. Therefore, they require individualized supports to help them to build their skills and abilities to reach their full potential in school. These additional services do not cost the students' parents any money and are funded by the local and federal governments.

the unique needs of students with disabilities in order to give them access to general education. Special education is therefore a part of general education, and we like to think of it as system of supports to help students learn the general education curriculum alongside their general education peers. This type of customized support and instruction may require a student to have accommodations or modifications to their class work. *Accommodations* are adaptations to the curriculum that do not fundamentally alter or lower standards (e.g., test location, student response method). Modifications, conversely, are changes to the curriculum that do alter the expectations. Examples of modifications include changes to course content, timing, or test presentation. Any student who receives special education services may receive specialized materials (e.g., audiobooks), services (e.g., speech and language services), equipment (e.g., a communication system), or different teaching strategies (e.g., visual notes) (IDEA 2004 [PL 108-446]). For example, a student who is deaf may require the services of a sign language interpreter so that they can follow along in the classroom. A student who has autism may require specialized materials such as a visual schedule to prepare them for the changing daily routines. A student with a learning disability may require additional reading instruction or extended time for completing their written assignments.

Related Special Education Services

Sometimes, the supports a student with a disability needs can be fully addressed by a special educator, other teaching personnel, and teaching assistants and paraprofessionals. However, sometimes, additional supports are required for a student to benefit from special education services. These additional supports are called *related services* in special education law. IDEA 2004 defines the term as follows:

> Transportation and such developmental, corrective, and other supportive services as are required to assist a child with a disability to benefit from special education, and includes speech-language pathology and audiology services, interpreting services, psychological services, physical and occupational therapy, recreation, including therapeutic recreation, early identification and assessment of disabilities in children, counseling services, including rehabilitation counseling, orientation and mobility services, and medical services . . . as may be required to assist a child with a disability to benefit from special education, and includes the early identification and assessment of disability conditions in children. (20 U.S.C. §1401 [602] [26] [A])

All related services are also provided at no cost to the students' parents. In other words, this variety of services is related services that allow students to receive the full benefits from special education.

Special Education Is a Service, Not a Place

In the past, when the term *special education* was used, a separate place came to mind. People thought of a room, a school, or other separate places to which students with disabilities went to receive different and special education. But special education has changed significantly over the past few decades and is now not limited to a specific location. All students—including students with autism, significant or multiple disabilities, and emotional or behavioral disabilities—learn best in classroom settings with their general education peers (Causton-Theoharis & Theoharis, 2008; Choi, Meisenheimer, McCart, & Sailor, 2017). Special education services are portable services (e.g., help with reading, math, social skills, or speech skills) that can be brought directly to individual students. Special education occurs in general education classrooms all over the United States and the rest of the world. As discussed in Chapter 2, when students with disabilities are educated primarily in general education settings, this is called *inclusive education.*

Who Receives Special Education?

Every year under IDEA 2004, roughly 7 million students in the United States between the ages of 3 and 21 receive special education services (U.S. Department of Education, 2019). In other words, roughly 14% of all school-age children qualify for special education services because they have some sort of disability. According to IDEA 2004, a student qualifies for special education because they have one or more disability (e.g., a physical or mental condition) that adversely affects the student's educational performance. Each of the different types of disabilities is defined and described later in this chapter.

What Does *Disability* Mean?

Disability categories are used to "classify and think about the problems developing children may encounter" (Contract Consultants, IAC, 1997, p. 8, as cited in Kluth, 2003). Understanding a student's label is only the beginning point in learning about a child. A disability label reveals nothing about the student's individual gifts, talents, and strengths. A disability is one of many parts of a student. A disability does not describe who a person is—it describes only one aspect of the person.

REFLECTIONS

To illustrate this point, take a moment to write down five descriptors about yourself. What did you include? You might include descriptors about who you are in relation to others, your profession, or your personality traits.

Our lists might include descriptors such as *mother, daughter, wife, educator, joyful,* or *to-do-list maker.* Interestingly, our lists did not include deficiencies, even though we have our fair share (e.g., trouble initiating nonpreferred tasks, following auditory directions without visual supports, sitting still during lectures). The same is true for any individual with a disability. That person's area of disability is one (likely very small) part of who they are.

Social Construction of Disabilities

It is also important to recognize that people create disability categories and that those categories shift and change over time. Medical professionals, teachers, and researchers, along with the federal government, have created these categories. However, these are not static categories—they do and have changed. An extreme example of how disability is constructed is that, at one point in time, to qualify for having an intellectual disability (ID), a person needed to have an IQ of 80 or below. In 1973, the federal government lowered the cutoff IQ score to 70 points or below. So, in essence, with the single swish of a pen, hundreds of thousands of people were cured of an ID (Ashby, 2008; Blatt, 1987). Once created, these categories are often reinforced. In other words, once a student is assigned a label, educators begin seeing the child largely through the lens of disability or deficit, rather than the whole child. As Julie was observing a high school 10th-grade English classroom, she witnessed this very notion. All of the students were busy working and talking as they completed partnered research projects. The room was bustling and busy. Suddenly, the teacher stated, "Jamie, that is the last time." The teacher walked to the chalkboard and wrote Jamie's name down. Nearly all of the students were talking, yet Jamie, who happened to have a label of *emotional disturbance (ED),* was noticed for being too talkative. From where Julie was sitting, Jamie's behavior looked no different than that of many of the other students.

When working as a paraprofessional, it is important to always be aware that disability categories are created, and then people determine who qualifies and who does not.

REFLECTIONS

Have you ever worked with someone who had a label even though you really did not think they had a disability? Have you ever seen a student who did not qualify for special education even though you thought they might? Disability labels are not hard-and-fast rules that describe people; they are indicators of patterns of difficulty for individuals and are determined by the perceptions of other people.

> Disability labels are not hard-and-fast rules that describe people; they are indicators of patterns of difficulty for individuals and are determined by the perceptions of other people.

Labels: Proceed With Caution

On the one hand, many in the field of education believe labels to be helpful for defining a common language for parents and professionals. This common language allows students access to certain supports and services that they need. In a way, a label is the necessary first step toward certain services—including the services of a paraprofessional.

On the other hand, there are real problems with the labeling or categorizing of individuals. Kliewer and Biklen (1996) stated that labeling students can be a "demeaning process frequently contributing to stigmatization and leading to social and educational isolation" (p. 83). The use of and overreliance on disability labels pose many problems. Disability labels can lead to stereotyping by enabling teachers to see certain students in one, and only one, way. Labeling tends to highlight the differences among people. For example, when a student is assigned a label, teachers and paraprofessionals begin to notice the differences between that student and their peers. Labels can lead to poor self-esteem as students begin to see themselves differently because of such labels. Lastly, labels convey the impression of permanence, even though, in some cases, students are only "disabled" when they are in school. Unfortunately, labels give professionals a real sense of security. They allow professionals to believe that "disability categories are static, meaningful, and well understood when in fact they are none of these things" (Kluth, 2003, p. 7).

In fact, educators and administrators in Iowa decided that labels can be so detrimental to student success that the Iowa State Department of Education adopted a noncategorical eligibility system for students with disabilities (State of Iowa Department of Education, 2019).

This means schools in Iowa do not use disability labels to determine the eligibility of a student for special education, and they do not refer to disability labels in student IEPs. Instead, students with disabilities in Iowa are referred to as "eligible individuals" (abbreviated as EI). The Iowa Special Education Eligibility and Evaluation Standards (2019) explains, "This is because labels, standing alone, do not provide parents and educators with information regarding instructional needs. This is also because labeling may be the basis for inappropriately restrictive placement decisions" (p. 49).

We are well aware of the real problem—and at times the dangers—of disability labels and thinking about difference in categorical or stagnant ways. So in this chapter, even while we provide you with language to understand commonly used disability labels in special education, we encourage you to think about ways you can eliminate using labels when you describe students.

REFLECTIONS

- Can you refer to students only by name and not by disability label?
- Rather than using a disability label to highlight the needs of a student, can you be very specific about what those needs truly are? For example, *Kim needs support with writing and support with communication.*
- How does it feel to think and write about students in these new ways?

What Are They Saying? Educational Terminology You Need to Know

Alphabet soup: that is how we sometimes describe the use of acronyms in the field of special education. Understanding the language of special education can take a long time. The following is an alphabetical listing of a number of educational terms that are often used as acronyms:

- ADD/ADHD: attention deficit disorder and/or attention-deficit/hyperactivity disorder
- BIP: behavior intervention plan
- CBI: community-based instruction
- DS: Down syndrome
- EBD: emotional behavioral disturbance
- ED: emotional disturbance
- ESY: extended school year
- FAPE: free appropriate public education
- FBA: functional behavioral assessment
- HI: hearing impaired

- ID: intellectual disability
- IDEA: Individuals with Disabilities Education Act
- IEP: individualized education program
- LRE: least restrictive environment
- OI: orthopedic impairment
- OT: occupational therapist
- PBS: positive behavior supports
- PT: physical therapist
- SL: speech and language
- SLD: specific learning disability
- SLP: speech-language pathologist
- TBI: traumatic brain injury
- VI: visual impairment

QUICK QUIZ

Without looking ahead, take a moment to jot down on a separate piece of paper as many of the 13 federal disability categories as you can. Compare your list with the information provided in that section.

Federally Recognized Categories of Disability

How many different categories of disability are you aware of? There are currently 13 federal categories of disability. Students who receive special education services receive a formal label representing 1 of the 13 categories under IDEA 2004.

The 13 categories of disability include the following:

1. Autism
2. Deafblindness
3. Deafness
4. Emotional disturbance
5. Hearing impairment
6. Intellectual disability
7. Multiple disabilities
8. Orthopedic impairments
9. Other health impairments
10. Specific learning disabilities
11. Speech and language impairments
12. Traumatic brain injury
13. Visual impairment including blindness

We have included the IDEA 2004 definition for each; however, the most useful way to understand each disability is to listen carefully to those people who have been labeled with the disability and therefore understand the disability deeply. In order to encourage this mindset when it comes to learning about disability labels, after each of the definitions we include supports that many individuals may find useful, as well as the voices of individuals who self-identify with the particular disability. These voices are not meant to be universal examples; one person cannot possibly represent the entire population of students who have the same disability. But we include them in order to note the differences between the legal definitions and the definitions or experiences that people themselves use and share. We find that the legal definitions focus on what students cannot do or the difficulties that they have, whereas the personal voices focus largely on the gifts and abilities of each individual.

Autism Spectrum Disorder

Legal Definition *Autism* is defined by IDEA as a developmental disability that significantly affects verbal and nonverbal communication and social interaction and adversely affects educational performance; autism is generally evident before age 3. Characteristics often associated with autism are engaging in repetitive activities and stereotyped movements, resistance to change in daily routines or the environment, and unusual responses to sensory experiences (34 C.F.R. § 300.8 [c][1][i]).

Useful Supports The supports used for people with autism are quite varied. However, many people with autism appreciate written words and visuals over auditory instructions only. Clear and concrete directions can be helpful. For students who do not have verbal speech, typed speech can be liberating.

Learn From the Experts   *I strongly believe that living with autism should not be any different from living without autism. All people actually have different strengths, weaknesses, and challenges. Instead of looking at us as a group with identical needs we should be viewed as individuals who have needs in certain areas. —Sue Rubin (Rubin, 2010)*

When I learned about the criteria for autism it was mind-blowing because it was like reading something I didn't know could be put into words. I thought every-body was just dealing with these things but hiding it better [than me] and I've practiced so much more self-love since I found out about my diagnosis.
—Shaine (Spectrum, 2020)

Deafblindness

Legal Definition   *Deafblindness* is defined by law as concomitant [simultane-ous] hearing and visual impairments, the combination of which causes such severe communication and other developmental and educational needs. These students typically cannot be accommodated in special education programs designed solely for children with deafness or children with blindness (34 C.F.R. § 300.8 [c][2]).

Useful Supports   Many students learn to use tactile sign, a form of sign lan-guage that is felt with the hands. Assistive technology devices used by students with visual impairments are often used by students who are deafblind. These include, but are not limited to, braille translation software, braille printers, speech to text and text to speech, screen readers that convert text on a com-puter screen to audible speech, or the use of a braille display that converts text on a computer to braille. Deafblind students often benefit from a total commu-nication approach, which includes spoken language, assistive technology, tac-tile information, and sign language.

Learn From the Experts   *As a deafblind person, I've had to fight for seemingly trivial things like the right to access cafeteria menus or participate in rock-climbing. Most of the barriers I have encountered stemmed from mis-understandings by people unfamiliar with accommodations for people with disabilities. We [deafblind] have a need for technology greater than the average person. These tools are necessary to facilitate communication and indepen-dence in our communities. I myself rely on technology for everything from communicating with store clerks, conducting my assignments, to chatting with friends. —Haben Girma (Girma, 2014)*

The best and most beautiful things in the world cannot be seen or even touched. They must be felt within the heart. —Helen Keller (Keller, 1903)

Deafness

Legal Definition   *Deafness* is legally defined as a hearing impairment so severe that a child's educational performance is adversely affected; people with deaf-ness have difficulty, with or without amplification, in processing linguistic information (34 C.F.R. § 300.8 [c][3]).

Useful Supports   Students who qualify for special education under the cat-egory of deafness typically use sign language. These individuals can access the general education curriculum through the use of a sign language interpreter, speech reading, or lip reading. Closed captioning for any video and transcripts for any audio are also critical accessibility supports.

Learn From the Experts   *What's wrong with being deaf? I'm deaf. I'm fine. I function fine. I drive. I have a family. I've made a baby. I make people laugh. I travel. What the hell is going on? Like, I have to hear? That has nothing to do with it. It's all about knowledge; it's about the heart. It's about abilities, about doing something you want and getting what you want out of life . . . Knowledge is the most powerful vehicle to success—not hearing, not speaking . . . —C. J. Jones (Hott et al., 2007)*

It is true. Every weekend, I ride my high-quality road racing bicycle at high speeds (sometimes as fast as 40 mph on the flats) with a bunch of men from my bicycle club. I am the only deaf person in that 500-member club. —Mavis (Mavis, 2003, p. 3)

Emotional Disturbance

Legal Definition   A condition exhibiting one or more of the following characteristics for a long period of time and to a marked degree that adversely affects a child's educational performance:

a. An inability to learn that cannot be explained by intellectual, sensory, or health factors.

b. An inability to build or maintain satisfactory interpersonal relationships with peers and teachers.

c. Inappropriate types of behavior or feelings under normal circumstances.

d. A general pervasive mood of unhappiness or depression.

e. A tendency to develop physical symptoms or fears associated with personal or school problems. (34 C.F.R. § 300.8 [c][4][i])

Useful Supports   Students with ED often experience withdrawal or anxiety, depression, issues with mood, feelings of low self-worth, aggression, hyperactivity, or impulsivity. Therefore, when working with students with ED it is important to remain calm and caring in your approach. Work hard on being a trusted adult in this student's life. Be clear with expectations and follow through with what you tell a student you will do. A student often has a behavior plan that will outline the team's strategy to support the individual student.

Learn From the Experts   *If we're pushing you away, it's because we really need you, we want you to ask us "how's your day going?" and actually care about the answer.' Cause we can tell when you don't really care about the answer. And if we push you and push you and push you, and you turn around and walk away, then that's it for you, like, you're not getting back into our head or into a relationship anymore. —Kelsey Carroll (Carroll, 2014)*

Hearing Impairment

Legal Definition   Hearing impairment is any difficulty in hearing, whether permanent or fluctuating, that adversely affects a child's educational performance but that is not included under the definition of *deafness* (34 C.F.R. §

300.8 [c][5]). Students with hearing impairments make up 1.1% of the special education population (U.S. Department of Education, National Center for Education Statistics, 2019).

Useful Supports   For students with a hearing impairment, you may be required to use an amplification system. This is often a microphone hung around the speaker's neck that goes directly into the student's hearing aids. Generally, it is useful to be clear with your speech. Ensure that you get the students' attention before speaking, and face the student with an unobstructed mouth if they are reading lips. It is also important to ensure that any video used in class has closed captioning engaged and that any audio files shared have accessible transcripts.

Learn From the Experts   *The way I tend to explain [hearing impairment] is that it's not necessarily that you can't hear the words that people are using, it's that you hear sounds that resemble words, but you can't quite figure out what the sounds are. Like, when a hearing person only just hears something, and asks someone to repeat themselves. Like that. Except for me it's way more frequent. So that's why I tend to use other strategies to figure out what's going on. I lip-read . . . But lip-reading isn't perfect. A lot of the words look the same and so it's hard for me to use it exclusively to talk to someone. I tend to guess a lot. I'll catch most of a sentence and then sort of try to fill in the gaps myself. Usually it works. Sometimes it doesn't . . . Every now and then I'll mis-hear an entire sentence and my brain will fill in the random words that sort of fit the syllables and sounds, but together those words do not make sense at all . . . It's just so normal for me to be hearing impaired. People ask me what it's like to be [hearing impaired] and I just don't have a perfect answer for them. "What's it like to be able to hear?" There's no real comparison and so I don't really know what is different about it. Obviously hearing people can hear more and understand more sounds, but what does that mean? It can be really hard to explain. It's all about perception.* —R. Williams (2008, para. 13)

Intellectual Disability

Legal Definition   *Intellectual disability* is assigned to students who have "significantly subaverage general intellectual functioning, existing concurrently with impairments in adaptive behavior and manifested during the developmental period, that adversely affects a child's educational performance" (34 C.F.R. § 300.8 [c][6]). The term *mental retardation* is cited in IDEA 2004 but was changed in 2010 under Rosa's Law (PL 111-256) to *intellectual disability*. Another term commonly used is *cognitive disability*.

Useful Supports   People with ID have a wide variety of abilities. Some students have speech and can write, whereas other students do not use speech and are unable to write. Lacking the ability to write or speak, however, does not mean that the person has no ideas or no desire to communicate with others. All people desire connections with others and, when given the tools to communicate, students who do not have speech or writing abilities can engage successfully with other students and with academic content. It is most useful to teach students with IDs in the context where they will be expected to use the skill. For example, teach social skills as students are expected to interact with other students, rather than a separate location. Many people with IDs also appreciate clear and concrete directions and examples. For example, in science class it would be more useful for the student to experience what happens to air when it enters a balloon than to merely read about it.

Learn From the Experts   *What I would like is for you to understand that my biggest problem is not a neurological dysfunction. It is being misunderstood by people who think my problems are due to poor parenting. My mom has really tried to teach me proper social behaviors, but it just does not click all the time. Sometimes I can't remember the social rules. —Anonymous (FAS Community Resource Center, 2008)*

Multiple Disabilities

Legal Definition   Legally, "multiple disabilities" means concomitant [simultaneous] impairments (such as intellectual disability-blindness, intellectual disability-orthopedic impairment, etc.), the combination of which causes such severe educational needs that they cannot be accommodated in a special education program solely for one of the impairments. The term does not include deaf-blindness. (§300.8[c][7])

Useful Supports   Because the individuals in this disability category range so greatly, it would be impossible to discuss general types of useful supports. However, it is important to determine the individual needs and the separate impairments as a starting point for creating and implementing useful supports.

Learn From the Experts   *Sabrina, an elementary student with multiple disabilities who does not yet have reliable access to communication but is included successfully in general education classes, was described this way by her teacher, Nancy: "Our expectations are changing as Sabrina progresses. Expectations for Sabrina always continue to grow and she is meeting them"* (MacLeod, Causton, & Nunes, 2017).

Orthopedic Impairments

Legal Definition   A severe orthopedic impairment is one that adversely affects a child's educational performance. The term includes congenital impairments (e.g., clubfoot, absence of a body part), impairments caused by disease (e.g., poliomyelitis, bone tuberculosis), and impairments from other causes (e.g., cerebral palsy, amputations, fractures or burns that cause contractures) (34 C.F.R. § 300.8 [c][8]).

Useful Supports   It is important to consider the mobility devices or tools that a person may use to be nearly like a part of their body. In other words, be respectful and don't touch. Ask the student what supports they want and how they wish to be supported.

Learn From the Experts   A high school student with cerebral palsy who uses a wheelchair describes herself and her experience in school as follows:

When you see me, I think the first thing you would notice is that I'm a pretty positive person. I love to listen to music, go horseback riding, and draw ... When I was in elementary school ... I had friends and liked to play the same games as everyone else, but the teachers were always worried that I was too fragile and would hurt myself. —Angela Gabel (Gabel, 2006, p. 35)

Other Health Impairments

Legal Definition   These include any disabilities in which the person has limited strength, vitality, or alertness to environmental stimuli, resulting in limited alertness with respect to the educational environment, that:

a. is due to chronic or acute health problems such as asthma, attention deficit disorder or attention-deficit/hyperactivity disorder, diabetes, epilepsy, a heart condition, hemophilia, lead poisoning, leukemia, nephritis, rheumatic fever, and sickle cell anemia; and

b. adversely affects a child's educational performance. (34 C.F.R. § 300.8 [c][9])

   This impairment includes students who have ADHD. The label *ADHD* is assigned to students who have difficulty maintaining attention, knowing when to slow down, or organizing themselves to finish tasks (American Psychiatric Association, 2000). Obviously, not everyone who has each of these disorders qualifies for special education, but if such a condition has been diagnosed by a medical professional and adversely affects a student's educational performance (and if the student needs additional supports), they are likely to qualify.

Useful Supports   The individual students would determine the type of support for these types of disabilities. For example, students with diabetes may need support with insulin injections from a nurse. Students with ADHD often share that being allowed to stand or to fidget is helpful support. Students who have limited capacity for staying awake may need more rest opportunities. In addition, students who require a feeding pump may need a dedicated person (perhaps, you, the paraprofessional) who is responsible for turning the pump on and off.

Learn From the Experts   Jonathan Mooney, an author and speaker who experienced multiple labels of disability growing up, including ADHD, explains:

What I do know is that there was a way out for me. I know that I don't feel stupid anymore. I don't believe I'm defective anymore. Normal must be resisted if you are ever going to live your life, as who you are, fully, in all your complexity.
—Jonathan Mooney (Mooney, 2019)

At first it made me so mad that no one ever believed me when I would try to explain that I just couldn't remember where I left my cellphone or why I could never remember to follow through on directions or how I felt. Sometimes I just wanted to cry because no one understood what I was going through, but then I realized that I should be proud because I'm learning lessons about hard work that most don't learn until later [in life]. Having ADHD makes me unique and different, and I should be proud of being different and not ashamed of it. Having ADHD has only made me stronger, and it may make things hard sometimes, but in the end, I just come out more confident in being different.
—Marie (LDOnline, 2020)

Specific Learning Disabilities

Legal Definition   These include a disorder in one or more of the basic psychological processes involved in understanding or using spoken or written language; it may manifest itself in an imperfect ability to listen, think, speak, read, write, spell, or do mathematical calculations. The term includes such conditions as perceptual disabilities, brain injury, minimal brain dysfunction, dyslexia, and developmental aphasia. The term does not include learning problems that are primarily the results of visual, hearing, or motor disabilities; of ID; of ED; or of environmental, cultural, or economic disadvantages (34 C.F.R. § 300.8 [c][10]).

Useful Supports   This is the most frequently occurring disability; thus, you are quite likely to work with students who have the label of *specific learning disability* (SLD). For students with SLD, it is important to provide appropriate accommodations, modifications, and assistive technologies and to use and focus on the student's strengths. For example, if the student you support is not a fluent reader but is a great auditory learner, ensure that the student has access to audiobooks.

Learn From the Experts   *Dysgraphia is a learning disability resulting in lots of trouble with writing. I have a very hard time with writing mechanics—those are things like grammar, punctuation, spelling, and others. I also have a hard time with organization, structure of written assignments, and getting thoughts down on paper. Even though I receive a lot of accommodations, some of my teachers don't use them. Although I have dysgraphia I still love to learn. I especially love history and geography. I want everyone to know that just because I have a learning disability does not mean I am stupid or can't learn. It means I am unique and special. —Anonymous (LDOnline, 2020)*

I believe one key idea is to find one's own definition of the dual identity within oneself as a learner and as a student. The learner is the one who makes an effort to be curious, involved, and motivated. Not all knowledge is taught in school. It is the student identity that gets labeled as the disabled. The "learning disability" should not be allowed to overwhelm one's desire to attain knowledge. The learner in you must prevent it. —Caitlin Norah Callahan (Callahan, 1997)

Speech and Language Impairments

Legal Definition   Speech and language disabilities can be defined as any communication disorder, such as stuttering, impaired articulation, a language impairment, or a voice impairment that adversely affects a child's educational performance (34 C.F.R. § 300.8 [c][11]).

This is the second most common disability category. Approximately 20% of students who qualify for special education are served under this category (U.S. Department of Education, National Center for Education Statistics, 2019).

Useful Supports   Students who qualify for this disability have a wide range of impairments. Some students who receive speech and language services have difficulty with articulation or fluency (e.g., stuttering). Other students might not use any speech for communication. A student who only has speech and language disabilities is not likely to be supported by a paraprofessional. However, many students have speech and language impairments and another disability

Not being able to speak is not the same as not having anything to say.
-R. Crossley

label that necessitates the support of a paraprofessional. Depending on the nature of the speech and language issue, you might be asked to follow through on communication programs or plans designed by a speech-language pathologist (SLP).

Learn From the Experts   *Not being able to speak is not the same thing as not having anything to say.* —Rosemary Crossley

We are the perfect example of intelligence working out itself in a much different way. —Tracy Thresher (Wurzburg, 2011)

Traumatic Brain Injury

Legal Definition   This is an acquired injury to the brain caused by an external physical force, resulting in total or partial functional disability or psychosocial impairment—or both—that adversely affects a child's educational performance. The term applies to open or closed head injuries resulting in impairments in one or more areas such as cognition; language; memory; attention; reasoning; abstract thinking; judgment; problem solving; sensory, perceptual, and motor abilities; psychosocial behavior; physical functions; information processing; and speech. The term does not include brain injuries that are congenital, degenerative, or induced by birth trauma (34 C.F.R. § 300.8 [c][12]).

Useful Supports   This type of disability differs from the others because it is acquired during the person's lifetime (e.g., car accident, blow to the head). People are not born with this condition—instead, they acquire the disability. The emotional adjustment to acquiring a disability is an issue not only for the student but also for parents/guardians and teachers. The location of the brain injury typically dictates the type of impairment that occurs. For students with TBI, get to know them and understand their strengths. Use their strengths whenever possible. In addition, sometimes student behavior is affected. So, remember to remain calm and caring in your demeanor toward the student.

Learn From the Experts   *It took me years to process . . . what had happened. While the physical disabilities and the brain damage that I have are inconvenient, a drag even, they're not as bad as the treatment by friends, social systems, and especially the "Do-Gooders."* —Billy Golfus (Golfus, n.d.)

The three-month coma that followed [the accident] and the years of rehabilitation are only a blur to me. I slowly awoke over the next two years becoming aware of my surroundings as well as myself and my inabilities, one being that I could no longer sing, as I was left with a severe speech impediment. —Kelley Parker (Parker, 2008)

Visual Impairment Including Blindness

Legal Definition   This includes any impairment in vision that, even with correction, adversely affects a child's educational performance. The term includes both partial sight and blindness (34 C.F.R. § 300.8 [c][13]).

Useful Supports   The services received by students under this category of disability differ depending on the severity or type of visual impairment. Some students with visual impairments use magnifiers and larger-print texts; stu-

Helpful Supports for Sam

- **Proximity is key.** In the classroom, Sam will need to sit close to see materials. When he reads or works on writing, he will put his head close to his work. This is normal for him and not uncomfortable. If he can hold information (e.g., books, worksheets, paper, manipulatives) close, he can see much better. He needs to get close to things and people—let him position his head and body in whatever way he chooses. He needs to get close to people to see facial expressions.

- **Visual fatigue.** This is a big issue. It is tiring to use so much extra effort to see. He may tire more easily when doing complex visual tasks (e.g., small font, fuzzy images, hidden pictures, word search). Let him take breaks as necessary. Hours of school followed by a lot of homework is exhausting.

- **Reading and writing.** We are continually learning what helps Sam with reading and writing. Enlarged font size and clarity of images are essential in providing Sam equal access. He is doing much of his independent reading on the tablet. He also needs print enlarged, and he sometimes uses the command center. We know he has difficulty with a font that is smaller than 24-36 point. He does most of his reading and writing on his tablet and sometimes uses a handheld magnifier. Using a magnifier is tiring and takes extra time. Typed or printed work is better than handwritten.

- **Optimal learning.** The best type of learning for Sam is active learning with hands-on experiences. Sitting in a large group is visually fatiguing for him. Sam does well with consistent routines and when concepts, themes, materials, and directions are clearly explained. Sam picks up oral direction quickly.

- **Whole-class instruction.** Allow Sam to preview books or visual materials before they are used in a large-group setting. The Join Me app has been very helpful. When you write on the board, read it out loud. Allow extra time for the effort of seeing. Use Sam's name when calling on him; he might miss a nod or a gesture. Reading expressions from a distance can be difficult. Seeing the board items can be difficult. Descriptive verbal instructions need to be paired with gestures or visuals. It is important that his command center be well integrated in the classroom space and routines.

- **Time to see.** Sam needs more time to see. Sometimes, it takes Sam a longer time to focus on what he is looking at. This is simply because the eye movement means his eyes are focused for less time.

- **Partner/small-group work.** Sam should be included in small-group instruction and partner work. When working with others, he will need his own copy of materials. It is nearly impossible for someone with nystagmus to share materials because he needs to position materials specifically so he can see.

- **Computer use.** Sam uses computers well. Enlarging the cursor helps Sam. Computers are very adjustable and by increasing the font size and being able to sit close to the screen, he can do most operations. Currently, he uses his tablet for much of his reading and writing.

- **Viewing movies and assemblies.** When Sam watches television at home, he sits very close—his eye doctors have informed us that this is very common for kids with nystagmus, and he should be allowed to sit as close as he needs. If he is separate from classmates, he should have a partner/friend of his choice. He also needs to sit in front for assemblies in order to see what is happening. We defer to him about how to make this not stigmatizing, and he should be able to bring a friend if this will require not being with the rest of the class.

- **Physical education.** Sam should be involved in all activities. Fast-moving objects and ball sports require explicit instruction and caution. Please let us know if he is having any difficulty with these. Sam is on the modified soccer team and enjoys skiing, running, swimming, and biking. He will often bike to school.

- **Music.** Music needs to be enlarged. Otherwise, Sam really likes music and is a strong auditory learner. He has excelled at the trombone, enjoyed drama and men's choir last year, and is enjoying singing in chorale this year.

- **Art.** Sam is creative and perceptive about the world. This can transfer to art if he receives instruction and encouragement to do detailed artwork.

- **Explaining to peers.** Over the years, Sam has found it helpful to have teachers explain his vision, accommodations, and tools to his peers. Sam will indicate when he is comfortable and ready to have this conversation with his peers. Mrs. Jones can help with this conversation. It is important that peers are allowed to touch and use Sam's vision aids (e.g., tablet, command center, magnifiers) so as not to stigmatize him.

- **Sam knows best.** The most important thing to know is that Sam is very comfortable telling people what he needs when he cannot see something. We have let him know it is okay to say that he cannot see something. Please encourage this by allowing him to move closer or visually inspect the materials. If you are not sure about something, ask Sam. He understands his own preferences and vision quite well.

- **Most important.** Please remember that in all ways, Sam is a typical 12-year-old. Be careful not to overdo it and provide undue attention to his visual needs. Vision is needed for socialization and friendships too. Help him navigate this.

We are open and appreciate any communication and/or questions about Sam and his vision. We look forward to being involved in his classroom. Do not hesitate to ask us for ideas or for help. Thank you!

Julie and George

Figure 3.1.   Helpful supports for Sam (a letter from Sam's parents).

dents who have no vision receive mobility training (or training on how to walk around their environment) and instruction in how to read braille.

Learn From the Experts   *Would I change my vision if I could? No, it makes me who I am, I am awesome! I have more technology, and of course less vision. But, I am proud of who I am and all I have accomplished.* —Sam *(personal communication, March 18, 2020)*

Figure 3.1 is an example of a letter that Sam's parents sent to his teacher every year to provide some guidance about how to best support him. Not all students require this, but these might be useful examples of supports.

Summary

Individuals may have a single disability or multiple disabilities, yet the most important thing to know about them is that they are people first and they experience disability second. Get to know the individual students, their strengths, their gifts, and what makes them light up. Consider the disability-specific knowledge second, and always be sure that the student and the team are helping you to design any supports you provide.

QUICK QUIZ

After learning about each of the categories of disabilities, how many of the 13 categories can you remember?

Distribution of Students With Disabilities in Each Category

How many students qualify for each of the different types of disabilities? The graph shown in Figure 3.2 depicts the percentages of students who receive special education services from ages 6 to 21 and the percentages of students who fall under each of the categories of disabilities. As Figure 3.2 indicates, the high-incidence (or most common) disabilities are SLDs, speech and language disabilities, autism, IDs, and other health impairments. The rest of the categories are considered low incidence (or not as common).

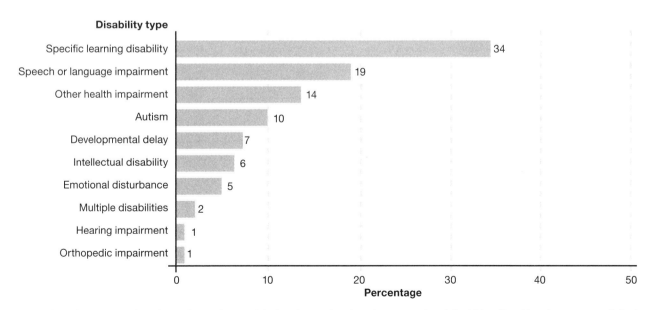

Figure 3.2.   Percentages of students who receive special education services based on categories of disabilities. Visual impairment, traumatic brain injury, and deafblindness are not shown because they each account for less than 0.5% of students served under the Individuals with Disabilities Education Act. (*Source:* U.S. Department of Education, Office of Special Education Programs, Individuals with Disabilities Education Act [IDEA] database and National Center for Education Statistics, National Elementary and Secondary Enrollment Projection Model, 1972 through 2029.)

REFLECTIONS

Think about the students you support. Do you know what special education label they have? Do you understand how that disability manifests in the child's day or life? Do you understand the unique gifts and talents of this student?

FAQs

Commonly Asked Questions About Special Education

Q. How can I learn about the students I am supporting?

A. Start by reading each student's IEP. Ask the teacher with whom you are working to show you a copy of the IEP. This document and its contents are confidential and not to be shared with others, but as the paraprofessional you can have access to a student's IEP. You can also get to know the student by asking questions about their likes, dislikes, interests, and struggles.

Here are some questions that would be helpful when getting to know a student:

- What do you want me to know about you?
- What do you like about school?
- What don't you like about school?
- What do you enjoy doing outside of school?
- Would you tell me about your friends?
- How do you prefer to be supported?
- What do you need from me?
- What don't you want me to do?

You can also ask the classroom teacher for insights about the type of support the student needs. Here are some questions you could ask:

- What is motivating for this student?
- What does this student enjoy?
- Would you tell me about this student's friends?
- How can we support this student's social needs?
- What are this student's academic needs?
- How can we best support this student's academic needs?
- Does this student have any challenging behavior?
- How can we best support this student's behavior?
- Does this student have sensory needs of which I need to be aware?
- Does this student have communication needs that I might need to know?

- What modifications does this student use?

- Does this student use assistive technology?

- What else do I need to know about this student?

Q. I do not feel that I am trained to do my job. How can I get some training?

A. The simple answer is, you should ask. Start with your building principal or the head of special education in your school. The following elements could be included in an e-mail, phone call, or letter to your supervisors:

- Be specific about the type of training you need. For example, you could say, "In my current position, I need to know more about working with students with autism."

- Ask whether they know of any training that is being offered, or ask whether they could hire someone to come in to work with the school or team.

> Understanding disability is critical to understanding the larger systems of special education.

Conclusion

Understanding disability is critical to understanding the larger systems of special education. Nonetheless, the only way to truly understand certain individual students and how their disability impacts them is to get to know each individual student. Reading the definitions of the 13 federal categories of disability is just the first step to beginning to understand the wonderful and complex students you support. Having covered some of the basics of inclusive and special education, we move next to the joyful work of helping you to learn about working with a team to support students effectively.

To Do

TO-DO LIST

After reading this chapter . . .

- Complete the reflections in the chapter.

- Review your responses to the quiz regarding the 13 federal categories of disability. Now, take some time to review the useful supports we have identified for each category. Do you notice any themes?

- In the Commonly Asked Questions section, review the questions we provide to help you get to know your student and understand how to best support them. Write down the answers you already know. Then, make a plan for asking the remaining questions.

- Write down all of your specific questions about this chapter. Then, identify who or what you might seek out to learn the answers.

Collaborating With Others

Working Within a Team

All students in a classroom community can benefit from a team of educators, which includes paraprofessionals and teachers working together in ways that promote meaningful learning and a sense of belonging for all students. In an inclusive classroom, the supporting adults all together can do something quite wonderful. In today's inclusive classrooms, it is quite common for general education teachers and special education teachers to work alongside paraprofessionals. This chapter provides information and tools that will enable paraprofessionals to engage in effective collaboration. In some cases, however, teachers and paraprofessionals work in isolation. Some common problems that arise from this are that paraprofessionals, who can sometimes have unclear roles in the classroom, feel undervalued or are left alone to determine student expectations and classroom policies.

This chapter will help you to clarify your role as a member of the larger teaching team and address the roles and responsibilities of each team member. We propose general ways to communicate with the whole teaching team, co-supporting structures, and strategies for handling conflict. Then, we discuss some of the ethical considerations of confidentiality inherent in the job of the paraprofessional. Finally, we address commonly asked questions about collaboration.

I ask those that teach, is it your ideal to provide what you love to teach to all who desire to learn? If so, basic steps are to presume every person able and anxious to learn, and then to strengthen the supportive systems they need to do so, and to always communicate and collaborate to vitally feel the sense of success and freedom that being a true teacher can bring. —Jamie (Syracuse University alumni who has autism) .

General Approach to Team Members

Remember that the team members you work with are your colleagues. They are as diverse and unique as the students you support. Be sure to approach each and every team member with respect and an understanding of the unique perspectives they bring. Each has a different type and level of education. See what you can learn from each and every colleague because everyone brings a unique skill set to the table.

Roles and Responsibilities

Roles and responsibilities of school staff vary among schools, districts, and even states. Despite these variations, there are generally accepted roles and responsibilities that hold true from school to school. The next section provides general guidelines for how school personnel can work effectively as a team to meet the needs of all students together.

The Teaching Team

Throughout an entire school day, I collaborate and work with dozens of people. I work closely with my fourth-grade team, the [general education] teacher, the special education teacher, and the program assistant. I also work with the speech and language clinician, the psychologist, the occupational therapist, the physical therapist, and, of course, I work closely with all of the special area teachers: music, art, physical education. Across the day, I have hundreds of interactions with adults. Sometimes that is the most challenging part of my job.
—Ted (paraprofessional)

The Paraprofessional

Paraprofessionals are expected to perform many different tasks, but supporting students and supporting instruction are the focus of the work you do. Some examples of the essential functions of paraprofessionals include the following:

- Working with a wide range of students with cognitive disabilities and/or multiple disabilities, including transfers, applying adaptive devices, tube feedings, diapering, bathroom assistance, and mobility training
- Maintaining records, including data collection (e.g., charting seizure activities)
- Providing instructional reinforcement to students in the classroom and at community-based sites under the direction of a teacher
- Assisting students individually and in small groups with academic and recreational programming under a teacher's direction
- Monitoring and managing student behavior consistent with behavior management programs
- Developing social skills under a teacher's direction
- Diffusing conflict situations
- Performing other related duties as assigned

The following is an example of a job description taken from a school district in Massachusetts, although your job description may differ. See your school's principal, special education director, or union representative to obtain a copy of your official job description.

Paraprofessionals are an incredible resource at Boston Public Schools, working directly with students of all abilities to support teaching. Paraprofessionals will assist teachers in providing an innovative, high quality education program designed to meet the needs of the children in the Boston Public Schools. Paraprofessionals will work with school staff to create an educational environment in which quality and continuity are key factors in educating the students of the Boston Public Schools.

Responsibilities:

- Supports direct instruction to children individually, in small groups, and in classroom settings
- Provides assistance with classroom activities
- Prepares instructional materials
- Assists in classroom set up and clean up
- Manages individual and classroom behavior, using prescribed approaches
- Supervises students on field trip activities
- Performs other related duties as requested by headmaster/principal

(Boston Public Schools, 2020)

We've also created a sample job description of a paraprofessional based on a comprehensive review of school districts across the country shown in Figure 4.1.

REFLECTIONS

Compare the sample job descriptions from Boston Public Schools and our example in Figure 4.1 to your current job description. What differs between them? Are there any specific questions you have about your own job description? What might you like to add to your job description?

The Special Educator

By definition, a special educator has earned a college degree in teaching. A special educator is partly responsible for designing each student's IEP. Each year, a team of teachers and parents determines each student's goals and objectives and the appropriate special education services. The special education teacher helps to ensure that the goals and objectives on each student's IEP are met. In collaboration with general education teachers and support staff, the special education teacher is responsible for helping to differentiate curricula and instruction and provides and recommends modifications and adaptations that would be appropriate for each student. Special education teachers are also responsible for solving problems that arise in the classroom, evaluating each student's services, and communicating student progress to the team.

The General Educator

A general educator, again, has earned a college degree in education. A general educator plans lessons, teaches these lessons, and assesses each student's skill. A general educator is responsible not only for each student with an IEP but also for all of the students who do not have disabilities. Typically, a general educator is considered the content expert for the particular grade level or subject being taught.

Example Job Description of the Paraprofessional

Reports To: Building Principal and/or designated administrator (e.g., Special Education Supervisor)

Takes Direction From: Principal, Special Education Supervisor, and Special and General Education Teachers

Summary of Job

The paraprofessional works closely with teachers, administrators, and other team members to improve learning for all students, foster inclusive environments, and carry out tasks associated with the teaching process and in meeting program needs. Work is performed under the supervision of general and special educators and the building principal.

Typical Work Responsibilities

- Uses lesson plans to assist in instruction and reinforcement of student learning for individual or small-group instruction as directed by the supervising teacher(s)

- Works with students to reinforce and support learning of materials or skills, including academic, social, and behavioral, initially introduced by the supervising teacher(s)

- Assists in data collection (behavioral, academic, and medical) including progress monitoring of individualized education program (IEP) goals for students

- Provides assistance to students with diverse needs including students with individualized education programs (IEPs), 504 plans, multilingual learners, etc.

- Modifies curriculum and/or instructional activities as directed by the supervising teacher(s) including locating, creating, copying, collating, distributing, and/or grouping materials to support instructional activities

- Assists identified students with transporting materials or supplies as needed

- Assists identified students with specific personal, medical, or physical needs

- Monitors, maintains, and reinforces behavior supports by following district, school, and class-wide behavior supports

- Monitors, maintains, and reinforces behavior supports for individual student behavior support plans created by supervising teacher(s) and other certified personnel (e.g., behavior specialists, inclusion facilitators)

- Supervises students in classrooms, hallways, cafeterias, schoolyards, and gymnasiums, or on field trips

- Provides support for individual students inside and outside the classroom to enable them to fully participate in activities

- Works with other professionals, such as such as a speech language pathologist, social worker, and occupational and physical therapist as directed and needed

- Assist with noninstructional classroom duties, such as snack time, toileting, class change, and clothing routines as directed by the supervising teacher(s)

- Demonstrates ethical behavior and confidentiality of information about students in school environment and community

- Participates in staff development opportunities provided by the district

Figure 4.1. Job description of the paraprofessional.

The Family

Family members are undoubtedly the most important people in a child's life. With the reauthorization of IDEA 2004, parents/guardians became equal members of students' IEP teams. Parents/guardians are expected to be active members of their children's education because they know their children better than anyone else. Teachers and paraprofessionals can help parents play active roles by communicating all that happens in the school setting and, furthermore, by listening closely to the wishes and concerns of family members. Remember that families are all different and unique. It is important to look at and see every family through a strengths-based perspective. Although a family may differ from your own family of origin, it is critical that you remain professional, positive, and caring when communicating directly with or about families.

Be open to the beauty of parent knowledge, vision, and undying motivation for their child to be included. Help parents learn to advocate without angry fighting. Assist parents in understanding the beauty of their teachers and schools and to be able to hear the viewpoint of school confines and restrictions. React to problems not with no's and can't, but with creativity! It is a process and a long-term relationship. —Kim (a parent of a student with a disability who is included in general education)

Occupational Therapists

Occupational therapy is a related service and is provided by a qualified and licensed occupational therapist (OT). OTs provide these services across the life span and focus on supporting their clients through everyday activities to participate in the things they want and need to do. For a student who requires the support of an OT, the student's disability typically necessitates support in motor functioning. The OT may evaluate the student's needs, provide therapy, modify classroom equipment, and generally help the student participate as fully as possible in school programs and activities. An OT may work with children individually or lead small groups. OTs also may consult with teachers and paraprofessionals to help students meet their goals within the context of general education settings. Specific types of therapies may include help with handwriting, typing, and computer work; fostering social play; and teaching life skills such as getting dressed or eating with utensils. The difference between the role of OT and physical therapist (PT) can be confusing; in general, OTs work more with fine motor skills, and PTs work more with gross motor skills.

Occupational Therapy Assistants

Some OTs have assistants who are responsible for carrying out therapy plans, supporting students in classrooms and the school environment, keeping track of data for the IEP goals, and supporting self-care needs. These assistants work under the direction of certified OTs.

Physical Therapists

Physical therapy, like occupational therapy, is a related service and is provided by a qualified and licensed PT. PTs address areas such as gross motor development skills, physical concerns, mobility, adaptive equipment, positioning needs, and other functional skills that may interfere with students' educational performance. Similar to an OT, a PT either works with individual students or leads small groups. PTs also consult with teachers and paraprofessionals. Specific types of therapies include stair safety, trunk support, stretching and standing after sitting in a wheelchair, or helping the student gain access to gross motor physical skills.

Speech-Language Pathologists

Speech-language pathologists (SLPs; sometimes called speech pathologists) help students with communication and with all of the skills required to communicate effectively. These skills include all issues related to language, the voice, swallowing, and fluency. Some students who work with SLPs have issues with stuttering. Others work on understanding and producing language. In schools, SLPs collaborate with teaching teams to support classroom activities and effective communication.

School Psychologists

The primary role of school psychologists is to help children and youth succeed academically, socially, and emotionally. School psychologists have graduate degrees in a specialist program or doctoral degrees and must be credentialed in the state where they work. School psychologists work closely with teaching teams, families, and other mental health professionals to improve academic achievement, promote positive behavior and mental health, create healthy and safe learning environments, and strengthen connections between each student's home and school. Psychologists assess students and are often involved in standardized testing to determine whether a student qualifies as having a disability. Psychologists also work directly with others on teaching teams by helping to problem solve and, at times, may provide direct support services to students.

Social Workers

Like psychologists, school social workers are trained mental health professionals whose primary role in schools is to help children and youth succeed academically, socially, and emotionally. Social workers help provide links connecting each student's home, school, and community. The services provided by social workers are intended to help enable students and families to overcome problems that may impede learning. School social workers provide individual and group counseling, consult with teachers, and teach or encourage social skills. They collaborate with community agencies and provide service coordination for students who require many different agencies or services.

Vision Teachers/Audiologists

Vision teachers support students who have visual impairments or blindness. Vision teachers typically work with classroom teachers to make modifications and adaptations to the curricula. They also help provide needed equipment like magnifiers and computer equipment.

QUICK QUIZ

Name all of the specialists you are likely to work with in your current position.

Audiologists typically work with students who have hearing impairments, providing amplification systems and sign language interpreters for students who are deaf.

ACTIVITIES

ACTIVITY: Service Providers Web Diagram

Create a specific team web for every student you support. Create a visual (web diagram) with the student in the middle and each of the student's related service providers and contact information. This will help you keep track of all of the individual team members that work with each individual student.

How Do All These People Work Together?

Coming together is a beginning; keeping together is progress; working together is a success. —Edward Everett Hale

Every school differs, but one thing is certain: all the adults on a teaching team must work together for the purpose of promoting student growth. One example of effective collaboration involves a seventh-grade team.

This team involves all of the staff who support Adam, a student with autism and a visual impairment. The core team of people supporting Adam in English class includes the English teacher, the vision teacher, the special education teacher, and a paraprofessional. This team meets monthly to discuss Adam's support in English class. Every week, the vision teacher and the English teacher meet with the paraprofessional to create enlarged materials or to upload digital materials on his tablet. In addition, the special education teacher and the English teacher plan lessons together with Adam in mind so that each lesson is designed to meet Adam's needs. For example, they planned a unit using a book from the Harry Potter series, which Adam particularly enjoys. In addition to having the paraprofessional enlarge the text in the packet of information, the teacher decided to have the entire class listen to a digital version of the book instead of reading silently. The paraprofessional receives written plans each day. This plan outlines the anticipated type and level of support that Adam needs during each activity.

Guiding Questions for Team Discussion

Getting to know your teammates on a personal level is necessary for real and true collaboration to occur. Understanding a bit about your colleagues' work styles and philosophies will help you to better understand how to collaborate effectively. Some questions that will help you as you sit down with a teacher or group of teachers are listed in this section. You may approach this list as some simple suggestions, or you may decide to go through each question with your team.

Work Styles

Understanding the preferred working styles of the educators you work alongside can help you to better understand how and when they prefer to communicate. This knowledge leads to more effective communication, feedback, and collaboration for you and them.

- What do you consider your strengths and weaknesses when working in a team situation?
- Are you a morning or an afternoon person?
- How direct are you?
- Do you like to do several things at once, or do you prefer doing one thing at a time?
- How do you prefer to get and give feedback to others on the team?

Philosophy

Understanding the educational philosophies of the educators you work alongside can help you to better understand the choices they make in lesson planning, during collaboration, and while supporting students. This knowledge will help you to support more effectively those colleagues and the students.

- To me, *advanced planning* means . . .
- All students learn best when . . .
- I think the best way to deal with challenging behavior is . . .
- I think it is important to increase student independence by . . .
- I think our team relationship needs to be . . .

Logistics

Understanding the logistics and setting expectations for your work with educators help to create much clearer and more effective collaboration. If neither you nor the educator knows the answer to these questions, it will be important to discuss them with an administrator who can provide guidance.

- How should we communicate about students' history and progress?
- How should we communicate about our roles and responsibilities?
- How and when should we communicate about lessons and modifications?
- If I do not know an answer in class, should I direct the student to you?
- Do we meet often enough? If not, when should we meet?
- How do we communicate with the families? What is each person's role in this?
- Are there other logistical concerns?

Questions for the Family

Understanding the family's expectations around communication as well as the hopes and dreams and concerns they have for their child is key to successfully supporting the student. As a paraprofessional, you can bring these questions to the teaching team so that the educators can share them directly with the family. And although you may not always be able to attend IEP meetings, it is critical that you are knowledgeable regarding the family's answers to these questions.

- How would you like to communicate about your child's progress?
- If we are using a communication notebook or e-mail, how often would you like to hear from the school?
- Are there things you are especially interested in hearing about?
- What are your long-term hopes and dreams for your child?
- What are your child's strengths and successes?
- Is there information that would be helpful for the school team to understand?

Questions for the Student

Understanding your students and their preferences for support is one of the most important aspects of your role as a paraprofessional. Discussing these questions with your students helps you to support them more effectively and appropriately and communicates to the students that you respect their autonomy and value their ideas.

- What are your greatest strengths?
- How do you learn best?
- What are your favorite activities in school? What about outside of school?
- How should we support you during a challenging moment?
- How can we support your connections with friends and classmates?
- How often would you like to check in about your progress?
- How would you like to communicate with teachers about progress (e.g., meetings, e-mail, text messages)?

After having personal discussions using these questions as a guide, teams are better able to negotiate the logistical and philosophical components of teamwork, allowing team members to feel more comfortable in knowing the roles and expectations within the classroom setting. In addition, before working with a specific student, you may need to directly ask for information from the team to help you to best support that student.

The next section describes some co-teaching and co-supporting arrangements that should give further clarity to the collaborative work of adults in and outside of the classroom.

ACTIVITY: 10 Questions

ACTIVITIES

What follows are 10 questions you should ask the special education or general education teacher before working with a particular student. Hold a meeting to be sure that you know the answer to each of these questions about each student you support.

10 questions you should ask before working with a student:

1. Can I read this student's IEP?
2. What other information should I know about this student?

3. Can you help me understand their academic strengths?

4. Can you help me understand their behavioral needs?

5. Are there any mobility issues to understand?

6. Are there any communication needs to consider?

7. What are the student's strengths, gifts, and talents?

8. What are this student's interests outside of school?

9. Are there any specific support needs this student has?

10. Is there any important background information that I should know?

Co-Supporting Arrangements for Paraprofessionals

Because paraprofessionals generally do not introduce or teach new content, we have adapted some co-teaching arrangements from Friend and Bursuck (2019) and have created some co-supporting arrangements that paraprofessionals can use in their work settings.

One Teach–One Observe

While the teacher is teaching, you might observe and take data on student performance. You could also collect information on the students' behavior.

One Teach–One Support

While the teacher is instructing the large group, you might provide support to all students in the class. You could answer questions or bring students back to attention. Consider writing or drawing examples on the chalkboard. If a student whom you support has significant needs (e.g., a seizure disorder, medical needs that require proximity), you will want to remain close to the student. For the most part, however, you should help all students even if you have been assigned to work with only one.

Station Facilitation

It is perfectly fine for a paraprofessional to run a small group or a station. It is important, however, for paraprofessionals first to receive instructions on how to run these stations (preferably in the form of a lesson plan, Google document, or task card). A paraprofessional should, at minimum, know the goal of the station, how to instruct the students, and what modifications or adaptations should be used with individual students.

Co-Support

Table 4.1. Ideas for providing engaged support

If the teacher is doing this:	You can be doing this:
Taking attendance	Collecting and reviewing homework
Providing large-group instruction	Collecting data on student behavior or engagement, or making modifications for an upcoming lesson
Giving a test	Reading the test to students who prefer to have the test read to them
Facilitating stations or small groups	Also facilitating stations or groups
Facilitating sustained, silent reading	Reading aloud quietly with a small group
Teaching a new concept	Providing visuals or models to enhance the whole group's understanding
Reteaching or pre-teaching with the small group	Monitoring the large group as they work independently

Source: Murawski and Dieker (2004).

Table 4.2. Multisensory co-support ideas

While one person . . .	The other . . .
Reads a book	• Acts it out dramatically • Creates a puppet show • Draws the action on the white board
Presents verbal information	• Holds up props or pictures to visually reinforce the content • Acts it out • Uses puppets or other manipulatives to bring the content to life • Draws it out on the white board
Conducts a discussion	• Writes or draws the ideas presented using sketch noting • Moves from student to student with a microphone so students can share their thoughts in an interview style
Explains directions to an activity	• Writes down each step clearly • Gives specific directions to peers or table captains • Creates visual cues • Uses puppets or manipulatives to act out the directions

Another common type of support is called *co-support.* While the teacher is leading the large group, you can ask clarifying questions or provide examples. Table 4.1 shows types of co-support you might provide in different situations as suggested by Murawski and Dieker (2004).

One Teach–One Make Multisensory

This new type of co-supporting structure first debuted in the book *30 Days to the Co-Taught Classroom* (Kluth & Causton, 2016), and it makes great use of an additional adult in a classroom by utilizing the second person to give students new access points of learning. Table 4.2 provides examples of options for one-teach–one-provides multisensory co-support.

ACTIVITY: Co-Support

Specifically ask your educators how they would like you to co-support students. If need be, show them the ideas discussed in this chapter.

ACTIVITIES

Addressing Conflict and Communication

The kids aren't the hard part of my job. It is working with other adults that I find most challenging. Sometimes I am not sure of my role. In some classrooms I feel like part of the class. In other classrooms it seems like [the teacher] doesn't know really what I should be doing. —Pam (paraprofessional)

Ideal team functioning is like a well-oiled machine in which every cog runs continually and smoothly, each harmoniously performing an individual function for the good of the entire machine. However, team functioning does not always feel this smooth. Conflicts among adults do arise.

DEFINITIONS

The Bonner Foundation has suggested eight steps for conflict resolution. *Conflict* is defined as "a mental or physical disagreement in which people's values or needs are in opposition to each or they think that they are opposed" (Bonner Foundation, 2008). The Bonner Foundation's suggestions for handling conflicts are listed here:

1. Identify positions (ask, "What are they saying?") of each side of the people involved in conflict. Write down your perspective and the other person's perspective.

2. Learn more about true needs and desires behind each side. Write down your beliefs about the other person's needs and desires. Write down your own needs and desires.

3. Ask clarifying questions for more information. Ask the other person, "Why do you feel the way you do?" "What do you feel you need in this situation?" Reframe the problem into a question.

4. Brainstorm possible solutions. Without judging the merit of the ideas, write down as many ideas as you can.

5. Discuss how each solution would affect each side and figure out possible compromises. Talk through each of the potential solutions. Discuss which solutions would work and would not work from your perspective and from the other person's perspective. Generate more ideas if necessary.

6. Agree on a solution. Determine which solution would work the best for both of you. Write out a plan for carrying out the solution, and determine how long you plan to implement the solution.

7. Implement solutions. Give your idea a try for the determined amount of time.

8. Reevaluate solutions if necessary. Come back together to discuss the solution and what is working or not working about this solution. Continue the process as necessary.

ACTIVITIES

ACTIVITY: Conflict Resolution

Think of a small conflict in your life. It can be personal or professional. Review the eight steps for handling conflict. Now, practice each step by writing down your responses.

When you use this in your school setting, you will be working with at least one other person. However, this individual activity will give you practice with the conflict-solving process.

Making Time to Communicate

We have worked with thousands of paraprofessionals across the country, and one of the most common problems they mention involves not having enough time to communicate or collaborate with the teachers with whom they work. Different teaching teams have solved this problem by using several strategies. Each strategy is described in the following list. Examine each strategy and determine whether it will help your team communicate more regularly and more effectively.

The following strategies have been successfully used to carve out more meeting time:

- *Independent work time*—Create a weekly meeting time during which students are expected to watch instructional videos or to work independently for 15 minutes while the team meets.

- *Use a parent volunteer*—As a parent volunteer reads a book to the students or leads a review game, meet together for 15 minutes.

- *Use another teacher team*—Put two classrooms together for a half hour each week for a certain portion of the curriculum or community-building activities. One teaching team supervises the students while the other team meets. The teams then switch and each has an opportunity to meet.

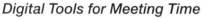

- *Meet during specials (e.g., music, physical education) time*—Ask the specials teachers whether their classes have any 15-minute periods that might not require paraprofessional support. Use that time to meet together.

- *Meet before or after school time*—Take 15 minutes before or after school to have a sacred meeting time for teaching teams.

Digital Tools for Meeting Time

If you simply cannot use any of these strategies to elicit more face-to-face times, some teams have come up with alternatives to meeting face to face.

STRATEGIES

- *Google Docs.* The team has a Google document that everyone checks each day. This way the team information is kept confidential and everyone gets the information they need.

- *Communication notebook.* Establish a notebook that all members of the team read and respond to each day. Team members can write questions in the notebook and obtain responses. Notebooks also can be used to discuss schedules or student-specific information.

- *E-mail.* E-mail can be substituted for the communication notebook; team members can contact each other with questions, comments, or schedule changes.

- *Proofread.* As notes are written that go home to the students' parents, have the teaching team proofread each of the notes. This way, not only are the notes proofread, but everyone receives all of the necessary information.

- *Lesson plan sharing.* Keep lesson plans electronically and share with all members of the team. Use the notes to communicate about upcoming content. Ask the person who writes the plans to delineate each team

What materials will be needed to adapt daily curriculum for students? Who will prepare those materials?	What is the process of instruction this week? • Small groups? • Computers? • Lecture? • Independent? Where will students sit so that they are most included?	What activities/days can Gloria come in to support David and Pat?	How will Pat co-support during the lesson and activities this week?
• For this week, I (David) have most already prepared. • It would be good if Pat prepares modified task cards for her students to use during the marshmallow project.	• Individual work Wednesday (9/5) • Group work Friday (9/7) • We are making catapults to launch marshmallows on Friday, and students will be in small groups. • I've put the two students Pat supports in separate groups with strong peers.	• Gloria, you may want to come in Friday because for half of the class it won't be structured time. During this unstructured time, students will be creating their marshmallow launchers. However, don't feel you need to—I think Pat and I have got it!	• Pat visualizes directions and big ideas during mini-lecture on 9/5. • Pat floats to support all small groups on Friday during project time.

Figure 4.2. Collaborative team weekly instructional plan. *Key:* Pat, paraprofessional; Gloria, special education teacher; David, general education science teacher.

member's role for each lesson in separate columns. Figure 4.2 provides an example of how one team we know uses a collaborative lesson plan for the week shared via Google Docs. We have also provided a reproducible version that you can download and/or photocopy (Figure 4.3).

Even with all of these possible communication strategies in mind, we know it can be difficult to take the first step to let your general and special education teachers know that you'd like to meet with them. We recommend asking to meet with the teachers you work with in order to discuss these possible communication structures so that you can plan to best support your teachers and students.

ACTIVITIES

ACTIVITY: Initiating Communication

Draft a brief e-mail you will send, or write out a script of the short conversation you will have with your teachers, about scheduling a meeting to discuss communication structures and options. Feel free to use the sample letter in Figure 4.4 as a template.

Ethical Considerations: Confidentiality

I work with a student who has had some pretty big behavioral blow-ups. Everyone in our town knows that I work with him. I often get questions in the grocery store or when I am out to dinner about the student I support. I want to tell the person it is none of their business. But instead I have to politely say, "I am not allowed to share information about the students that I support." There is a fair amount of pressure to gossip about students. I have to remain very professional and keep the student's information confidential. —Donna (paraprofessional)

Confidentiality is one of the most crucial aspects of the job of a paraprofessional. You are an ambassador of the school district. As you do your job, you will have to be careful when others ask questions about school situations. Many parents and community members might ask for details about

Hi Gloria and David,

I'm currently reading **The Paraprofessional's Handbook** and learning all sorts of great ways we could regularly communicate about how I can support you and our students. Would we be able to meet for 15 or 30 minutes during RISE time to develop a plan for communication and supports?

Looking forward to it!

Pat

Figure 4.4. Sample letter for initiating conversations.

Collaborative Team Weekly Instructional Plan

What materials are needed to adapt the daily curriculum for students? Who will prepare those materials?	What is the process of instruction this week? • Small groups? • Computers? • Lecture? • Independent? Where will students sit so that they are most included?	How will the paraprofessional co-support teacher(s) during the lessons this week?	Are any other supports needed?

Figure 4.3. Blank collaborative team weekly instructional plan.

You are an ambassador of the school district.

student behavior, disability, or activities. Think of ways to deflect potentially inappropriate personal questions. For example, a parent approaches you and says, "I notice you work with Lucy. Why does she need a walker?" What would you say in response? Consider saying something such as, "I am sorry, but school confidentiality does not allow me to talk about that." Then, direct the parent to someone with whom they can talk: "Feel free to ask the general education teacher, special education teacher, or principal."

REFLECTIONS

What confidentiality questions can you anticipate?
Script an answer to those questions.

FAQs

Commonly Asked Questions About Collaboration

Q. **I am not sure what I am supposed to be doing in art class. I have never had a conversation with the art teacher, so mostly I just sit and support two students. What should I do?**

A. Set up a time to meet with the art teacher. Ask questions such as, "How can I be most useful to the students in this class?" "When you are giving directions, how can I best support you?" "When the students are working on a project, what would you like me to do, and what would you like me not to do?" These kinds of conversations are crucial in any classroom in which you will be providing support.

Q. **I have read about common support arrangements, but we do not use any of them; instead, I just sit and support or walk around and support. How can I suggest that we use these strategies?**

A. Show your teacher the arrangements. Begin a conversation asking whether the arrangements might be useful to your team.

Q. **What if I feel uncomfortable with a role I have been assigned?**

A. Communicate your concerns to your teaching team. The role might not have to be changed; it could be shared. If you feel you are being asked to do something outside the scope of your job, talk to the teaching team first and then to your principal or director of special education.

Q. **What is confidential about my job?**

A. Consider this question: If this were me, or my child, would I want this information shared with others? Err on the side of always maintaining confidentiality. As a guideline, sharing anything about your student (e.g., academic performance, behavior, stories, or otherwise) is a violation of their privacy. If you are not sure, check to see what is outlined in your school policy and what your team deems confidential.

Q. **What do I do on the spot when someone asks me something that is confidential?**

A. Prepare and practice catch phrases in advance, such as, "Mrs. Keen would be the person to ask."

Conclusion

Working as a team member and within a school setting can be challenging, but it also can be rewarding. Understanding each team member's roles, including your own, can bring clarity to your work. Learning more information about each of your teammates is essential to building trust among your team. Furthermore, using common co-supporting arrangements can clarify specific roles and responsibilities within the classroom. Communication is key. The more effectively you communicate and solve conflicts as you work together, the better your team will function, enabling you to deliver more seamless support to students. The next chapter focuses on how to rethink students in terms of their strengths, gifts, and talents so that they can reach their full academic potential.

TO-DO LIST

To Do

After reading this chapter . . .

- Complete the activities and reflections in the chapter.
- Ask the appropriate team members any questions you have so that you are certain of everyone's roles and responsibilities.
- Reread your own job description and be sure you are clear on all that it requires of you.
- Discuss co-supporting with your teachers.
- Create a team web for each of the students you work with and all their related service providers.
- Make sure you have asked the 10 important questions for each student you support.

5

Rethinking Your Students

Presuming Competence

A lot of different flowers make a bouquet.

—Muslim Proverb

I have been a paraprofessional for 23 years. The biggest surprise to me is that these students are really smart. When I began working . . . we would have them practice writing their name and address every day, they would work on matching colors to these plastic bears—and the kids hated doing the same things over and over.

Then we got a new teacher, and things changed! We were now expected to take these same kids into classrooms like algebra and physics. I thought [the teacher] was crazy (laughing) . . . But, I will never forget the day I was supporting Daniel. I gave him the calculator to figure out the problem . . . and it was a hard problem too. He pushed the calculator away, refusing to use it, and he wrote the answer down. I checked it. He was right! It made me want to cry. Who knows what we have done to kids like Daniel in the past, and who knows just what kids like Daniel can do!? —Chantel (paraprofessional)

This chapter introduces the concept of *rethinking students*. Rethinking a student entails getting to know as much as you can about the student and then reflecting on how you see, treat, and work with them. First, we discuss the importance of rethinking our students, particularly those who are marginalized and most vulnerable. Then, we describe how to talk about students with others, such as your colleagues, using student strengths and multiple intelligences. This chapter also shares the important concepts of presumption of competence and using age-appropriate and person-first language. Finally, we conclude by discussing ways to celebrate diversity.

Supporting Our Most Vulnerable Students

Across our nation's schools, our most vulnerable student groups are at greater risk for poorer academic, behavioral, and social and emotional outcomes than many of their peers. Students with disabilities, students of color, and LGBTQIA+ students are graduating at lower rates and are suspended, excluded, and expelled at higher rates than their nondisabled, white, and cisgendered peers (U.S. Department of Education Office of Civil Rights, 2016). These same vulnerable populations of students are also subjected to bias-based bullying, which puts them at a higher risk for negative emotional and physical health effects (Rosenthal et al., 2015). Even though these educational issues are overwhelming, we can begin to retrain ourselves on how we think about our students in order to better support them throughout the school day. Our students deserve adults who care deeply about positive, holistic outcomes and who are ready to celebrate diversity, rethink negative descriptors, and approach students from a strength-based perspective.

ACTIVITIES

ACTIVITY: Student Descriptions

You are about to read two different descriptions of the same student. Take a look at these next two paragraphs. What are the differences in the two descriptions? What do you notice?

Description 1

Shawntell Strully is a 22-year-old who lives in her own home with roommates, attends classes at Colorado State University, volunteers on campus, travels during spring break, gets around in her own car, has her own interests, likes, and desires, has a boyfriend, and speaks out on issues of concern to her. (Strully & Strully, 1996, pp. 144–145)

Description 2

Shawntell Strully is 22 years old, is severely/profoundly mentally retarded, is hearing impaired, visually impaired, has cerebral palsy, has a seizure disorder, does not chew her food (and sometimes chokes), is not toilet trained, has no verbal communication, has no reliable communication system, and has a developmental age of 17–24 months. (Strully & Strully, 1996, pp. 144–145)

These two radically different descriptions of Shawntell come from two different groups of people. The first description comes from her parents. The second comes from her teachers and other school support personnel. Although not all teachers would describe Shawntell in these ways, this is how her team described her in her IEP. It is surprising to compare these statements side by side. The stark contrast raises the question of how the same person can be described in such disparate ways.

The principal reason for these radically different descriptions is that each group of people looks for different things and approaches Shawntell from a different perspective. Shawntell's parents know her deeply. They have spent a great deal of time with her, know her intimately, and understand her as a person who has wide interests and capabilities. Their description of her cites her interests, gifts, and talents. Conversely, the description generated by Shawntell's teachers reflects a more distant understanding of her; it is a clinical account that focuses exclusively on her challenges and impairments.

Rethink Your Descriptions

As a paraprofessional working with students with disabilities, you will hear impairment-driven descriptions of students, and thus you will need to work instead to understand these students through their strengths, gifts, and talents. You may read a student's IEP, and it might abound with phrases such as

When I approach a child, [s]he inspires in me two sentiments: tenderness for what [s]he is, and respect for what [s]he may become.
—Louis Pasteur
(Institut Pasteur, n.d.)

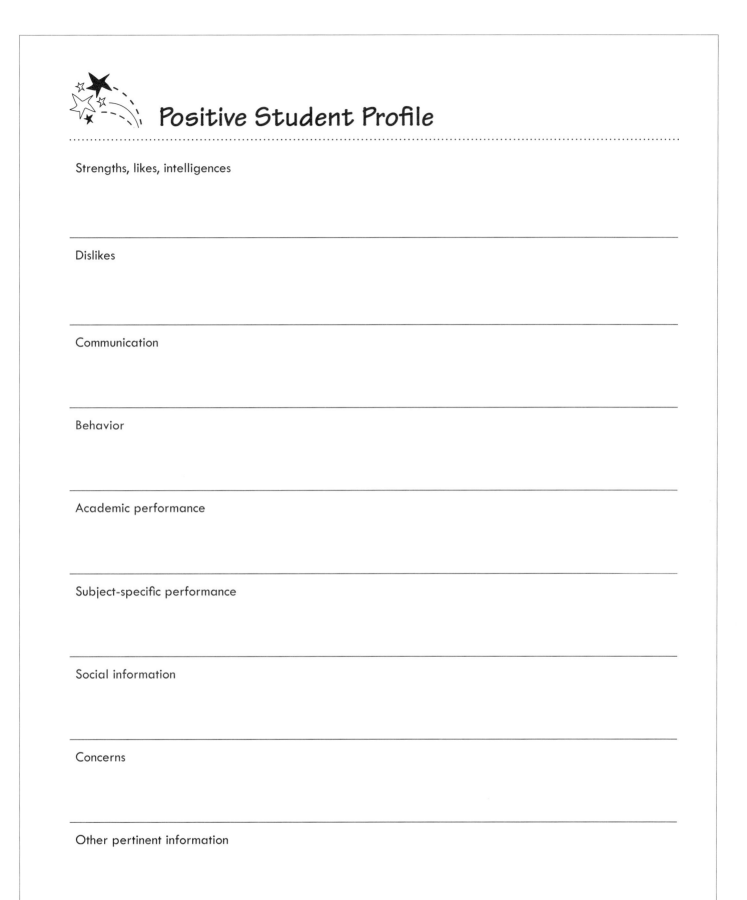

Positive Student Profile

Strengths, likes, intelligences

_____

Dislikes

_____

Communication

_____

Behavior

_____

Academic performance

_____

Subject-specific performance

_____

Social information

_____

Concerns

_____

Other pertinent information

_____

Figure 5.1. Positive student profile.

mental age of 2, phobic, or *aggressive*. Reading those descriptors, you will need to realize that you are getting only one perspective on the student. Get to know the student yourself and learn about what they can actually do. Hopefully, your descriptions of a student would look much closer to the parents' perspective on Shawntell than that of the teachers. Develop a Positive Student Profile (see Figure 5.1) that provides a person-centered, strength-based understanding of the individual.

I like LEGOs. I like Minecraft. I like Star Wars. I like them to do lessons in a fun way. Not just teach it. I like it when teachers give us partners. I want teachers to learn about me as a person, not just a student. —Allyah (middle school student)

I am not a series of deficits to be remediated. —Jamie (Syracuse University student with autism)

Begin With Strengths

We were recently working with a group of paraprofessionals at a middle school and asked them to describe a particular student they were supporting. We would like you to do the same.

ACTIVITIES

ACTIVITY: Descriptors

Think of a student you support, and write down 10 descriptors of this student in the first column in the table.

Student descriptor (before)	Student descriptor (after)

Now, look over the list. Were your descriptors positive, negative, or a combination of both? Circle each of the descriptors that could be considered negative.

If you are not sure, consider if you would like the descriptor to be used when someone is speaking about you. Now rewrite any negative descriptors into the second column of the table by changing them from negative to positive or neutral. For example:

A student who could be considered . . .	Could also be considered . . .
Hyper	An active learner
Lazy	Relaxed
Unfocused	Creative
Demanding	Assertive
Immature	Developing
Emotional	Sensitive
Scattered	A divergent thinker
Anxious	Cautious

Many paraprofessionals shared descriptors such as *autistic, hyperactive, sweet, nonverbal, stubborn,* and *bright.* These descriptions speak to the paraprofessionals' beliefs about their students.

Your beliefs about a student will affect how you support and work with that student. For example, if you believe a student is lazy or defiant, you will approach them in a different way than you will if you believe that the child is motivated or cooperative. You can alter your beliefs about students by spending some time rethinking those beliefs or assumptions. Reframing your conceptions of students in positive ways creates more opportunities for growth.

Thomas Armstrong, an educator, psychologist, and writer (2000a, 2000b), recommended that education professionals purposefully rethink the ways they describe students. Regardless of what field you work in—but especially when working with vulnerable populations—when workers (educators) change their language, they begin to change their impressions. Armstrong emphasized that all behavior is part of the human experience and that behavior is based on a multitude of influences (e.g., environment, sense of safety, personal well-being). Armstrong has proposed that instead of considering a child to be *learning disabled,* people should view the child as *learning differently.*

What would happen if all education professionals changed how they viewed and spoke about students? What if every student were viewed as a capable learner? What if every student was viewed as resourceful and whole? One of the best ways to think about the students whom you support is to look at each child through the lens of their strengths. Ask yourself the following questions: "What can this student do?" "What are this person's strengths?" "How would a parent, who deeply loves this student, speak about them?" Now, return to your list and take a moment to develop a list of strengths, gifts, and interests.

During this same middle school workshop, Kathy, a paraprofessional, did just that. First, she wrote a list of descriptors. Then, after spending some time rethinking her student, she came up with a completely different list. She had originally described the student, Brian, as "lazy, smart, sneaky, a liar, cute, cunning, and mean (at times)." After talking about viewing students differently, she got a new piece of paper. She wrote, "relaxed, intelligent, good in math, cute, needs support with creating positive peer relationships, a great sense of humor, needs support to understand his actions, and has a great smile." We asked Kathy whether this still accurately described Brian. She said that the second list was a much *more* accurate description of him.

Multiple Intelligences

QUICK QUIZ

Without referencing Table 5.1, how many of the intelligences can you recall?

There is a pervasive myth in education that some people are smart and that others are not. *Intelligence, academic potential,* and *competence* are words often used to describe "smartness." In education, this belief can be understood through the system of labeling people with disabilities via IQ testing. Students take IQ tests, and if a student's IQ score falls below 70 and they have other issues with functional skills, the student receives the label of "intellectual disability." Howard Gardner proposed his multiple intelligences (MI) theory (1983), challenging the way psychologists and educators defined *intelligence.* MI theory identifies multiple types of human intelligence that each represent different ways humans process information.

Gardner viewed each of the MIs as a capacity that is inherent in the human brain and that is developed and expressed in social and cultural contexts. Instead of viewing intelligence as a fixed number on an aptitude test, like the IQ test, Gardner argued that every person—regardless of disability label—is smart in different ways. Some people can have incredible abilities in a particular intelligence while experiencing underdeveloped abilities in another intelligence. This theory is extraordinarily useful when educators commit to viewing students in a positive and holistic perspective, similarly to Armstrong's perspective and the positive student profile we discussed earlier in this chapter. MI theory also provides educators with important opportunities to consider all of the different ways that information can be presented to and processed by students. Howard Gardner's eight intelligences are described in Table 5.1. We have also added a column titled "Support Using," which might help you think of the students you support.

ACTIVITY: Multiple Intelligences

ACTIVITIES

Think about a student or students you work with. Write down whether they prefer to learn in a certain intelligence area or whether they have strengths in a certain area. Consider some of the suggested activities and teaching styles from Table 5.1. Make a list of supports that might work for those students.

Presume Competence

In the school setting, assumptions about students can affect their education. Take Sue Rubin, for instance:

Table 5.1.　Multiple intelligences and support ideas

Intelligence	Which means . . .	Support using . . .
Verbal/linguistic intelligence	Good with words and language—written and spoken	Jokes, speeches, readings, stories, essays, the Internet, books, and biographies
Logical mathematical intelligence	Preference for reasoning, numbers, and patterns	Mazes, puzzles, timelines, analogies, formulas, calculations, codes, games, and probabilities
Spatial intelligence	Ability to visualize an object or to create mental images or pictures	Mosaics, drawings, illustrations, models, maps, videos, and posters
Bodily kinesthetic intelligence	Knowledge or wisdom of the body and movement	Role playing, skits, facial expressions, experiments, field trips, sports, and games
Musical intelligence	Ability to recognize tonal patterns including sensitivity to rhythms or beats	Performances, songs, instruments, rhythms, compositions, melodies, raps, jingles, and choral readings
Interpersonal intelligence	Good with person-to-person interactions and relationships	Group projects, group tasks, observation dialogs, conversation, debate, games, and interviews
Intrapersonal intelligence	Knowledge of an inner state of being; effective and aware	Journals, meditation, self-assessment, recording, creative expression, goal setting, affirmation, and poetry
Naturalistic intelligence	Knowledge of the outside world (e.g., plants, animals, weather patterns)	Field trips, observation, nature walks, forecasting, star gazing, fishing, exploring, categorizing, collecting, and identifying

Sue, a student with autism, had no formal way of communicating until she was 13 years old. Before that time, she had been treated and educated as if she had a mental age of 2 years old. Mental age is often based on a person's score on an IQ test. For example, if a 14-year-old girl's score on an IQ were the score of a "typical" or "normal" 3-year-old, she would be labeled as having the mental age of a 3-year-old. This is not a useful way to think about intelligence. When Sue acquired a form of communication called facilitated communication, those long-held assumptions were no longer valid. People began to realize that she was very smart. She subsequently took advanced placement classes all through her high school career, and she is now in college. (Biklen, 2005; Rubin, 2003)

Because education professionals have no real way of determining what a student understands, they should presume that every student is competent and capable of learning. Anne Donnellan, an educational researcher and teacher who specializes in autism, uses the term *least dangerous assumption* to describe this idea: "Least dangerous assumption states that in the absence of absolute evidence, it is essential to make the assumption that, if proven to be false, would be least dangerous to the individual" (Donnellan, 1984, p. 24). In other words, it is always better to presume that students are competent and that they can learn than to expect that they cannot learn.

Biklen and Burke (2006) have described this idea of presuming competence by explaining that outside observers (e.g., teachers, parents, paraprofessionals) have a choice: they can determine either that a person is competent or incompetent. The presumption of competence recognizes that no person can definitively know another person's thinking unless the other person can (accurately) reveal it. As Biklen and Burke put it, "Presuming competence refuses to limit opportunity . . . it casts the teachers, parents, and other [professionals] in the role of finding ways to support the person to demonstrate his or her agency" (p. 167). See Figure 5.2 for a list of strategies for presuming competence.

In addition, because students without reliable communication offer educators and paraprofessionals unique challenges, we have included Figure 5.3 which provides ideas about how to support students who do not communicate verbally.

Developing a Flexible Mindset

Presuming competence goes hand in hand with developing a flexible, or growth, mindset. Mindsets are the assumptions and beliefs that guide our interactions and behaviors with others. According to neurological research (Sapolsky, 2017), our mindsets begin to develop at an early age when our brain's frontal lobes are summarizing and storing our interactions with family, friends, and society at large. All humans develop mindsets about ourselves, our families, the future, jobs, education, politics, religion, and other people. As adults, our mindsets can become very engrained, or fixed, and therefore difficult to change. Depending on your experiences, you may have a particular mindset about what education should look like (e.g., all students in rows, sitting still, listening quietly) or which individuals are considered intelligent (e.g., students who communicate verbally and excel at reading and writing). However, these fixed mindsets limit our students and perpetuate stereotypes. When educational professionals underestimate a student's capacity because of their fixed mindset about disability label, socioeconomic status, gender, language, race, or culture, these professionals are doing significant harm instead of good.

In contrast, one of the most important foundational supports for student success is an educational mentor that believes in the student. Effective teachers and paraprofessionals who develop flexible, or growth, mindsets approach education with the belief that *all* students can succeed. Educators who use a flexible mindset in their work with students are also typically more creative in their support, more understanding of what they need to do to help move a student forward, and more effective at encouraging students to believe in themselves. When you approach students in this way, the students receive consistent signals from you that they can succeed and will be supported. Students who may have previously seen themselves as "not smart" or "not capable" begin to view themselves in a more positive light. This can lead to greater academic, socio-emotional and behavioral outcomes.

Using Age-Appropriate Language

There is a tendency for people to speak down to individuals with disabilities (as if they were younger than they actually are) because of assumptions that people with disabilities are at younger developmental levels. For example, we've heard education professionals ask a high school student, "Do you have to use the potty?" but we would not ask a high school student who did not have a disability that same question in that way. We have also overheard someone describe a young man with Down syndrome who attends college as

Strategies for Presuming Competence

- *Examine your attitude.* Practice saying, "How can this work?" or "How can this child be successful?"

- *Question your stereotypes.* How someone looks, walks, or talks does not tell you about how they think and feel.

- *Use age-appropriate language.* Examine your tone of voice and topic.

- *Support communication.*

- *Listen openly.* Actively work to shed judgments.

- *Teach peers and others how to interpret potentially confusing behavior.*

- *Do not speak in front of someone as if they were not there.*

- *Be inclusive.* In conversation, refer to the person in a way that includes them in the conversation.

- *Ask permission to share information with others.*

- *Be humble.*

- *Allow the student to speak.* If possible, always let the person explain for him- or herself and do not speak for them.

- *Assume that intellectual age is in line with physical age.* Assume that every student will benefit from learning age-appropriate academic curriculum.

- *Look for evidence of understanding.*

- *Allow students to use their individual strengths to demonstrate understanding.* Support students' comprehension by providing opportunities to use individual strengths to master academic topics.

- *Design adaptations and accommodations to support access to academics.*

- *Always acknowledge your student(s).* Be sure to acknowledge the presence of a person with a disability in the same way you would acknowledge others.

Remember, if you want to see competence, it helps if you look for it.

—Douglas Biklen

STRATEGIES

Figure 5.2. Strategies for presuming competence. (*Source:* Kasa-Hendrickson & Buswell, 2007.)

Eleven Tips for Supporting Students Who Do Not Use Verbal Speech

1. *Communication is for everyone.* All students who struggle with communication deserve to have a system in place that allows them to express anything they wish. This system may be sign language, an augmentative communication, or ways to help someone type, point, or direct their gaze to indicate choices.

2. *Presume competence.* All students can benefit from schooling, learn high levels of academics, and desire friendships and connection.

3. *Give students choices all day long.* Allow them to learn that their choices have an impact in their life (e.g., "Do you want water or milk?", "Is this going to be red or purple?").

4. *Always acknowledge the person's presence.* Do not talk about someone as if they were not there; assume they are listening and always assume they understand.

5. *Include students in conversation.* For example, when discussing the sinking and floating lab, the paraprofessional said, "Maya, you are going to love this book. It is all about swimming." The acknowledgment of Maya and her interests was a very inclusive connection to make.

6. *Use a strength-based approach.* Even though this person does not use verbal language, what do they use to communicate? What can this person do? What are this person's gifts?

7. *Use an age-appropriate tone and demeaner.* In other words, talk to this person like you would to anyone of their same age.

8. *Provide chances for them to encounter age-appropriate experiences.* Give them enough space and support so they can have similar experiences to their peers (e.g., struggling, failing, goofing around, or even getting into trouble).

9. *Teach peers how to talk to students with communication differences.*

10. *Program devices with content before each lesson.* If a student uses a yes or no only, create yes or no type questions. "Do you think that 6×6 is 37?"

11. *Look for evidence of understanding.* What you look for, you are likely to find.

Figure 5.3. Eleven tips for supporting students who do not use verbal speech.

REFLECTIONS

Take a moment to consider your own mindset.

Do you believe we all have a certain amount of intelligence that can't be changed? Or do you believe intelligence can be increased with effort and time?

Do you consider an individual's poor performance to be inevitable due to their disability, home life, or cultural background? If so, this might be evidence of a fixed mindset you developed growing up. How might you reframe this belief to become more flexible and supportive?

Do you believe that discovery and insight stem from failures and setbacks, or from successes?

If you have discovered you might have a fixed mindset, there's no need to worry! Many people find they can learn to be more flexible with effort and time. The following are some statements that you can say to yourself to help cultivate a more flexible mindset about the students you support.

- Students can only succeed if I first let them know I believe in their value and potential.
- I will set high expectations for all of my students.
- I will give students the support they need to succeed.
- I understand that success will not look the same for all students.
- Success, in part, is defined by a student's individual growth.
- Students gain discovery and insight from setbacks and failures, rather than successes.

These statements can help lead you to a flexible mindset about your students. The next step is to put them into practice. Table 5.2 provides suggestions to help you practice a flexible mindset with students rather than a fixed mindset. Take a moment to consider how you can implement flexible mindset practices with your students right away.

Table 5.2. Fixed and flexible mindset practices

Fixed mindset	Flexible mindset
You find you teach down to students because of disability, language, culture, or economic status.	You set high expectations and communicate them clearly with your students. You always look for ways to provide opportunities for challenge and growth.
You emphasize/praise students for being smart.	You emphasize/praise students for hard work and effort.
You emphasize/praise only natural talents.	You emphasize/praise students for having inherent value and potential.
You hide your own failures and setbacks.	You share your failures and setbacks with students and highlight how you persisted with hard work and effort.

"a real cutie." Individuals with disabilities should be described in accordance with their chronological ages.

Paraprofessionals should treat and work with students in age-appropriate ways. Julie once witnessed a paraprofessional holding hands with a sixth-grade student in the hall. We doubt that the paraprofessional would have thought it appropriate to hold the hand of a sixth-grade student who did not have a disability. For that very reason, it is inappropriate to hold any student's hand. This same logic holds true for having students sit on your lap, play with age-inappropriate toys, sing age-inappropriate songs, and so forth. Ask yourself how you would talk to or work with the student if she or he did not have a disability, and proceed in that manner.

Person-First Language

When describing, speaking, or writing respectfully about people who have disabilities, many people use a common language. It is called *person-first language* and is something that you can easily integrate into the way you speak about the students with whom you work. The concept is simple and is detailed in the following subsections.

> If thoughts corrupt language, language can also corrupt thought.
> —George Orwell (1981)

Avoid the Label

Although there has been much progress in the language used by educators and other professionals, unfortunately students with disabilities are invariably described with labels instead of person-first language. Have you ever heard phrases such as *the learning-disabled student, the autistic boy, that Downs child, the resource room kids,* or *the inclusion kids?*

It is important to understand the preferences of people with disabilities regarding how they would like others to speak about them. The following guidelines listed in Table 5.3 come from several different self-advocacy groups (Disability Is Natural and TASH).

If you ever have a question about how to describe a student's disability to your colleagues or other professionals who support the student, try to remember this general rule: put the person's name or pronoun before the disability (e.g., "I work with a student who has a learning disability" is preferable to "I work with a learning disabled student").

The Same as Anyone Else

Another way to retrain how you use person-first language to describe students with disabilities is to think first about how you might introduce someone who does not have a disability. You might use the person's name, say how you know them, or describe what he or she does. The same is true for individuals with disabilities. Instead of saying, "Chelsea who has Down syndrome," you might say, "Chelsea who is in biology during 1st period." No one should be identified by one aspect of who they are—especially if that aspect represents a difficulty or struggle for someone. Words are powerful. The ways we talk about and describe

Table 5.3.   Examples of person-first language

Say . . .	Instead of . . .	Because . . .
People with disabilities	The disabled or handicapped	Place emphasis on the person.
People without disabilities	Normal/healthy/typical	The nonpreferred terms assume the opposite for students with disabilities (i.e., abnormal, unhealthy, atypical).
Ella, the fourth-grade student	Ella, the student with Down syndrome	Omit the label whenever possible; it is most often not relevant.
Communicates with their eyes/ device, etc.	Is nonverbal	Focus on strengths.
Uses a wheelchair	Is confined to a wheelchair	Use possessive language to refer to assistive technologies; the nonpreferred language implies the person is stuck.
Accessible parking spot	Handicapped parking spot	Use accurate representation.
Beth has autism.	Beth is autistic.	Emphasize that disability is one attribute—not a defining characteristic.
Gail has a learning disability.	Gail is learning disabled.	Emphasize that disability is one attribute—not a defining characteristic.
Jeff has a cognitive disability.	Jeff is retarded.	Emphasize that disability is one attribute—not a defining characteristic; also, cognitive disability is a preferred term.
Ben receives special education services.	Ben is in special education.	Special education is a service, not a place.
The student who is blind	The blind student	Place the person before the disability.
Denis writes by using the computer.	Denis cannot write with a pencil.	Focus on strengths.
Needs a magnifier, laptop, or cane	Problems with vision; cannot write or walk	Focus on needs, not problems.

Source: Snow (2008).

people with disabilities do not just affect our beliefs and interactions with our students; they also provide models for others who hear these descriptions.

If your own child broke his arm, would you introduce him to someone new as "my broken-armed child"? If one of the students in the school had cancer, would you expect to hear a teacher state, "She is my cancerous student"? Of course not! No one should feel ashamed about having a broken arm, cancer, or a disability of any kind—a broken bone or malfunctioning cells do not define the essence of a person.

Celebrate Diversity

Across disciplines, such as medicine, business, psychology, and education, research evidences that diversity is critical for success (U.S. Department of Energy, 2012; Gomez & Bernet, 2019; Gurin, Nagda, & Lopez, 2004; Tadmor, Satterstrom, Jang, & Polzer, 2012). For example, studies show that diverse groups have better problem-solving and decision-making skills (U.S. Department of Energy, 2012; Page, 2008), and diversity increases innovation, productivity, and growth in workplaces (Lorenzo & Reeves, 2018). Education-specific research shows evidence that diversity in schools improves student academic achievement (National Assessment for Educational Progress, 2017), increases student enrollment in college (Palordy, 2013) and prevents dropouts for students (Balfanz & Letgers, 2004). In fact, educational researchers Peck and colleagues (Peck, Staub, Gallucci, & Schwartz, 2004) explained that membership in a diverse class community is one of the most important domains that contribute to increased participation for students.

However, in our society and in our schools, we often overvalue uniformity and perfection. Consider standardized tests, standardized curriculum, the value placed on valedictorians, and more broadly in society, norms of family structures, beauty, and success. But if all of the research suggests that diversity leads to happier, more positive, more productive, more innovative outcomes for all—we encourage you to celebrate the diversity of your students. Focus on valuing all the ways students vary academically and behaviorally but also in their many races and ethnicities, abilities, communication styles, life experiences, language experiences, and beyond. Celebrating those differences is one important way that we can better support our students, our school communities, and each other.

Commonly Asked Questions About Students

FAQs

Q. What if a student prefers an age-inappropriate toy or game?

A. Often, people with disabilities have been treated as if they were younger than they are. As a result, they have been exposed to cartoons, toys, or games that their same-age peers may have outgrown; their peers are not likely to think these activities are "cool." One option, then, is to expose the student to more age-appropriate music and activities.

Q.   Are there any exceptions to person-first language?

A.   Yes, people who are deaf often prefer the term *deaf* instead of *person with deafness*. A group called Deaf First suggests that deafness is a major component of identity, and this group prefers disability-first language. Similarly, some people with autism prefer to be called *autistic*, or *neurodivergent*, and some use insider language such as *autie* to describe themselves. It is not accurate to say that all people with disabilities prefer one way over another. However, person-first language serves as a helpful guideline because many advocacy groups consider it a more respectful way to refer to people.

Q.   I do not think the student I work with is smart. This student has a label of intellectual disability. How can I presume competence?

A.   This person may not perform well on standardized tests of intelligence. However, your responsibility when working with this student is to identify the student's strengths. Keep those strengths in mind when working with them in academic settings. Every person is intelligent in different ways. Work on developing your flexible mindset about this student. Commit to the idea that this student has inherent value and potential, and that you can uncover that potential with a little time and patience.

Conclusion

Diversity ensures that our classrooms, schools, and communities are richer and more successful. Labels are not accurate descriptors of people. Children who have disabilities are unique individuals with unlimited potential just like everyone else (Snow, 2008). This recognition is not only about having a good attitude or believing that all students are smart; it will also allow you to treat, support, and work with all students in ways that promote dignity and respect. In the next chapter, we discuss how the ideas of dignity and respect can help facilitate social relationships.

TO-DO LIST

To Do

After reading this chapter . . .
- Complete the activities and reflections for this chapter.
- Identify ways to celebrate diversity and cultivate a flexible mindset in your daily life.
- Practice those ways to celebrate diversity and flexible mindset.
- Write all of your specific questions about this chapter down.

6

Providing Academic Supports

I was surprised to find out that it doesn't take much to support Steven. By allowing him to draw his answer instead of writing it, he was able to represent the big ideas from the science lesson. Modifying can be surprisingly simple. It just takes some creativity and guidance from the special education teacher. But with Andrea, I needed to learn a lot of new skills to keep her focused and engaged. I also had to learn to program her device and keep it loaded with everything she might need for each lesson. —Meghan (paraprofessional)

We, your authors, personally use a variety of supports throughout our daily routines. For example, Julie sets her alarm to wake up and ride her bike in the morning to be sure she can fit in a workout. Kate uses her Google calendar to keep a daily schedule. Julie writes a daily priority list on a single piece of card stock and prioritizes each item by writing numbers in the left-hand margin of the list. When we have a shared task to complete—like writing this chapter—we use a video-conferencing platform (e.g., FaceTime, Zoom) to support each other to get motivated. We then set a timer with a smartphone or smart home device (e.g., Alexa, Google Home) for 30, 15, 10, or even 5 minutes at a time. When the timer goes off, we check in with each other to see what we accomplished or what we might need to stay focused, or to answer each other's writing questions. The point is this: *All* people need their environments, time schedules, and behavior modified or adapted to allow them to be successful members of society. This chapter discusses the adaptations, accommodations, and modification that can be made to support students with disabilities. We describe general and content-specific strategies, and then we discuss the topic of assistive technology and digital tools.

As a paraprofessional, you will provide modifications or accommodations to students and help them navigate the academic terrain of schooling. This can

REFLECTIONS

What supports do you routinely use throughout your day to feel more successful?

LEGAL INFORMATION

be a formidable task. NCLB of 2001 also requires paraprofessionals to work with students, "under the direct supervision of a certified staff member." The law stipulates that it is not the responsibility of paraprofessionals to decide the best modifications or adaptations to use with students. Instead, you should simply carry out plans designed by a certified teacher. Specifically, the regulations for paraprofessionals state the following:

Paraprofessionals who provide instructional support must work under the direct supervision of a highly qualified teacher. (§§ 1119 [g][3][A])

A paraprofessional works under the direct supervision of a teacher if (1) the teacher prepares the lessons and plans the instructional support activities the paraprofessional carries out, and evaluates the achievement of the students with whom the paraprofessional is working, and (2) the paraprofessional works in close and frequent proximity with the teacher. (§ 200.59 [c][2] of the Title I regulations)

As a result, programs staffed entirely by paraprofessionals are not permitted. A certified teacher should design the lessons, and you should help students during the lesson, review or reinforce the material, and provide feedback and input to the team about what seems to be successful for the student(s) you support. You should not be responsible for designing or teaching new content.

This chapter will familiarize you with several different types of modifications and specific ways to modify and adapt, using teachers' instructions, to meet the needs of the students in your care. It first describes general strategies that will enable you to support students, then discusses content-specific ideas, and, finally, suggests strategies that can help you work across all content areas. Consider reading this chapter with your teaching team. Figure 6.1 shows a general cycle of support, which has been adapted from one developed by Mary Beth Doyle (2008), a special education professor who specializes in curriculum design and paraprofessional training and support.

Adaptations: Accommodations and Modifications

Adaptation is the umbrella that encompasses the accommodations and modifications educators use with students. Accommodations and modifications are changes made to the environment, curriculum, instruction, or assessment practices that enable students with disabilities to be successful learners and to participate actively with other students in the general education classroom and in schoolwide activities. The following information about the differences between accommodations and modifications comes from the PEAK Parent Center (n.d.) in Colorado Springs, Colorado.

Accommodations

Accommodations are changes in *how* a student accesses information and demonstrates learning. Accommodations do not substantially change the instructional level, content, or performance criteria. The changes are made to provide a student with equal access to learning and equal opportunity to show what they know and can do. Accommodations can include changes in presentation, response format and procedures, instructional strategies, time and scheduling, environment, equipment, and architecture.

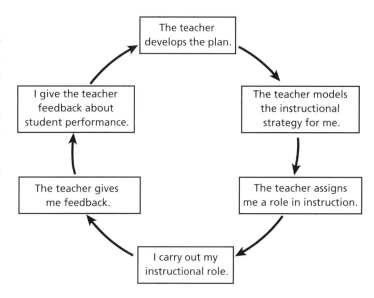

Figure 6.1. Cycle of support. From Doyle, M. B. (2009). *The paraprofessional's guide to the inclusive classroom: working as a team* (3rd ed., p. 58). Baltimore, MD: Paul H. Brookes Publishing Co.; adapted with permission.

Accommodation Samples

- Test taken orally
- Large-print textbooks
- Additional time to take tests
- A locker with an adapted lock
- Weekly home–school communication tool(s)
- Peer support for note taking
- Lab sheets with highlighted instructions
- Graph paper to assist in organizing and lining up math problems
- Digital lectures
- Use of a computer for writing
- Highlighted directions

Modifications

Modifications are changes in *what* a student is expected to learn. These changes are made to provide a student with opportunities to participate meaningfully and productively along with other students in classroom and other school learning experiences. Modifications include changes in instructional level, content, and performance criteria.

The following list contains examples of modifications that can be provided in general education classrooms. IEP teams determine accommodations and modifications that meet the unique and individual needs of their students.

QUICK QUIZ

Now that you are clear on the differences between accommodations and modifications, how would you describe the difference to someone else? Let's say you're discussing your job as a paraprofessional with someone in an elevator or over dinner and this person asked you, "What is the difference between accommodations and modifications?" How might you respond?

Modification Samples

- An outline in place of an essay for a major project
- Choices of Picture Communication Symbols on tests
- Alternative books or materials on the same theme or topic
- Spelling support from word prediction software
- Word bank of choices for answers to test questions
- Use of a calculator on a math test
- Video supplements in place of text
- Questions reworded using simpler language
- Projects substituted for written reports

Deciding which accommodations and/or modifications to use is a process that depends on the class assignment and needs of each individual student. This process is determined by a teacher, but a paraprofessional will have input on how adaptations are carried out. When the appropriate adaptations are made, all students can have access to the general education curriculum (PEAK Parent Center, n.d.).

STRATEGIES

General Strategies for Academic Supports

As soon as you assume they can't do something, the student won't be able to prove you wrong. We have to keep expectations high. Students surprise me every day. I start with the notion that Jenna **can** *and provide supports when and if she needs it. —Jay (paraprofessional)*

Focus on Strengths

When providing support to students, it is easy to become overwhelmed by what they cannot do. For example, when I (Julie) was providing support to Steven, a third grader with Down syndrome, it was easy to think, "Steven does not read; how am I to help him understand the science content in this chapter?" It helps to reframe your thinking and ask yourself about what the student can do. Focus instead on the student's strengths; with Steven, you might think, "Steven is quite social. He can easily comprehend big ideas. He is masterful at drawing what he knows and labeling parts. He also can answer questions."

We focused on Steven's strengths of listening, social interaction, and understanding main ideas. When other students were required to quietly read the chapter from the science book, Steven's partner read the chapter aloud. At the end of each section in the text, Steven and his partner were required to say something about the section, and Steven, as he listened, worked on a drawing depicting the big ideas involving cell division. Steven and his partner then asked each other questions about the section and the drawing. This worked so well for Steven and his partner that the teacher decided to have the entire class read the science text in the same manner the rest of the year.

This strengths-based approach works for students in secondary settings, as well. Kayla, a high school junior that I (Kate) worked with, received many accommodations and supports due to multiple physical disabilities. She had experienced many health issues and surgeries in her lifetime, used a wheelchair, and was often fatigued. She required extended time to finish assignments and projects and also needed all of her texts to be available digitally so she could easily enlarge the text or use audio or text-to-speech programs to accommodate her visual impairment.

Some of Kayla's teachers viewed her as a bit fragile—both physically and emotionally—and assumed that "not pushing her too hard" was the best way to support her. However, when I talked with Kayla, I learned that she believed teachers just "let her skate by," which led her to skip out on homework deadlines or turn in incomplete assignments because "they didn't really expect much anyway." When we made a list of all of her strengths and skills together, I learned that because of her complicated medical history and many accommodations, she was very interested in advocacy and wanted to learn how to share information about disability awareness and advocacy. Tapping into this interest, Kayla's teachers helped her to practice self-advocacy in her daily academic work, such as requesting accommodations and setting deadlines and goals with teachers. With clear and high expectations from her teachers and an interest in practicing to advocate for herself, Kayla became a much more empowered and conscientious student.

Ask the Student

If you are unsure about how to provide support, when to provide support, or how much support to provide, you do not need to make that decision alone. Consider reviewing Chapter 4 to gather the big questions you want to bring to the team regarding your student. Or, revisit the positive student profile in Chapter 5 with the team to discuss the types of accommodations, modifications, and other supports that will most benefit your student. After discussing the student's support requirements with the general education and special education teachers, you should also consult the student. Asking students about the types and levels of supports they want or need is of the utmost importance. Not only does asking directly keep them at the center of the work, it also helps them—and you—to better understand their learning needs; it provides opportunities to make decisions about their learning and advocate for themselves; and helps you to co-create a support that is much more likely to be accepted by the individual student and is therefore much more likely to be effective.

Keep Expectations High

Having a disability does not mean that a student cannot complete assignments and projects in the same way as anyone else. Before attempting to modify or alter a student's assignment, ask yourself whether the assignment actually needs any changes. Too often, education professionals overmodify for students or decide to make the same modification for every student with the same disability. Sometimes, the best thing to do for a student is not to change your expectations for them but, instead, to change the type or level of support.

Break Tasks into Smaller Steps

For some students, it might be useful to break tasks into smaller parts. For example, one student, Chelsea, preferred having a to-do list posted on her desk for any independent work time. The paraprofessional would write down the big tasks that needed to be completed, and Chelsea would complete them independently and cross out each task. If you have a student who does not read, you could draw a picture list and have the student cross out the picture as they complete each task. Another student, Sam, likes to have his task list on his tablet. The teacher loads everything that needs to be completed onto the device, and it helps him independently stay on track.

Extend Time on Tasks

Many students require extra time for certain tasks, including tests and exams. For example, some students need more time to process written text (e.g., a student with a reading disability) or to write (e.g., a student who requires support with fine motor functions), or to use specific accommodations or equipment (e.g., audio text, screen reader). Students who have difficulty concentrating for long periods of time (e.g., a student with ADHD) can benefit from extended time to not only increase productivity but also decrease stress and anxiety. Other students with health-related disabilities may require extended time to combat the fatigue that comes with engaging in activities for a certain length of time. When provided these time accommodations, students are able to complete the same high-quality work as their peers.

Flexible timing or scheduling can also be considered for students. For example, if students have an hour to complete a test, allow the student to take the test in parts—one part on the first day, the second part on the next. One student we know selects only two of the four choices during center time because it simply takes her longer to do each task at the centers. This way she can completely finish both of the tasks. As the student experiences success with extended time as an accommodation, it may be helpful to slowly decrease the time allotted for certain tasks to learn whether their focus or stamina has improved.

Present Limited Amounts of Information on a Page

Some students prefer to see less information at once. The layout of information should be clean and free of distraction. Adequate white space, for example, can make an assignment appear less confusing or overwhelming. This modification can be made easily by copying different segments of an assignment onto different pages. In addition, white-out tape helps limit certain distracting information or pictures so that the student has less information to wade through. In addition, an index card or a *word window*—a piece of cardboard with a small rectangular window cutout covered by cellophane that allows students to see one line of text or one word at a time—can also help students eliminate information as they read by themselves. For digital work, the highlighting feature of many types of software can help focus the student to limited amount of information at a time.

Offer Support, Do Not Just Give It

Do not assume that a student needs help. If a student is struggling, encourage them to ask a peer first. If the student is still struggling, ask, "Can I help you get started?" If the student says "No," respect their wishes. It is okay for a student to sit for a minute or even struggle to get started. Just think if you had someone with you all day making sure you were getting started without wasting any time. After a while you would start to feel the overwhelming pressure. It is human nature to be distracted or resistant to starting a difficult task, so give the student space to prepare him- or herself to mentally prepare for the task.

Make Things Concrete

Many students need concrete examples, such as pictures or videos, that support the concepts taught in class. Jill, a paraprofessional with whom I (Kate) worked, would use downtime to search the school library and Internet for pictures and videos to support learning. The teacher would then incorporate these teaching aids into her mini-lectures and teaching centers. This helped not only the students with disabilities; everyone in the class benefited from these visual supports. It is much easier to understand photosynthesis when seeing an animated video about it than it is to learn the concept only through reading.

Teach Organizational Skills to Everyone

It is common for students with and without disabilities to struggle with organization and executive functioning skills. Executive functioning skills are mental processes that help us to plan, focus our attention, remember instructions, and manage multiple tasks effectively. Unfortunately, we are not born with these skills, so we must have the opportunity to develop these skills over time in order to help us prioritize tasks, set and achieve goals, control impulses, and minimize distractions. In one seventh-grade classroom, the paraprofessional helped everyone with their executive functioning skills by doing binder checks at the end of each class. She made sure the notes were in the correct color-coded spot as students left the room. This helped not only Adam, who chronically struggled with keeping things organized, but countless others who needed similar support. Another paraprofessional typed a digital reminder of all the items students needed to take home each day. These lists were made available as a checklist or as a text message sent to the student.

Change the Materials

Sometimes, a different type of material is all a student needs for success. A change in the type of writing utensil, or a different size or stock of paper, or lined paper, can make a substantial difference for a student. For example, I (Julie) used to work with a student named Brett. Every time Brett was expected to write, he would put his head down on the desk or angrily scribble or break pencils. The team of teachers and paraprofessional who supported the classroom met and discussed the potential reasons for Brett's behavior and how they might make writing more pleasant for him. As a result of this conversation, the team decided to let all students choose their writing instruments and paper size. When this choice was offered, Brett chose a black felt-tip marker and a half-sheet of paper. For some reason, the change of materials proved much better for him, and he wrote for longer periods of time. He later explained that he would get nervous if he saw "a whole blank piece of paper" and that he hated, "the feel of the pencil on the paper" but loved how the marker "glided across [the paper] and made perfect marks."

Use a Timer

Timers can be useful for students who like to know how long tasks will take or who need help organizing their time. For some students, visual timers, or timers on which you can actually see how much time is left, can be particularly useful.

Izzy was a kindergarten student. Whenever transitions (e.g., moving from rug to work time, or math to music time) occurred in the classroom, he had loud, tearful tantrums. Because of Izzy's difficulty with transitions, his team decided to use a timer to alert him when transitions were coming. Izzy's teacher handed him a digital timer and told him that he was in charge of letting the other students know when it was cleanup time.

After first practicing with the timer, Izzy took his responsibility very seriously. He walked around from group to group, reminding the kindergartners that there were only "5 minutes until cleanup time ... 4 minutes ... 3 ...." He continued to remind his friends until the timer went off. He then shouted happily, "Clean up, everyone!" For Izzy, the timer helped him know when the transition occurred and also gave him an important responsibility.

After a few weeks with this transition support, Izzy was able to increase his flexibility around transitions, and instead of holding the timer and counting down the time, he was able to set the timer on the smartboard for the whole class to see.

Pre-Teach

Pre-teaching big ideas such as vocabulary or major concepts can be useful for many students who have learning disabilities, processing delays, or intellectual disabilities. Pre-teaching should be done before a concept is officially taught to the rest of the class. You may introduce a concept, term, or idea to a student before the rest of the students learn it. For example, as the students were preparing for a magnet lab, Mr. Marco, a paraprofessional, taught some of the key science vocabulary to Kenny, a student with a nonverbal processing disorder, before the lesson. Kenny entered the magnet lab understanding the terms *attract* and *repel*. This allowed Kenny to come to the class prepared and more confident. Similarly, Stephanie, a student with a reading disability, benefited from her paraprofessional teaching her how to read the elements on the periodic table of elements before they were required to memorize them for chemistry class. This allowed Stephanie to not only get the additional academic support she would need to learn the elements and do well on the quizzes but it also gave her additional confidence when answering questions during the science lecture.

For students who have difficulty learning or retaining new concepts, struggle with memorization, or face a particular reading, writing, or mathematical disability, pre-teaching can be transformative for them. One elementary school teacher describes pre-teaching transformation for students like this: "[Pre-teaching] can make reading an act of pleasure instead of torture. Math can become fun instead of frustrating. The feeling of confidence can linger long after the class has moved on to the next concept" (Minkel, 2015).

Peer Support

Peer support is one of the best ways to support students. Have all of the students work in teams or partnerships. Tell students that their job is to help each other. However, some caution is necessary regarding peer support. Do not set up "helping relationships"—for example, Sonja *always* helps José. Instead, encourage students to help each other. Using the information you know about students' individual strengths, figure out times when José can help Sonja and his other peers to allow for more equal relationships to form in the classroom.

Use Movement

All human beings need more movement during the day. When memorizing concepts or pieces of information, use visual cues, signs, or move-

ments. Challenge students to come up with their own movements that match the concepts of specific words. For example, I (Kate) was recently in a middle school science class as students learned how amino acids come together to form proteins. As the teacher explained the process, Susan, a paraprofessional, showed students how to use both hands to float in the air as if they were amino acids and then clap their hands to join together as a protein. Not only might this help students with certain disabilities, it also benefits English language learners (ELLs), kinesthetic and visual learners, and students who struggle with abstract concepts.

Another example comes from a paraprofessional who practiced spelling aerobics with his elementary students. When spelling words, if the letters were "tall letters" (e.g., *t, l, b*), he would lead the students to stand up tall and put their arms up; if letters were "short" (e.g., *o, e, a*), the students would put their hands on their hips; and, if letters hung below the line (e.g., *p, g, q*), the students would touch their toes. For instance, to spell the word *stop*, the students would touch their waists (*s*), reach up (*t*), touch their waists again (*o*), and then touch their toes (*p*). What makes this particular example so powerful is that the movement is purposeful and helps the students remember the content.

Content-Specific Strategies

STRATEGIES

The following section discusses various ways to approach different types of content and activities that are commonly used across content areas. Remember, you will not be responsible for coming up with these ideas—that is the teacher's job. However, you should know these types of modifications and how best to use them with students. If you see an idea in Table 6.1 that you would like to try with a student, talk to the team to decide whether it would be an effective strategy. Discuss how to use it, when to use it, and when you might fade the strategy or idea.

Causton-Theoharis and colleagues (2007), in their educational study about effective paraprofessional supports, determined at least five elements associated with the successful use of paraprofessionals to improve student outcomes.

1. The paraprofessional provides supplementary instruction (not primary instruction).

2. Instruction is designed in a way that does not require significant instructional decision making by the paraprofessional.

3. Proven instructional methods are used.

4. Paraprofessionals are trained in the instructional approach that they are expected to implement.

5. Paraprofessionals are supervised and monitored to ensure consistency of instruction.

If any of these conditions for providing content-specific instruction are not present, talk with your team to discuss how these elements could be implemented.

Table 6.1. Content-specific modifications

In this subject	Consider these modifications, adaptations, and accommodations
Reading/language arts	Listen to audiobooks. Read with a peer. Follow along with a word window. Read from a computer with headphones. Work with a peer and have them summarize. Read enlarged print. Use closed circuit television (CCTV)—a video magnifier that enlarges the font. Read adapted stories with simplified language. Use books with repetitive texts.
Mathematics	Calculators Touch math (each numeral has the corresponding number of dots to represent the numeral) Hundreds charts Number lines Flash cards Count stickers Manipulatives (e.g., Unifix cubes, counting chips) Worksheet modified with easier-to-read numbers Pictures or visuals Larger cubes Chart paper to keep track of columns Talking calculator Numbered dice instead of dotted dice Real-world problems—problems with students' names in them
Physical education	Different-size sporting equipment Silent activities (for those who are sensitive to noise) Choice stations Change the size of the court
Art	Choice of materials Bigger/smaller materials Slant board Precut materials Stencils Smocks and aprons with pockets Gloves for students who don't like to get messy Wiki sticks Posted steps about the process Adaptive scissors
Science	Hands-on experiences Teacher demonstration A role play Guest speaker Posted steps indicating the process
Social studies	Highlighters or highlighting tape A way to connect the content to self Videos Visuals Maps A written task card (a card with a step-by-step process on it)
Music	Songs in the student's native language Instruments Signs while singing Rhythms to clap out MP3s or CDs of music to practice at home Music videos to watch

Commonly Occurring Activities Across Content Areas

Sometimes, a different teacher is responsible for each content area, and this can result in different expectations for students. Some students prefer certain subjects and perform better in them. For example, Ricky enjoyed music, so he needed almost no support in that class. He would enter the music room, gather his folder and instrument, and be ready to go. In science, he did not seem fond of the teacher or the subject, and he therefore needed more support not only to get to class but also to get started with tasks. Although a student's support might look different from class to class, teachers use similar activities across different subject areas. Table 6.2 highlights activities that are used commonly across subjects. Teachers may require students to do any number of these things throughout the day. Nonetheless, different students may have difficulty with each of these activities, for different reasons. The considerations listed on the right side of Table 6.2 have proven helpful for many students of all abilities.

Table 6.2.   Common activities and supports

When the students are asked to . . .	Consider providing . . .
Sit and listen	Visuals Movement breaks A frequency modulation (FM) system that amplifies the teacher's voice A rug or mat to help students determine where to be An object to signify who is speaking (e.g., a talking stick) A ball to sit on Choice about where to sit A focus object for students to hold or manipulate A signal to start listening The book that is being read A topic bag (i.e., filled with objects that relate to the content) A job to do (e.g., help another student, write ideas on the board)
Present orally	Choice about the supports necessary Note cards Visuals A handout A voice recorder A video A microphone Slides (e.g., PowerPoint, Google) Preprogrammed communication device
Take a test	A review of test strategies A review of the information A practice test A double-spaced test Easy questions first A reader for the test A reduced number of choices by eliminating one or two choices In matching, divide a long column into smaller sections A computer As much time as needed A flexible schedule (e.g., half one day and half the next) An oral exam A performance-based test The option of drawing or labeling Simplified language
Complete worksheets	A word bank Clear directions Sticker labels with answers Highlighted directions Fewer problems or questions Choice about type of writing instrument
Discuss	A talking object Note cards with students' ideas written on them Peer support A preprogrammed communication device with a question on it A piece of paper to draw ideas or concepts Choice about how to participate in the discussion The text the students are discussing A highlighted section of the text—have the student read and others discuss

(continued)

Table 6.2.   *(continued)*

When the students are asked to . . .	Consider providing . . .
Take notes	A lecture outline to complete during the lecture A chart A graphic organizer The teacher's notes from the day before A word processor (e.g., AlphaSmart) A digital voice recorder or pen Choice about how to take notes A copy of the teacher's notes with key words eliminated Lecture notes with pictures Photocopies or carbon copies from another student A laptop computer
Use a computer	A task card for how to start up the program Adaptive keyboard Large keyboard An alphabetical keyboard Enlarged font Programmable alternative keyboard (e.g., IntelliKeys) An adjusted delay on the mouse A screen reader Touchscreen Choice about what to work on
Read a text	Audiobook Electronic book Larger print font Highlighter Choral reading Background information about the text Bullets of the main ideas Sticky notes to write questions on Books at the appropriate level (i.e., "just-right books") Puppets Reading light Choice about what to read
Be organized	Color-coded folders A planner An agenda written on the board Assignments written on the board in the same place Assignments that are already three-hole punched A picture schedule An online calendar An accountability peer partner A sticky note with to-do lists on students' desks A homework folder A desk check Clock or timer on desk A verbal rehearsal of the schedule A consistent routine
Write	Tell a friend your story before writing it Discuss as a whole group Use graphic organizers Use bullet writing Use pencil grips Type instead of hand write Student dictates the story to you or a peer Teacher writes words on a separate piece of paper, then student rewrites Use stickers to fill in blanks Draw instead of write Use raised-line paper so students can feel lines

ACTIVITY: Student Supports

Take a look at Table 6.2. Star the supports you are already providing your student(s) and highlight the supports you think would benefit your student.

ACTIVITIES

Assistive Technology

Assistive technology is any type of technology that helps people with disabilities perform functions that might otherwise be difficult or impossible. The official definition of *assistive technology* is as follows:

DEFINITIONS

Assistive technology in special education refers to any devices or services that are necessary for a child to benefit from special education or related services or to enable the child to be educated in the least restrictive environment (IDEA 2004, 34 C.F.R. § 300.308).

The term *assistive technology device* as outlined in IDEA 2004 means any item, piece of equipment, or product system, whether acquired commercially off the shelf, modified, or customized, that is used to increase, maintain, or improve functional capabilities of children with disabilities (20 U.S.C. § 1401 [a][25]).

The term *assistive technology service* means any service that directly assists a child with disabilities in the selection, acquisition, or use of an assistive technology device. The term includes:

- The evaluation of the needs of a child with a disability, including a functional evaluation of the child in the child's customary environment;
- Purchasing, leasing, or otherwise providing for the acquisition of assistive technology devices by children with disabilities;
- Selecting, designing, fitting, customizing, adapting, applying, maintaining, repairing, or replacing of assistive technology devices;
- Coordinating and using other therapies, interventions, or services with assistive technology devices, such as those associated with existing education and rehabilitation plans and programs;
- Training or technical assistance for a child with disabilities or, where appropriate, the family of a child with disabilities;
- Training or technical assistance for professionals (including individuals providing education or rehabilitation services), employers, or other individuals who provide services to, employ, or are otherwise substantially involved in the major life functions of individuals with disabilities. (20 U.S.C. § 1401 [a][26])

Assistive technology includes mobility devices (e.g., walkers, wheelchairs), software, keyboards with large keys, software enabling students who are blind to use computers, or amplification systems to allow a student with hearing loss to access the teacher's voice. A student who struggles with the fine motor skills involved with writing might use a tablet, and a student who struggles to communicate might use the text-to-speech function. If a student uses one type of assistive technology or another, you should learn as much as you can about the technology. If possible, ask the special educator you work with or the special education director in your district for specific training on the technology so that you can assist the student in using the device, programming it, or fixing it if necessary

Not all support needs to be highly technical. In fact, as mentioned previously, a new writing utensil or different size paper might be all that a student needs to become successful with a task. We challenge you to think of any type of office supply as a way to support a student. For example, a clipboard can give support to a student who prefers to write in a bean bag chair. A paperclip might be used to keep important papers together for a student who struggles with fine motor skills. Tape might be used to hold down a paper for a student who struggles to use that guide hand. Table 6.3 provides some examples, from low-tech to high-tech options, of various supports that can be used in classroom for children with and without disabilities.

Twenty-One Ways to Use a Sticky Note

A paraprofessional we know wrote a positive message on a sticky note every day for the student she supported. The student brought the notes home and read them with his grandma. The purpose of these notes was to provide only positive comments to the student. These kind notes helped the student feel good about his performance at school. Sticky notes are amazingly versatile.

ACTIVITIES

ACTIVITY: Office Supplies

Think of an everyday office item, or pick it up and hold it in your hand. Consider 10 uses for that particular item as a way to provide support to a student. For example, try to determine 10 ways to support students using a file folder label, scissors, or glitter glue. We use a simple sticky note as an example to guide you through this activity. In addition, we went ahead and thought of 21 ways to use that sticky note—just for fun. See Figure 6.2 for the full list.

FAQs

Commonly Asked Questions About Academic Support

Q. One student asks me to "go away" when I work with him. I cannot just let him sit there and fail. What should I do?

A. Listen to the student. If a student requests that you not work with them, do not support the student at that time. Instead, figure out how you might provide support without being physically next to the student.

Table 6.3.   Assistive technology

Type	Example or function
No Tech/Low Tech	
Calendar	Organize or track tasks
Sensory input items (e.g., fidgets)	Provide self-regulation and focus
Magnifying glass	Enlarge text or image
Mid Tech	
Audiobooks	Listen to books
Calculator	Complete math problems
Digital recorder	Device that records lectures or dictates student responses
High Tech	
Screen readers	Access screen via voice or touch
Voice-recognition software	Alternative to typing or keyboard use
Text-to-speech software	Augmentative communication or to turn printed material to speech
Word-prediction programs	Program anticipates what students will write or say on the computer or phone

Q. **When a direction is given, a student just calls my name and asks me to come and help. I am trying to fade my support, but the student will not do anything without me by her side. What should I do?**

A. This student has become very dependent on adult support. We would suggest talking to the student about the need to try things by herself or asking peers for help. Encourage all students in the class to use and provide help to one another. Also be sure to involve your team in determining ways to increase the student's independence. You want the solutions to make the student feel empowered to become more independent—not punished for his or her dependence. Consider having different student roles at the table groups. One person can be responsible for fielding any questions the tablemates may have.

Q. **I am really struggling to understand the content of the class. What should I do?**

A. First, work with the classroom teacher or your case manager to better understand the content. Try to stay a step ahead of the students. Take things home and study them or learn them. On occasion, such as when I (Kate) was supporting a student with autism in AP Chemistry, I didn't necessarily need to be an expert in the content, but having some foundational knowledge helped. However, your role as the paraprofessional is to provide support in helping the student access the curriculum content, not teaching it; the student can access the general education teacher when they get stuck on content-specific concepts or ideas.

Q. **I am really just left to figure out how to support my students. What should I do if I receive almost no direction from a teacher?**

A. This is unfortunately a common and major problem. You should first set aside time with the teacher who is directing your work. Be prepared with a list of questions. Refer back to Chapter 4 for help with this conversation. Ask for the support you need to do your job. Here are some questions to get you started:

- Could I have a written plan to follow throughout my day?
- Could you please tell me specifically what to do when the student gets anxious, gets out of his or her desk, or [fill in a concerning behavior here]?
- When I support the students in math, could you give me an outline telling me what to do?
- Can I shadow you for a day to get a better sense of what I am expected to do?

When you meet with the teacher, be specific and ask your questions directly. If you still do not get the answers you need to effectively support the student, consider going to someone else (e.g., the director of special education, the principal) and letting them know you need more support. The bottom line is that you are required by law to receive support and supervision by a certified teacher, so you may be responsible to ensure that this is happening.

21 WAYS TO USE A STICKY NOTE

1. As an individual agenda

2. As a to-do list

3. For a positive note in a pocket

4. To mark page numbers

5. As a reading guide

6. To highlight sections of text

7. To place under the directions

8. To write questions to the students in their reading books

9. As a written reminder about behavior

10. As a way to monitor raising hand (every time they raise their hand and answer, they mark the note)

11. To cover up sections of a worksheet

12. As a word bank (so students don't have to write but can, instead, place word in blank)

13. For students who have a lot to say and blurt out a lot—have them write their questions on sticky notes and select one or two to ask

14. To add ideas to a brainstormed list

15. For students to give feedback to each other on projects or papers

16. To label parts of a diagram

17. To create a matching game

18. To put students into groups

19. For students to write questions or comments and then to give to their teacher as a ticket out the door

20. To ask a question to a peer, such as "Do you want to sit with me at lunch?"

21. To summarize the main idea of a lesson, story, or activity

Figure 6.2. Twenty-one ways to use a sticky note.

Conclusion

As a paraprofessional, you will not decide which modifications, adaptations, assistive technology, or data collection procedures are used. Nevertheless, it is very helpful to become familiar with the multitude of ways students can be supported. Careful support is critical when providing support to students during academic work time. The time that a teaching team spends discussing the types of support necessary to enable students to learn certain subjects or perform certain activities, how to fade support, and how to best adapt material and instruction across curricular areas is time well spent. Interestingly, when teams make these changes for specific students, they can end up making improvements to teaching for all students. This chapter has focused on the many ways you can use strategies to support academics. The next chapter highlights behavioral support strategies.

To Do

TO-DO LIST

After reading this chapter . . .

- Complete the activities and reflections in the chapter.
- Follow up with any specific content that is new to you by highlighting, reflecting on, and even asking colleagues to discuss the ideas with you.
- Look at each of your student's IEPs and learn about any required accommodations and modifications.
- Talk with your teacher(s) about each of the new ideas you have.
- Reread Tables 6.1 and 6.2; do they give you any new ideas?
- Complete the office supply challenge.

7

Providing Social Supports

Connection is the energy that exists between people when they feel seen, heard, and valued.

—Brené Brown

Seth sits down at the lunch table all by himself. Five minutes later, a few students sit at the same table. The distance between the other students and Seth makes it clear that they are not sitting with him. Seth quietly eats his lunch. Chewing carefully and using his napkin, Seth finishes his lunch and slowly packs up his belongings. He looks over at the other students. They are engaged in a conversation about their soccer team. No one says a word to Seth during lunch, and he does not talk with anyone during the entire lunch period. He puts his head down on his arm and closely examines the threads on his sweatshirt until the bell rings to indicate that lunch is over. Seth stands up and walks over to Judy, the paraprofessional who will walk him to his next class.

There are kids like Seth at every school and in many classrooms. Often, when a student has a disability or receives support from a paraprofessional, the student's social isolation can be significant. Students with disabilities—even those supported by paraprofessionals—can undeniably have rich social lives, friendships, and social relationships. This chapter is intended to help improve the social lives of students such as Seth who are supported by paraprofessionals. Specifically, this chapter focuses on 1) the importance of friendships, 2) the Velcro phenomenon, 3) subtle and gentle supports, 4) natural supports, 5) your role as a bridge, 6) supporting unstructured time, 7) supporting structured time, 8) teaching the rules of social interaction, and 9) commonly asked questions.

The Importance of Friendships

Think about your own life. How important are friendships? What do friends add to your life? For all people, friendships are critical to quality of life. Friends provide connection, love, and entertainment; they seek fun with us; they are our travel partners; they are sounding boards to help us deal with the trials of life; and they share in our joys and successes. Our friends support us, and we, in turn, support them. We, the authors, have both always relied on friendships—

We humans want to be together. We only isolate ourselves when we are hurt by others, but alone is not our natural state (Wheatley, 2002, p. 19).

even when in school. When we think back on our schooling experiences, some of our most important memories include friends. (Dare we say we were even more excited about seeing friends than we were about the social studies lecture or chemistry lab?) Similarly, friendships and relationships are a key part in every student's life. This chapter focuses on how paraprofessionals can facilitate students' relationships with their peers and bring people together instead of hindering the students' social interactions.

REFLECTIONS

Think how it would be if someone were paid to be with you 8 hours a day, 5 days a week. How would your relationships change?

Would you notice a loss of privacy, freedom, or intimacy?

What do you think your friends and coworkers would think of this new addition to your life?

Do you think they would flock to you? Avoid you?

Now, imagine this from a student's perspective. How do you think your presence affects the students whom you support?

Paraprofessional Proximity and Supporting Independence

Sometimes, a paraprofessional is a magnet. Other students (particularly those in younger grades) want to connect with the adult and interact. But, the unintended consequence of paraprofessional support has been widely documented—specifically, the interference with peer relationships and friendships. Michael Giangreco, an educational researcher who is an expert in understanding effective paraprofessional support, and his colleagues Edelman, Luiselli, and MacFarland (1997), have identified several ways in which paraprofessional proximity (or the closeness of you to the student) can actually hinder students with disabilities.

Ownership and Responsibility of General Educators

Many teachers in the previously referenced study viewed a student with a disability in their classroom as the paraprofessional's responsibility rather than their own. This also meant that the teachers interacted very little with the student with a disability and the education for that student came primarily from the paraprofessional.

Most of the classroom teachers in this sample did not describe their role as including responsibility for educating the student with disabilities who was placed in their class. Team members reported that the proximity and availability of the instructional assistants created a readily accessible opportunity for professional staff to avoid assuming responsibility and ownership for the education of students with disabilities placed in general education classrooms.

Separation from Classmates

Paraprofessionals were frequently observed separating the student from classmates for an activity or transition, even when the activity was achievable or even well-suited for the student. For example, students were asked to get in small groups for a hands-on science lab, but three students with disabilities were taken by the paraprofessional to an adjacent smaller room to complete an alternative worksheet activity. However, all three students would have benefitted significantly from hands-on, tactile learning and peer support.

Dependence on Adults

Paraprofessionals in the study were observed prompting the student for every behavior rather than fading their direct cues and allowing for more natural supports like peers, teacher, and materials. Students therefore become reliant on the paraprofessional and their prompts. For example, a student's paraprofessional was sitting in the back of the classroom during a whole-group literacy instruction, but the student kept looking back to check in with the paraprofessional and eventually left the group to go sit on her paraprofessional's lap.

Loss of Personal Control

The study found that because paraprofessionals often make so many decisions for the student rather than *with* the student, the student loses personal control more quickly than her nondisabled peers who do not have full-time adult support.

Impact on Peer Interactions

In the study, many teachers viewed paraprofessionals as barriers to peer interactions. For example, some peers did not choose to volunteer to work with the student who had a paraprofessional because they saw the student and the para as a package deal. And when typically developing students were partnered up with students who received paraprofessional support, often the paraprofessional was observed to dominate the interactions, diminishing the possibility for peer connections and collaboration. Other studies have also determined that the close proximity of a paraprofessional hinders the amount of peer interaction that would naturally occur in the classroom (Malmgren & Causton-Theoharis, 2006).

Embarrassment can be another factor. In a different study about paraprofessional support by Giangreco and colleagues (Broer, Doyle, & Giangreco, 2005), one student spoke of the embarrassment he felt at times over having a paraprofessional. He felt it was similar to having his mother with him:

I was kind of getting embarrassed because I always had, like, a mother right there. People were like looking at me and stuff, and saying, "Why do you always have this person with you who is twice as old as you?" (p. 420)

Even though paraprofessionals often provide side-by-side support in order to increase access and success for the student, that very support can still translate into a negative experiences for the embarrassed student. The placement of one student directly next to a paraprofessional (nearly attached) can be described as the *Velcro phenomenon*. As a paraprofessional, it is important to avoid being Velcroed to a student. Velcroing might include holding hands, walking next to a student, sitting next to a student, having a student on your lap, walking together in the halls, and so forth. There are many different alternatives to such close proximity; several suggestions are provided in this chapter. See the sections "Five Ways to Naturally Support Students" and "Six Ways to Facilitate Relationships" in this chapter.

The Velcro Phenomenon

In a study about paraprofessional support in the classroom (Malmgren & Causton-Theoharis, 2006), a second-grade student named Gary was observed as he worked in his classroom and played with his friends. Gary was supported by a paraprofessional throughout his day. During a 4-week period, Gary participated in only 32 interactions with his peers. Twenty-nine of those interactions occurred on the day when the paraprofessional was absent. Only three interactions occurred when the paraprofessional was with him, and the paraprofessional ended two of those three interactions by asking him to get back to work. Clearly, the presence of the paraprofessional had a significant impact on Gary's ability or willingness to connect with other students.

What do kids report about having paraprofessionals? Another important study examined the perspectives of high school students with disabilities attending general education classes with paraprofessional support. These students described their paraprofessionals' roles primarily in four ways: as 1) mother, 2) friend, 3) protector, and 4) primary teacher (Broer et al., 2005). The majority of the students in the study further, "expressed powerful messages of disenfranchisement, embarrassment, loneliness, rejection, fear, and stigmatization" (Broer et al., 2005, p. 427). These students can be powerful teachers to those responsible for their education. Paraprofessionals can learn from their voices and from those of other students to create supports that are not stigmatizing but that, instead, help students make friends and feel socially successful in school.

Hiding in Full View: Subtle, Gentle, and Respectful Support

I think I've helped Ian the most by giving him space and letting him do more on his own and stepping in when needed. He wouldn't be as successful as he is if I was always right next to him. —Jane (middle school paraprofessional)

At this point in the book, we will move to the art of paraprofessional support. There is a great deal of finesse, subtlety, and elegance that goes into excellent paraprofessional support. This part of the job requires the most nuance, careful action, and, at times, inaction. As Jamie Burke—a high school student with autism—spoke about adult support and its impact on his social interactions, he emphasized that the support he received should be subtle so that it would not interfere with his desire for a social life. He stated, "We are willing and ready to connect with other kids, and adults must quietly step into the background, camouflaging their help as a tiger who may hide in full view" (Tashie, Shapiro-Barnard, & Rossetti, 2006, p. 185).

Five Ways to Naturally Support Students

All students need to move toward independence as they grow. Providing support in natural ways is one way to help reduce dependence on support personnel. The following suggestions from Causton-Theoharis and Malmgren (2005) can help you maximize student independence and interdependence with peers and minimize student dependence on adults.

Physical Proximity

Always consider your physical proximity to the students you support: do not sit or place a chair meant for adult support next to a student. Where you position yourself during instruction is very important. There is rarely a reason to sit directly next to a student. Even if a student needs close support because of behavior or physical support, that student likely does not need you next to them 100% of the time. Never have a space permanently reserved for a paraprofessional next to a student. Remove the empty chair next to the student. Do not have any students sit on your lap or hold your hand unless that is commonly done for all students (e.g., in a preschool setting). If you feel that the expectation in a particular school or classroom is for you to sit next to a student, ask your team the following questions:

- When is it absolutely necessary to sit next to a student to provide one-to-one support? (Examples of this type of necessary support are when providing medical assistance, lifting/transferring a student, or scribing for a student.)
- Are there times during the day when I could provide the student with less support? If so, when?
- When and how can we help this student increase independence?
- When should I move away from this student?
- Could a peer provide key supports to this student?

Keep Students in Class

Friendships and relationships occur because of common experiences over long periods of time. Every time a student is removed from an inclusive classroom, that student loses potential time to interact, socialize, and learn with and from other students. If a student leaves for a sensory break, consider putting the sensory materials in the classroom; if a student is leaving because of challenging behavior, try to determine strategies that will help the student stay in the classroom (for strategies for working with students who have challenging behavior, see Chapter 8).

Encourage Peer Support

If a student asks for your help with something, encourage the student to ask a peer first. Make this the norm for all students. One useful way to set this up is to have all students follow the rule "ask 3 before me" (all students seek help from three peers before asking a paraprofessional or the teacher). Set up partnerships during instructional time. Have students work together. Set up play partners, transition partners (partners for walking to and from classes), choice-time partners, lunchtime partners, math partners, and so forth. Make sure the student you are supporting has a choice about whom they select as a partner. Giving students the skills to seek peer support is a valid and important lifelong skill.

If a peer approaches you with a question or comment that impacts your student, instead of responding to the peer yourself, facilitate a conversation so that the peer can share directly with your student. For example, if you enter the classroom late with your student, and a peer approaches you to say, "We're doing the Kid City graphic organizer now," you might respond with the following, "Great, can you bring Taylor up to speed?" and take a step back.

Encourage Independence and Interdependence

If a student is able to complete a task in your presence without adult support, have them complete the task without supervision the next time. For example, Andrea had been having trouble getting her lunch tray to the lunch table, so the paraprofessional had been carrying it to the table for her. The paraprofessional soon realized that the issue was the weight of the tray and the drink. So, the paraprofessional took the drink off the tray, and Andrea was able to carry her tray to her table independently. Andrea then decided she would just take two trips (one with her tray and one with the beverage) without the paraprofessional helping.

Continually ask yourself what the next step is that will enable a student to become more independent and less dependent on adult support. If a student will still need assistance, consider having peer interdependence, which is successfully completing the task with other students, be the goal. By the end of the year, sometimes Andrea's friend, Will, would carry her drink. Therefore, she would get to the table without any adult support and, instead, have the support of a friend. We provide more ideas for developing independence and interdependence in Chapter 8.

Fade Your Cues

One of the simplest, yet most effective ways to increase peer interaction for students is to fade the assistance of paraprofessionals. Fading assistance means actually reducing the type and level of support given to a student in a systematic way. Reducing support promotes independence, interdependence, and interaction with peers. Take a look at the cuing structure list shown in Table 7.1. The goal with this structure is always to move away from the most obtrusive (those on top) and toward the least obtrusive supports (those on the bottom) (Doyle, 2008). Chapter 9 provides more ideas and tools for fading cues and supports.

Providing natural or nonobtrusive supports is a very important first step toward helping students in need of support feel like everyone else. The next step in helping students connect with one another is to facilitate relationships and assist students with positive social interactions by becoming a bridge that links students and their peers.

Your Role as a Bridge Between Students With Disabilities and Their Peers

The next step in helping students connect with one another is to actually facilitate relationships and assist students with positive social interactions by becoming a bridge linking students and their peers. As a paraprofessional, you are in a unique position to become a bridge connecting students; you can blend in, provide more natural supports, and facilitate relationships among students in ways that general or special educators cannot.

Table 7.1. Types of support

Type of support (listed from most to least intrusive)	Definition	Example
Full physical	Direct and physical assistance used to support a student	Provide hand-over-hand assistance while a student writes their name.
Partial physical	Physical assistance provided for some of the total movement required for the activity	Begin to zip a student's coat; the student then pulls the zipper up the rest of the way.
Modeling	A demonstration of what the student is to do	The paraprofessional does an art project; the student uses the art project as a model.
Direct verbal	Verbal information provided directly to the student	"Josh, stand up now."
Indirect verbal	A verbal reminder that prompts the student to attend to or think about what is expected	"Josh, what should happen next?"
Gestural	A physical movement to communicate or accentuate a cue (e.g., head nod, thumbs up, pointing)	Paraprofessional points to the agenda written on the board.
Natural	Providing no cue; allowing the ordinary cues that exist in the environment help the student know what to do	The bell rings for class. The teacher asks students to move to the rug. A message on the chalkboard reads, "Turn to page 74."

Source: Doyle (2008).

Six Ways to Facilitate Relationships

The following section offers six ways to help students relate to one another to form lasting friendships. These ideas have been modified from Causton-Theoharis and Malmgren's (2005) article about increasing peer interactions for students with disabilities.

Highlight Similarities Among Students

In a general education classroom, students are continually talking and sharing stories about things not related to the curriculum (e.g., hobbies, extracurricular activities). Become conscious of conversations going on around the student, and point out similarities. For example, as students are talking about baseball, you might say, "Oh, Josh loves baseball." Or, as students are settling down with their library books, you might point out similarities among their books: "The two of you both selected books about computers. You can sit together and compare your books."

Help Students Invite Each Other to Socialize

Some students are very eager to socialize but do not know how to approach other students. It can be helpful for a paraprofessional to be proactive about all of the potential social situations that occur throughout the school day. Think ahead about social possibilities, and ask the student questions such as, "Who do you want to play with at recess today?" "How can you ask them?" "Who do you want to sit next to in study hall?"

If you have a student who is nonverbal, provide a picture list of the students in the class or load a class list with photos onto an available tablet or laptop. Make sure the student's communication device is programmed to be able to ask a friend to join them in activities. You could also create low-tech support using index card(s) that say things like, "Do you want to play with me?" or "Will you be my partner?" for such situations. It is important to empower students with opportunities to make their own decisions and to independently select the student with whom they want to work.

Provide Behavioral Supports That Are Social in Nature

When a student is rewarded for doing a good job, make the reception of the reward something social. This way, the reward can be more fun for all involved, and it will have the added benefit of allowing students to learn and practice social interaction. Some examples of these types of interactive behavioral supports follow:

- Encouraging your student to play basketball with a friend
- Encouraging your student to eat lunch with a friend
- Encouraging your student to make bead necklaces with a friend during study hall
- Encouraging your student to a computer game with a friend
- Encouraging your student to go to the library and read with a friend
- Encouraging your student to make an art project before school with a friend

Provide Your Student With Responsibilities That Are Interactive, Collaborative, and Strengths-Based

Students are commonly assigned responsibilities within the classroom and school environments. This is done to help students contribute to the classroom community and to build a sense of belonging. Paraprofessionals can be key participants in helping create partners for these tasks. For example, change the job responsibilities in the classroom so that all jobs are done with partners. When jobs arise in the classroom, ask students to do the jobs together: "Sue and Joryann, can you please pass out these papers?" You might also work with the teacher to create an Expert Wall on which students list their strengths in terms of how they can help the class community (e.g., spelling support, math support, organizational support, tech support, emotional/cheering up support). Make sure your student has a way to shine.

Help Other Students Understand

Peers are much more likely to interact with students if they understand necessary information about each other. Provide honest answers to students' questions. I (Julie) once heard a little girl ask a paraprofessional, in reference to another student's frequency modulation (FM) device, "Why does he wear that thing on his head?" The paraprofessional said that it was private and that she should get back to work. The student got back to work, but an important question had been left unanswered. In the mind of the little girl, the subject was not to be talked about. As an unintended result, that girl may perceive the FM system to be a taboo subject. Your job is not to share confidential information about students with their peers; however, there are times when providing basic information about a student or the type of support they are receiving may be helpful to other students. If you are unsure about whether to share information, ask the student in question and the special education service coordinator. As a more proactive way of addressing such subjects, some teaching teams have decided to bring their classes together to talk about what makes everyone diverse and how we can celebrate and value those differences. For example, the students in one middle school classroom all listed things that made them unique. Then, they posted this information on a bulletin board. Some students included things like, "I live with my grandmother" or "I speak two languages." One student in this class wrote, "I know sign language." This type of conversation can be used to describe specific behaviors or the accommodations that a student receives. Information can be shared about how and when to assist a particular student (e.g., do not talk in a baby voice, do ask whether they need help). Before initiating a discussion of this type, make sure the student is comfortable with the plan, and involve students and parents in deciding what information the student wants to share with their peers.

Get Out of the Way!

When a conversation among students has begun, give the students space so that a natural conversation can occur; eventually, a relationship may evolve. Think about where you should stand; try to be as unobtrusive to the student as possible. When we work with paraprofessionals to fade their support, a common mistake is to stand 3 or 4 feet away, keeping their eyes directly focused on the student. If you remain this close, it will be clear to everyone around that you are there, creating an invisible barrier between other students and the one you are supporting. Instead, while fading, move away and focus your attention on something else. Connect with other students and offer help in other ways to the class community.

Supporting Unstructured Time

Social interaction occurs at all times during the school day. Unstructured times are some of the most important to provide support that will help students connect with one another. Examples of key times are listed in the following sections, with some suggestions that should be useful.

Before and After School

Students spend a lot of time traveling to and from school. This is a perfect time to facilitate social interaction. Before and after school, help the student's family find a travel partner or someone in the neighborhood to walk to school or ride the bus with the student. Encourage students to attend events and join groups at school and in the community. Clubs, sporting events, and community programs are excellent opportunities for students to socialize, meet new people, and connect over shared interests and experiences. It is also an opportunity for peers to see students outside the academic classroom in new ways. For example, Trina was a freshman in high school who felt socially isolated and shy at school but felt comfortable and confident during her youth group meetings through her church. Her paraprofessional encouraged Trina to tell her peers at school about the youth group, emphasizing the fun activities they did together such as karaoke, songwriting, photography, and video game nights. Her peers' interest was piqued, and two girls decided to attend alongside Trina one week. Fast forward 3 years later, and Trina and those two girls are close friends who all went to prom together.

In the Hallway

Have walking partners in the hallway between classes. A teacher we know had her students go on talk walks as they traveled to and from class. Each student would receive an index card containing a quote from the book the class was reading, and the student would have to talk about the particular quote on their card. Or, the teacher would give each student a number and a partner, and the students would have to come up with as many mathematical equations that equal their numbers as possible. Another paraprofessional had a student push a student named Samantha in her wheelchair while another student walked alongside them. This allowed Samantha to have some space from an adult and a chance to converse. If a student does not use speech, program the student's device to have common chatty phrases such as, "How's it going?" As the student moves through the hallway, they can initiate interactions.

At Lunchtime

Do not have students with disabilities sit together at one table. Instead, help students select lunch places at which they will feel the most comfortable and, at the same time, have increased likelihood of interacting with peers. Some schools create interest tables at which students' interests are printed on table tent cards (e.g., TikTok, chess, Animal Crossing, rainforest animals). Students then sit at tables that interest them and can freely converse about their preferred topic. Other schools have lunch bunches. Organizing a lunch bunch is a useful way to help a student who struggles with social interaction during the lunch period. A lunch bunch involves gathering a group of students to get together during the lunch period for a particular purpose (e.g., planning the end-of-year picnic, creating a class yearbook). This mixed group of students (not all students with disabilities) can meet weekly to complete the task. At the end of the year, the lunch bunch might celebrate the accomplishments with a pizza party. The goal is to bring students together in a more intimate setting, foster social interaction, and help form friendships. Music can also be provided at lunchtime to create a calming atmosphere. A paraprofessional in one school employed this strategy because Jonah, the student with autism whom she supported, had found the lunchroom to be overwhelming to his senses. After asking him what kind of music he would like to have on, she piped Beatles music into the lunchroom, providing a calming atmosphere for all students. And, best of all, Jonah was able to stay in the lunchroom and connect with other students.

At Free or Choice Time

Help students choose the activities in which they want to take part and which peers they would like to invite to participate. In high school, where a student sits is crucial. Have each student select a location in the room by asking the student where they would prefer to sit, and respect that choice. During recess time, or during any other downtime outside of class, bring an activity that is particularly interesting to the student. For example, an elementary student, Chelsea, loved to make beaded necklaces at home. So, the paraprofessional working with her brought a beading kit to class and told the students that they could use the kit as long as they shared it. She put it on Chelsea's desk and asked her to be responsible for it. At recess, four girls and two boys had formed a semicircle around Chelsea and the beading kit, and all of them were making necklaces.

This may seem more difficult at the secondary level, but in fact, there are often more ways to connect students during free time in middle and high school. For example, Alex was a high school student who was skilled at interacting with younger students but had difficulty connecting with same-age peers. His paraprofessional suggested that he join the Reading Buddy program, in which high-school students visited the district elementary school to read to the students during free study hall time. Over the next few months, not only did Alex feel successful as part of the Reading Buddy program, he developed a friendship with a peer his age who had also joined the group.

To Select Partners

We have supported students in classrooms for a long time, and three words we—and most students—dread hearing are, "Find a partner." Inevitably, as students clamor to work with their friends, someone will be left without a partner. If that happens, do not become the student's partner. Instead, help the student find a friend. However, to create a more sustainable solution that helps every student feel that they belong, there are many effective inclusive partnering strategies to use. For example, one very thoughtful paraprofessional, Corrie, grew disheartened seeing the same scenario occur repeatedly during math class: One of Corrie's students, Caleb, felt so bad every time partner selection occurred that he would not participate in the activity. Corrie worked with the math teacher to create partners who would remain constant so that this type of disruption would not have to occur. She found a Clock Buddies sheet online (see Figure 7.1) and, with the teacher's help, set up partners for the rest of the year by having students sign up on the Clock Buddies sheet. From that point on, when the teacher would say, "Find your 4:00 partner," Caleb knew exactly who his partner would be, and he was able to participate successfully in the math center.

CLOCK BUDDIES

Figure 7.1.   Clock Buddies. From Jones (1998–2006). Copyright © Raymond C. Jones. All Rights Reserved. http://www.ReadingQuest.org

Another wonderful paraprofessional, Jenn, worked with middle schoolers and noted similar issues for her students whenever teachers asked the class to find a partner or get with a small group; her students stood or sat alone, slumping against walls or chairs as they noticed peers had not approached them to work together. Jenn spoke with the teacher about her concerns and together they came up with more effective ways to partner all students:

- *Vocabulary Match-up*—Jenn created a class set of content-specific cards that included a vocabulary word and matching definitions. The teacher passed the cards out to the class and students had to match up based on the vocabulary word and correct definition.

- *Expert List Connection*—Jenn and the teacher used a student Expert List to match students up. They each began their partnerships by learning about their partner's unique expertise.

- *Playing Card Partners*—The teacher brought in a set of playing cards and Jenn passed them out to the class, and students had to find a small group based on the same suit, color, or number.

Support During Instructional Time

During instructional time, walk around the room, supporting all students and answering everyone's questions. It can be very stigmatizing to be the only one receiving help. The best scenario is one in which you provide support to the entire class, with none of the students thinking that you are there to help a specific student. Avoid calling yourself "Claire's helper or assistant." Instead, refer to yourself as someone who supports everyone who needs help. As soon as a student has gotten started, do not hover. Give the student space to work and make mistakes, just like everyone else. Have the student request help in the same way that everyone else does. If you must redirect a student, do so quietly. Also praise quietly. Each of these aspects is important, and your support should be as unobtrusive and gentle as possible.

To ensure that all students come into contact with a student with disabilities, you can move instructional materials to the student instead of asking the other students to go to a certain station or object. Julie once observed a paraprofessional do this beautifully with Jonah, a student in kindergarten who used a wheelchair. All of the students were moving over to a globe to gather information. The paraprofessional decided to move the globe over to Jonah's desk, and, as the students came over to look at it, many of them interacted with Jonah. For more examples of supporting students with social interactions—both in and out of the classroom—see Table 7.2.

Don't Forget Familiar Technology

Students today are skilled at connecting with peers via text messaging, social media, and video platforms. Help students to connect with peers this way by introducing the idea of video chatting (e.g., FaceTime), texting, or using social media to connect with peers after school hours. Social networking, video calls, and texts can open up a new world of communication, inclusion, and community participation. It allows students to connect socially with peers even if they are not able to leave home, or if social situations can feel difficult in person (e.g., Ben likes using Twitter to communicate with friends instead of attending crowded social situations where eye contact is difficult). Be sure to communicate with the student's family to ensure their consent in allowing the child to participate on social media and other platforms; ensure that you know all of the boundaries surrounding the child's use to respect family rules and expectations.

QUICK QUIZ

What are three ways to provide social supports to students during unstructured times?

1.

2.

3.

What are three ways to provide social supports during structured times like academics?

1.

2.

3.

Table 7.2.   Social supports across activities

When the student is asked to do . . .	Try this . . .
Transition to another location	Ask the student and a peer of they want to walk to the next class together, or give your student a job as line leader for the whole class.
Play with a peer	Create a game or activity on the playground that can be played by many students.
Work in a small group	Provide specific roles for students in the small group that require students to work together and use each other's strengths. For example, a student can be the task manager if they like organization, and another student can be the notetaker if they are self-conscious about talking with his peers.
Express ideas	Ask your student and a peer to talk through the concept together. If your student likes to talk but has difficulty writing, the peer can be the scribe. If your student has difficulty expressing thoughts verbally, they can be the scribe or notetaker.
Follow directions	Ask your student to check in with a peer about the directions, or ask a peer if they could talk your student through the directions for the assignment.

Specific Strategies for Facilitating Support From Peers

STRATEGIES

Peer support is a highly recommended strategy for improving social outcomes for students with disabilities. But have you ever felt unsure about how to direct a peer to support your student? This is common, as paraprofessionals and educators do not always have explicit training regarding how to facilitate peer support for students. Recent research by Brock and Carter (2016), however, provides evidence that students with disabilities experience increased social outcomes when paraprofessionals use particular behaviors to clearly communicate with peers how to support a student with a disability. Those facilitation behaviors range from prompting academic support to reinforcing social interaction. Review Brock and Carter's ideas and examples in Table 7.3.

REFLECTIONS

Do you already use any of the peer support facilitation behaviors? Which ones can you begin to use?

Teach the Rules of Social Interaction

Many students struggle with *how* to interact with others. They feel they are playing a game for which they do not know the rules. If you are working with a student who feels this way, teach them the rules explicitly. But, do not teach the rules in isolation or in a separate room with only students who have disabilities. Instead, use everyday moments in the classroom and hallways, and on the playground, to artfully teach students how to interact with one another. Examples of supporting your student's social education might take place in the following situations: during a natural interaction between a student and a peer; in connection to class literature and videos, which can be filled with topics about making new friends; experiencing and handling bullying behavior; and experiencing and processing new social situations at every age. Research (Lavoie, 2005) shows that immediately after a social interaction it can be useful to discuss what actions or social skills the student practiced, and determine whether or not the outcome was what they wanted to happen (i.e., positive or negative) and whether the student would repeat the action or skill in a similar future situation. There are many other resources and tools available to help you teach social skills to students who need additional support are outlined in the following section.

Using Assistive Technology to Support Socialization

Assistive technology devices, both low tech and high tech, are incredibly effective for supporting socialization for many students who need additional support and scaffolding to interact with peers. Often, the easiest way is to use low-tech supports in the form of pictures and symbols.

Table 7.3. Paraprofessional behaviors, definitions, and examples

Behavior	Definition	Example
Prompt social interaction	Paraprofessional encourages or suggests a way for the focal student to interact with a peer, or a peer with the focal student.	Paraprofessional points to a symbol on augmentative communication device to prompt the focal student to answer a question from a peer.
Reinforce social interaction	Paraprofessional praises the focal student or peer with social interactions (verbally or with gestures).	The paraprofessional gives the focal student a thumbs-up when he greets a peer.
Provide information for social interaction	Paraprofessional provides information to peers that might help peers better interact with the student. This includes information about how the focal student communicates, interpreting the focal student's, behavior, the focal student's interest, and possible conversation topics.	Paraprofessional says to peer, "When Dylan tries to stroke your hair, that is his way of trying to interact with you. Just let him know that you don't like it, but you would love to give him a fist bump and talk with him."
Prompt academic support	Paraprofessional encourages or suggests a way for peers to work with the focal student to help them participate in class.	Paraprofessional says to peer, "Maybe after the lecture, you could explain to Sarah in a few sentences what it was about."
Reinforce academic support	Paraprofessional praises the peers for the way they are working with the focal student to help them participate in class.	Paraprofessional says to peer, "That was really smart to think of helping Marty outline his paper so he could go back and fill in the information."
Provide information for academic support	Paraprofessional provides information to peers so that they might better support the student. This includes information about strengths and needs related to class participation, accommodations and modifications, and instructional strategies.	Paraprofessional says to peer, "Olivia has a really hard time writing. Maybe she could tell you the answer and you could write it down."
Prompt proximity	Paraprofessional prompts the focal student and peers to be in close proximity (verbally or with gestures).	Paraprofessional asks the focal student to sit by a peer so they can partner for an activity.
Check in with peers	Paraprofessional communicates with peers to see if they are comfortable in their role providing support, if there is anything they want to talk about or discuss, or if they would like assistance from the paraprofessional.	Paraprofessional says to peer, "You look frustrated. Is there something I can do to help?"

Source: Brock, M. E., & Carter, E. W. (2016). Efficacy of teachers training paraprofessionals to implement peer support arrangements. *Exceptional Children, 82,* 354–371. doi: 10.1177/0014402915585564

Social Stories

Social stories were originally developed as a way to teach children with ASD social skills through story and images, but they are now used to support students of all kinds who would benefit from additional communication support. The social story typically describes a social situation from the perspective of the student. The story should describe what happens during the social situation and provide a variety of scenarios and responses. We recommend using language, symbols, and pictures, or create a video if that works best for the student. Students should also have the opportunity to participate in co-writing the social story. Once the story is complete, review the story with the student before they enter that particular social scenario (e.g., at lunchtime or recess). The social story is one example. To review additional examples of social stories, we recommend Carol Gray's web site: www.carolgraysocialstories.com.

SOCIAL STORY: GOING to the LIBRARY

Some days we walk to the Library as a class.

When I get to the Library, I am quiet. (SHHH...)

I can choose 5 books to check out.

I walk back to class with my teacher.

Going to the Library can be fun! ☺♥

Visual Schedules

Visual schedules can be created on paper or on a laptop, tablet, or phone. Visual schedules typically combine pictures and words that represent the schedule of expected classroom activities in the exact order they will be completed. They can also be created as a First–Then activity; for example, first, the student says, "Hi, will you be my partner?" and then the student and their peer work side by side. Visual schedules can be created for an individual student you work with, or you can create one for an entire classroom (see Figure 7.2).

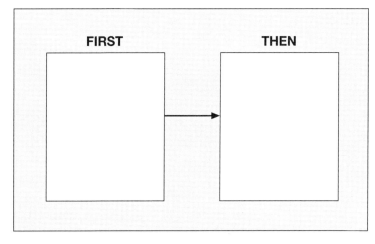

Figure 7.2.   First–then example.

Feelings Chart, Books, or Posters

We can help students recognize and learn to recognize emotions using a feelings chart, poster, or book. This tool visualizes emotions through cartoon faces or faces of real people, whichever is more beneficial to the student. The tool can be created as a laminated chart to carry in the student's binder, a small book to flip through, or a visual to pull up on a tablet or phone. You can also create a feelings poster for the whole class. These tools help students understand emotional responses from peers and adults and can help them to express their own feelings too.

Teaching Social Skills in Culturally Relevant Ways

Students come to school with incredibly diverse home lives in which, over time, they have learned the language, traditions, attitudes, behaviors, and norms associated with their family culture. These particular cultural norms are also influenced greatly by where the student lives, their socioeconomic backgrounds, family levels of education, religion, and other unique experiences. Upon entering school, however, students are often expected to behave and socialize in ways that are accepted by the *majority* culture present in the school or community. When there is a discrepancy between a student's cultural norms and the majority culture's norms, the student can often experience stigmatization, stereotyping, and bias from peers and staff.

To avoid this danger for a student, it is so important for staff to learn about students' backgrounds rather than making assumptions. Then, staff must take student backgrounds into account when teaching social skills at school.

Gloria Ladson-Billings, an educational researcher who studies culturally relevant teaching, explained that staff must raise questions about *what* they are teaching (Fay, 2019). For example, you could ask, "What's the cultural implication of teaching this social skill?" or "What do I want this student to do with this skill?" Often, we believe we must teach students a particular skill because they need to know it. However, it is very important for us to ask *why* they might need to know it. Researchers who study social skills—and cultural relevancy in particular—explain that after first recognizing and honoring students' cultural backgrounds when it comes to social behaviors and attitudes, it is then important to identify appropriate opportunities to teach students social norms from

THERE'S AN APP FOR THAT
Social Stories
• Story Maker
• ConnectABILITY
Visual Schedules
• First Then Visual Schedule
• Choiceworks
Feelings Books, Posters, Charts
• Emotions & Feelings Chart

within the majority culture to help students feel empowered to operate within and participate in that majority culture (Richardson, 1998).

For example, if a student comes from a cultural background in which eye contact is seen as intrusive, simply teaching a student "Look someone in the eye when they are speaking to you" does not honor their cultural norm and does not help them understand why it might be important for them to learn the skill. Instead, you might say, "I know at home you look down when someone is speaking to show them respect. But Johnny uses eye contact at home with his family to show that he is listening and respects what they say." This type of conversation can help students understand that differences in cultural norms is common and expected, and that learning each other's cultural norms can be important for social relationships and friendships.

REFLECTIONS

Stop and reflect about your own cultural background. What do you know about your own cultural identity? What social norms do you practice with your family and within your culture? What is important to you regarding these practices? What is less important? Have you ever been the target of discrimination due to your cultural background and the cultural norms you practice?

FAQs

Commonly Asked Questions About Social Supports

Q. **This student's challenging behavior makes other kids not want to be around them. What do I do about that?**

A. First, you have to understand that the student is worthy of friendships and relationships. Help support the student in a way that will both minimize the behavior *and* help others understand the behavior. One student, Kenny, used to rock back and forth when he felt anxious, and this behavior looked strange to Kenny's peers. Simply explaining to the other students what the behavior meant allowed one bright student to ask Kenny, "What can I do to help you stop rocking?" Kenny typed out a response: "Let me put my hand on your shoulder." From that moment on, Kenny's peers helped him to manage his rocking behavior by asking, "Do you want to lean on me?"

Q. **You suggest that I should not remove the learner from the classroom, but one student has sensory issues that do not allow them to be in the lunchroom. What do I do about that?**

A. Consider some of the lunchroom ideas discussed in this chapter. Make the lunchroom fit the student. Consider music, lunch partners, interest centers, or a quieter lunch space with fewer peers.

Q. **I understand why I should fade my support, but I worry that people will think I am not doing my job. What can I do while I am fading my support?**

A.   This is a common concern. When moving away from a student, you can support other students, prepare for an upcoming class by creating modifications, take data on social interactions or behavior, read the student's IEP, help the teacher prepare for an upcoming task, or search the school library and Internet for pictures and videos to support learning. You also can ask your team to brainstorm a list of ideas that fit your particular situation. The best practice is to be open and communicate frequently with your colleagues so that everyone is on the same page about fading support.

Conclusion

Seth was introduced at the beginning of this chapter. Seth is a student who struggles with social interactions. The biggest detriment to his social life is that he has an adult supporting him for the entire school day. Friendships and relationships are critical to Seth's development and quality of life. This is true for all students, and for those who are supported by a paraprofessional, care needs to be taken to ensure maximum social interaction. The suggestions mentioned in this chapter are meant to support your efforts to include students in the social aspects of school. The previous chapter focused on providing support during academic instructional time. However, be mindful that you often will need to provide both social and academic supports at the same time. It is also crucial for paraprofessionals to take a holistic approach when supporting their students, so the next chapter discusses ways to provide behavioral support along with academic and social supports.

ACTIVITY:
Social Support Strategies

ACTIVITIES

Throughout this chapter, we have provided you with many strategies, ideas, and resources for supporting and encouraging a student to connect with peers and learn social interaction rules. Take some time to write down which strategies and ideas you will want to use with your students. Ask your team of teachers to support you and give you feedback on your ideas. Educators should not assume that loneliness or isolation are part of the schooling experience; we can intervene and help students make and maintain friendships.

To Do

TO-DO LIST

After reading this chapter ...

• Complete the activites and reflections in this chapter.

• Write down three new ways you can commit to facilitating peer relationships for your students. Discuss your ideas with your colleagues, and try them out as soon as possible.

- Observe and write down what happens when you facilitate peer relationships between your student and peers. Share this information with your team.

- Take some time to research any supports or ideas in this chapter that you want to learn more about.

8

Providing Behavior Supports

I haven't had enough training to handle this kid. If I tell him to stop, he continues. If I try to make him stop, he screams. I literally don't know what to do when he is out of control. Maybe this is not the job for me... —Ben (paraprofessional)

I recently learned that at school they were restraining my child. They were actually lying on top of him. It made me sick to think about how powerless he must have felt. I marched in the next day, and that situation has changed... But I think about that every day, and I worry that he does too. —Tracy (parent)

Consider Your Mindset on Challenging Behavior

Before we begin this chapter about supporting students with challenging behavior, we invite you to read this mantra. Take time meditating on each line.

- This is someone's child.
- This is a good person.
- This student wants to be successful.
- This student is communicating something with their behavior.
- I can figure out what this student needs.
- I can set this student up for success.
- I can choose to respond with care.
- I can welcome this student into this space.
- I can forgive past mistakes.
- I can start fresh each day.

The Most Challenging Behaviors

We were once giving a presentation to a large group of teachers. We asked them to list the most challenging behaviors they had seen among their students. The teachers thought about it for a while and then shared their lists as we wrote their ideas on chart paper. The lists included swearing, fighting, yelling, shutting down, becoming silent, running out of the room, hitting, and injuring oneself (e.g., biting one's own arm).

Do You Ever Exhibit Challenging Behaviors?

We then asked this same group of teachers whether they ever had participated in those behaviors themselves. I told them to raise their hands if they ever had sworn, fought, yelled, shut down, become silent, run out of a room, hit someone, or done anything to hurt themselves. The sound of nervous laughter filled the room as almost everyone raised their hands. This is no reflection about that particular group of teachers. On occasion, most people behave in ways that would be considered challenging, concerning, or at least unbecoming. When we then asked the teachers to distinguish the students' challenging behaviors from their own behavior, one teacher responded, in a half-joking manner, "When I have bad behavior, I have a darn good reason!" Guess what? So do students.

What Do You Need?

We next asked the group to think about what they needed when they behaved poorly. They brainstormed this list: a hug, time away, someone to listen, a glass of wine, a nap, a cool-off period, changing the subject, talking to someone, a walk, or fresh air.

We personally consider this a great list. Many of those things also help us calm down when we are angry or upset. Notice, however, not only what they suggested but also what was *not* suggested. No teacher reported needing a sticker chart. No one said they needed to be lectured or kicked out of the room. Instead, like most people, these adults needed support, comfort, and calm, gentle understanding. Students need that, too.

Students Need the Same Things

Take a look back at that list. Students who are in crisis—who are upset or out of control—need comfort and understanding. The same exact strategies or ideas you use with yourself can be used with students. It might take some creativity to figure out how and when to support, but a hug, a rest, a cool-off period, a walk, or someone to listen are some of the best ways to provide support.

You will likely work with students who have challenging behaviors. These may range from relatively nonconfrontational behaviors, such as skipping class or shutting down, to more significant or externalizing behaviors, such as fighting with other classmates, running out of the school, or hurting oneself. This chapter begins with a discussion of ways to think about students, typical responses to challenging behaviors. Then, we present a series of recommendations of what to do before, during, and after students demonstrate these types of challenging behaviors. At the end of the chapter, we answer some commonly asked questions.

All Students Are Naturally Good and Whole: No Student Is Bad or Broken

Our students are not challenging or bad. Student actions and behaviors might present as challenging or disruptive. However, we must remember that students themselves are good and whole. And challenging behavior is evidence of our students asking us for help, for new tools, for connection, for support, or for guidance. The more significant the behaviors, the more we need to let our students know that we do not believe they are bad or broken. We need to let those students know we are there to support them.

ALL students are naturally GOOD & WHOLE.

Students Want to Succeed

No matter how challenging the student's behavior, all students want the same thing: to be loved, valued, and understood. They want to hold a conversation with peers without running away. They want to have a good relationship with you and their teachers. They want to complete their homework.

However, students might not yet have the skills, knowledge, or opportunities to succeed. For example, if we assume that a student is manipulative because their challenging behavior helped them to get out of class, this manipulation would also require the student to use forethought, planning, and organization. However, most students with challenging behavior do not have those planning and organizational skills. If the student did have those skills, she would most likely already be succeeding at the tasks in class. So, it comes down to you and her teachers to help her gain the necessary skills so she can succeed.

> No matter how challenging the student's behavior, all students want the same thing: to be loved, valued, and understood.

Responses to Challenging Behavior

In schools across the country, there are a variety of responses to students who express challenging behavior. In this section, we will review two common approaches: the control approach and the PBS approach.

The Typical Response: Control

Herb Lovett, a researcher who was at the University of New Hampshire's Institute of Disability, described the typical response to challenging behavior:

Our initial response to an unwanted behavior is to react, to correct what we perceive to be unacceptable, inappropriate behavior. The thinking behind this perception is that the person exhibiting the behavior has lost control and that those who are in charge—in control—are responsible for regaining it through the application of methods and technologies specifically designed for this purpose. (1996, p. 136)

A major issue with this type of response is that when the chosen method of control does not work, the teacher or paraprofessional tends to become frustrated and, consequently, uses more punitive methods for control. The intentions backfire, and, through the need to control and correct, teachers and paraprofessionals often create formidable barriers that further alienate them from those they are supposed to support and teach (Lovett, 1996). This way of thinking involves a negative connotation of behavior: "What is wrong with this student?" instead of "How can I support more effectively?" When educators use more humanistic behavior supports, they do not blame students. Instead, they reflect on the curriculum, environment, social space, and necessary skills the student might need to acquire in order to better understand the behaviors.

A Different Approach: Positive Behavior Support

PBS has been developed "as a movement away from the traditional mechanistic, and even aversive behavior management practices that were being applied to individuals with disabilities" (Bambara, Janney, & Snell, 2015, p. 4). This approach "emphasizes the use of collaborative teaming and problem-solving processes to create support[s] that stress prevention and remediation of problem behaviors through the provision of effective educational programming and the creation of a supportive environment" (Bambara et al., 2015, p. 5). Ultimately, behavior is a form of communication, and educators should approach situations with a problem-solving mindset.

The basic tenets of PBS are as follows:

1. Behavior is learned and can change.
2. Intervention is based on studying the behavior.
3. The response emphasizes prevention and teaching new behaviors.
4. Outcomes are personally and socially valued.
5. Intervention requires comprehensive, integrated supports. (Bambara et al., 2015)

Note that approaching challenging behaviors with a PBS framework requires a team approach. As a paraprofessional, you should not be expected to design a PBS program. Nevertheless, understanding the basic tenets of the framework is important because you will likely be responsible for helping to carry out behavior plans for some students. Having a clear understanding of your approach with students is central to the success of the student.

Proactive Behavior Support

Most challenging behaviors can be avoided or managed by thinking ahead. Thinking ahead involves determining what might work well for the specific student.

Gabe, a student with autism, has a very difficult time with changes in his schedule. He needs to know when transitions will occur. If he is surprised by a change in the schedule, he hides in his locker, paces, or runs around the room. One way to avoid this issue is to prepare Gabe for each day's schedule. The teaching team does this by having a peer greet Gabe's bus in the morning. Gabe and his peer then walk to the room together; when they reach the classroom, they review the agenda for the day. Gabe also has an individual copy of the schedule in his planner and he reviews it as frequently as he needs. This strategy represents one of the most successful ways to prepare Gabe for the day ahead and to reduce his anxiety—and therefore the anxious behavioral responses—about the schedule.

Building and Maintaining a Relationship

In his research, Lovett has also highlighted the importance of relationships and connections as more central than anything else related to supporting students behaviorally:

A positive approach [to behavior] invites people to enter into the same sort of relationship that most of us have and treasure: ongoing, with mutual affection and regard. In such relationships, we all make mistakes, are all in some ways inadequate and yet it is not the level of success that is the ongoing commitment. In the context of relationships, the success and failure of our work becomes harder to assess because the key elements no longer involve simply quantity but the more complex issues of quality. We professionals have routinely overlooked the significance of relationships. (1996, p. 137)

Getting to know your students and learning what they enjoy can be a truly helpful way to address challenging behaviors. As Tim Knoster says in his book *The Teacher's Pocket Guide to Effective Classroom Management*, "Creating a suitable level of rapport with students is an absolute essential prerequisite for helping students behave" (Knoster, 2008, p. 25).

Lisa, a paraprofessional working with Connie, a high school student with Down syndrome, was having a difficult time getting to know Connie. Lisa decided to go to Connie's cheerleading competition after school to watch her perform in order to get to know her better. After the routine was over, Connie introduced Lisa to several of her cheerleading teammates. In addition, when Connie's mom came to pick up her daughter, their dog Max was in the car, so Lisa got to meet Max. Lisa indicated that this experience helped her to break down Connie's walls and to see how very important Connie's friends were to her. Lisa said that up until that time, "I did not see how important just being a typical teenager was. This helped me give her more distance." When Connie was interviewed about her relationship with Lisa, Connie said, "I trust her. Even my dog Max likes her!"

Lisa created an opportunity for Connie to begin to trust her. She achieved this through making an outside connection and by continuing to be a respectful and trustworthy figure in Connie's life. However, there are many different ways to form relationships and to let students know that you trust them and that they can trust you. Some different methods include giving students space, having fun with the student, learning more about the student's interests, seeing the same movies that the student enjoys, participating in the same activities the student likes, and talking to the student about their friends and hobbies. The next section discusses additional ways to build rapport each day with students.

An important thing to remember is that you want to have a warm, trustworthy, and professional relationship with the student. However, it is important to note that this is not about becoming friends with the student. The goal is to be a trustworthy support but also to help the student connect to other students. Peer relationships are incredibly important; therefore, watch to be sure that the relationship is professional and warm but does not replace any typical peer connections.

How Do I Build Rapport With Students?

Latham (1999), an educational scholar and professor who was considered an expert in human behavior, provided steps for parents to build rapport with

REFLECTIONS

In what ways do you already build a positive, trusting relationship with students? In what ways do you hope to build a positive relationship with students?

their children. These steps have been modified for paraprofessional use with students and are as follows:

1. Demonstrate age-appropriate touch (e.g., high-five, handshake), facial expressions (reflect the nature of the situation), tone of voice (e.g., your voice also should match the situation), and body language (e.g., appear relaxed, keep your arms open, be attentive, look at the student).

2. Ask open-ended questions (e.g., "What are you doing after school?" "What do you think about that book?" "What was your favorite part of the movie?").

3. Listen while the student is speaking. Ideally, talk much less than the student (do not interrupt or change the subject).

4. Demonstrate the use of empathetic statements. Act like a mirror and reflect the child's feelings by expressing your understanding and caring (e.g., "I know this feels really discouraging right now" or "I know you must be so angry, and I am here for you if you want to talk about it or just sit here together").

5. Ignore nuisance behavior, such as talking out of turn, tapping a pencil, or doodling, and let the little stuff slide so it doesn't escalate into a larger issue.

REFLECTIONS

In what specific ways do you currently build rapport with students? In what specific ways would you like to build rapport with students?

Matching Instructional Practices to Student Strengths

One of the simplest ways to support students' positive behavior is to match instructional techniques to student strengths. For example, when a student who is a successful artist is allowed to draw their ideas during a social studies lecture, the student is more likely to be engaged and have positive behavior. As a paraprofessional, you may not have a lot of control regarding how the instruction is planned. However, some paraprofessionals have very successfully helped teachers integrate new instructional techniques that support student learning. By trying out ideas and putting new plans in place, you can discover alternative approaches that others on the team can also try. You can always suggest new ideas. Never underestimate your power and creativity in supporting the students with whom you work.

Paraprofessional Sue supports a student, Alex, who needs to move around the room often. Sue asks the general education teacher whether they can put chart paper on the wall and have all students stand and use markers to do a brainstorming activity instead of doing it at their desks. The teacher is willing to try it. Alex is more successful, and the other students seem to really enjoy this approach. Before this, Alex was considered a problem because he never sat still. He was always out of his seat, wiggling and moving. What Sue sensed was that Alex's misbehavior indicated a learning preference—a bodily kinesthetic learning preference. Sue had an idea for putting more movement into Alex's learning.

Knowing and understanding why and how students misbehave can help you identify what they need. Research has demonstrated that aligning instruction with students' strengths can effectively decrease negative behavior and increase on-task behaviors (Kornhaber, Fierros, & Veenema, 2004). See the connections between behaviors and strengths along with examples of support outlined in Table 8.1.

> Knowing and understanding why and how students misbehave can help you identify what they need.

Table 8.1. Connections between behaviors and strengths

Student behaviors	Student strengths	What the student needs	Example
Student is constantly moving and fidgeting.	Bodily kinesthetic learners	Student needs more movement during instruction.	EunYoung needs to move during instruction. So, when the teacher reads aloud to the class, EunYoung is allowed to sit in a rocking chair. The teachers in EunYoung's class let the students sit however they like during certain class activities.
Student is continually talking.	Interpersonal learners or verbal/linguistic learners	Student needs more interaction during learning.	Gwen works best when she is able to talk with peers. So, before writing a journal entry, she is given a few minutes to talk to a friend about what she plans to write.
Student is constantly singing, tapping, or drumming.	Musical learners/musically gifted	Student needs more musical access in school.	Lucy enjoys music, so the teacher uses music during writing workshops. The music helps Lucy stay focused, and other students also enjoy it.
Student often daydreams or does not pay attention in class.	Intrapersonal learners; enjoy making connections to their own lives	Student needs more time during school to make personal connections to the content.	Jerry enjoys making personal connections. So, during the *Little House on the Prairie* (Wilder, 1932–1943, 1971) unit, Jerry's assignment is to determine how each of the settlers is like him and different from him.
Student draws or doodles instead of taking notes or listening.	Spatial or visual learners; artistically gifted	Make art part of the learning process.	Rubin likes to draw. So, while he listens to a mini-lecture about cellular division, Rubin has the option of drawing the concepts.
Student does not engage in activities unless they are highly structured or logical.	Logical, mathematical; enjoy mathematical calculations	Use math and logic to strengthen student's learning in other subjects.	Jorge loves math and struggles during English. So, the paraprofessional has Jorge make Venn diagrams, timelines, and graphs about the characters in *Romeo and Juliet*. This helps him keep track of all of the characters, and, during discussion, he shares his charts with other students to help them remember the details of the book.

REFLECTIONS

Consider your students' challenging behaviors. What type of intelligences or strengths do they likely have? What might they need more of?

Set Up the Environment in a Way That Promotes Positive Behavior

Have you ever walked into a classroom that felt controlled and stiff? Have you ever been in a learning environment from which you wanted to escape? Alternatively, have you ever entered a learning space that felt warm and welcoming? What type of learning environment promotes learning? The following list offers ideas to help promote a more comfortable classroom environment for positive behavior outcomes during class:

- Arrange desks in a way that allows for easy student interaction. Desks grouped into small tables are more likely to promote interaction than are rows and columns of desks.
- Seat students with disabilities in different locations in the room. Do not group students with disabilities together. It can be quite stigmatizing to group students by disability or ability. Instead, mix up the groups so that everyone has a chance to learn from their peers.
- Create a calm, relaxed place in which students feel comfortable moving around and engaging with others.
- Create structure by posting the agenda or daily schedule.
- Do not isolate any student by seating them in a separate location.
- Make the room feel like a unique space for students by adorning the walls with student work.
- Have music playing softly in the background at appropriate times.
- If students are expected to sit on the floor, a soft, carpeted place will make them feel more comfortable.
- If a student struggles with personal space, have all students sit on carpet squares, or in their own space if the students are older.
- If a student does not like to be called on in class without warning, set up a system to let the student know when the teacher might call on them. For example, the teacher tells the student what question she will ask before class starts. That gives ample time to prepare an answer.

REFLECTIONS

What environmental supports are in place in the classrooms you work in? Can you think of other ways to make the school environment more relaxed and comfortable?

Although paraprofessionals are often deployed after challenging behaviors have started, a better use of paraprofessional time and energy is in helping to create comfortable and relaxed environments so that problematic behaviors are less likely to occur.

Meet Students' Needs

All human beings require certain things to be happy and, therefore, well behaved. These things have been called *universal desires* (Lovett, 1996). Autonomy, relationships, interdependence, safety, trust, self-esteem, belonging, self-regulation, accomplishment, communication, happiness, and joy are needs for all human beings. Helping students meet these needs is essential to creating learning environments in which students feel comfortable and safe; such feelings, in turn, help resolve behavioral issues.

Autonomy

Autonomy means the right or power to govern oneself or to be self-determined. To help students feel autonomous, provide choices and allow them to make as many decisions as possible throughout the school day. Examples include choice in location of seat, whom to sit by, the materials to use for a project, the topic of a project, the type of writing instrument, whether to have something modified, or what to eat. Allowing students more choices enhances their ability to make decisions and become independent people.

Relationships and Interdependence

The entirety of the previous chapter of this book was dedicated to relationships. This is because relationships are deeply important. Students need to be allowed to have relationships and connections with their peers. Opportunities should be created for students to help one another. Chapter 7 suggested several strategies for facilitating relationships and building connections among students. When these needs are not met, students will invariably try to gain each other's attention. This occurs in a variety of ways: it may be through hitting, teasing, tapping, or pestering. Students might also seem lonely and choose to sit by themselves. They may seem angry and intentionally act out to try to get removed from certain settings. If you notice that a student is exhibiting challenging behaviors, be sure to observe them when interacting with peers. You may learn that the student needs support or encouragement in the area of building friendships with their peers.

Safety and Trust

Creating a safe, trusting relationship requires you to follow through when you say you are going to do something. Demonstrate that you can be trusted and that you are not there to punish or hurt any students. Keep your promises to students; it has been found that "many people who engage in difficult behaviors have too much experience with broken promises" (Pitonyak, 2007, p. 18). Continually send the message that you can be trusted to help and support, not to punish and manage. Do not remove students from the learning environment. Every time a student is removed for a time-out or a brief stint in the hall, a clear message is sent to that student. The message is, "You are not welcome here.

Your membership in this community is contingent on your behavior." This tends to create a vicious cycle; students feel that they do not belong, and they act in ways to demonstrate such feelings—if they are removed, their suspicions are reinforced.

Happiness and Joy

All students need happiness and joy in their learning environments. When supporting a student, ask yourself, "How often does this student experience genuine happiness or joy in the classroom?" "How often does this student laugh or have fun with others?" "How can more time be devoted to joy in the environment?"

Communication

All students deserve the right to communicate their needs and wants. Once, when I (Kate) was observing students in a classroom, the teacher asked about the weather and date. One student using a communication device pushed a button to make the device say, "I know the answer." He pushed the button again and pushed it three more times during the morning meeting. He was never called on to answer. It seemed that the teacher was beginning to feel frustrated by the noise of the device, and she eventually walked over and took the device away from him. He later found the device and pushed the button to make the device say, "I feel sad." This story illustrates an important point. Communication is not something to be earned and taken away. Any attempt to communicate should be honored because all people need to be heard.

If students do not feel as if they are being heard by teachers and other adult staff, they will attempt to communicate their thoughts, feelings, and needs through their behavior—and often with undesirable behavior. Students will assert their own independence by acting out when they do not feel safe or feel unable to communicate something; they may also simply act out to create more happiness and joy in their lives. Purposefully creating such opportunities is essential to helping students avoid negative behavior. Students might be communicating something such as, "I am lonely," "I do not feel safe," or "I do not know how to tell you what I need." The behavior they exhibit might not immediately identify a need to communicate, but in those moments it is important to remember that *all* behavior is communication. Part of the job of educators and paraprofessionals is to figure out what students are attempting to communicate through their behavior.

Anticipating Students' Needs

For each individual student, make a plan to help that student receive more of the things that will fulfill their needs. Invite the student into a discussion about what is needed to help them learn or participate in class. For example, if you believe a student needs more choice, you should provide more choice as soon as possible.

We are aware that this recommendation contradicts most behavior systems and plans. Many people believe that if you give students what they need, they will act out more. The opposite, however, has been found to be true. If you help meet students' needs, they will not need to display challenging behavior to get what they want (Kluth, 2010; Lovett, 1996; Pitonyak, 2007). Here are some great questions to ask yourself:

- What might this person need?
- Does this person need more pleasure and joy in their school day?
- Does this person need more choice or control over what happens to them? See the box titled "Suggestions for Providing Choice" for ideas.
- Does this person need to feel more as if they belong?
- Does this person need more relationships and interdependence?
- Does this person need more autonomy?
- Does this person need more access to communication?

You must first determine each student's possible needs, and then work with your team to determine avenues to meet those needs. Whenever possible, include the student in this discussion. Table 8.2 details common challenges

REFLECTIONS

Consider a student you work with. Highlight the behaviors the student exhibits and the possible supports that might be effective. Can you implement any of these supports right away? Can you schedule to meet with the student's team to discuss possible ideas?

Table 8.2.   Give them what they need

For students who ..	Give them . . .	For example . . .
Talk a lot	More opportunity to talk	Talk walk, think-pair-share, debate, turn and talk
Move a lot	More opportunity to move	Stand and write, do graffiti-style work, write Michelangelo style, dance party, back to back
Want to lead	More opportunity to lead	Line leader, paper passer, helper, pointer
Appear shy	More support with social interactions	Write ideas before joining the group, clock partners
Are resistant	More choices	Choice of writing utensil, type or color of paper, types of manipulatives
Have tantrums	Time to calm down and then a plan when finished	"When you're ready, let's write down your first step."
Bully others	More opportunities to strengthen friendships	Tables at lunch based on interest, supported conversations with peers
Shut down	More ways to express frustration	"I need a break" card, a whiteboard to write feelings down
Make noise	Opportunities to make noise	A mouse pad to drum on, repetitive lines in read aloud
Interrupt	Opportunities to share during lessons	Turn and talk, say something, social break, cooperative learning groups
Have issues with assigned seating	Opportunities to select the best way to work	Use a clipboard on the floor, use a music stand, write Michelangelo style, do graffiti-style work

SUGGESTIONS FOR PROVIDING CHOICE

PIG grouping: Work in a Partnership, as an Individual, or in a Group
Marker or pencil
Window marker on table or window
Computer or laptop
Small paper or chart paper
Standing or sitting
On the floor with a clipboard or on grass outside the classroom
Listening or reading
Draw it or write it
Use sidewalk chalk or pencil and paper
Keep going or take a 5-minute break
Use a music stand or an easel
"Graffiti style" or "Michelangelo style"
Use a chair or therapy ball

you may face with a student, provides ideas to determine what a behavior might mean, and gives details on how to support each need along with helpful examples.

Provide Choice

Providing students choices in how to complete tasks is an important way to help students succeed, decrease challenging behavior, and build confidence. For a student who moves a lot when learning, we found that giving her and her classmates the choice to use window markers was an excellent way to get everyone engaged in writing lists, brainstorming ideas, and planning writing assignments. Providing tablets and laptops for written tasks can also increase student access and success. We've also found that giving students personal whiteboards and whiteboard markers to use at their desks or while seated on the floor can engage students in new ways as they practice solving math problems or brainstorm topics for an upcoming essay.

Providing choice in body positioning, or providing what we like to call a "Working Ways Menu," is another strategy we like to use when supporting students. Students can choose to sit on the floor to do work, set up music stands to create standing desks, use clipboards to move easily about the room with work, or tape papers to the wall—graffiti style—to complete the assignment.

Students might also choose to use a therapy ball for a chair or use a sit disc at their chair. Some students have access to comfortable beanbags or couches in their classrooms. We find that flexible seating arrangements can help students to focus and engage in tasks for longer periods of time. See the box titled "Suggestions for Providing Choice" for other examples of ways to seamlessly provide students with choice throughout their day.

Weathering the Storm

When confronting challenging behavior, school personnel often react by imposing consequences, threatening to impose consequences, removing rewards, or ignoring the behavior; in some instances, school personnel might force students to behave. Forcing a student to behave might involve physically moving a student or providing hand-over-hand assistance. None of these strategies is good for students or for the adults involved.

We remember a student who was having particularly difficult behavior in a classroom. The student was supposed to be working with the OT with Unifix cubes. Instead, the student began running and throwing the cubes at the OT. The therapist responded by saying, "If you do not stop, I will write your name on the board and you will lose recess time." The student did not stop. The OT walked over and wrote the student's name on the board in large letters. The student became loud and continued running around. The therapist then put a checkmark next to the student's name as more Unifix cubes rained down on her head. She eventually said, "You are going to the time-out room!" She brought the student kicking and screaming to the time-out room, where he spent 2 hours screaming until he eventually fell asleep.

These types of situations are very difficult; you may have witnessed similar situations before. There might not be easy solutions in these cases, but educators often use consequences—or threaten consequences—that can be isolating before trying other, more positive approaches. Isolation of any kind needs to be the very last solution; isolation is never a decision that should be made by a paraprofessional. Researchers have determined that although negative reinforcement like isolation may stop a behavior in the short term, it is not an effective or humane way to stop the behavior for the long term (Kohn, 2006).

Certainly, it is easy for us to suggest alternatives—we were not the ones frustrated by the behavior of the student who ran around throwing things. Nonetheless, consider different reactions that the therapist might have had. How do you think the interaction between the OT and the boy throwing cubes might have changed had the therapist done any of the following?

- Walked over to the student and quietly asked, "What do you need right now?"
- Gave the student a piece of paper and said, "Draw for me what is wrong."
- Calmly asked the student whether he needed a break or a drink of water.
- Asked the student to help clean up the mess.
- Changed the activity entirely and asked the student to help her get ready for the next activity.
- Interpreted the student's behavior and asked, "Are you finished?" or "Something seems wrong. Can you help me understand what it is?"

Had the OT responded with any of these reactions, we doubt that the student would have ended up in the time-out room with so much instructional time lost and with major trauma and significant personal cost to the student and the OT.

Alfie Kohn, a thoughtful researcher on rewards and punishments, suggested that rewards and punishments work in the short term. However, all educators need to ask themselves, "Work to do what?" and "At what cost?" When educators think big about what they want for their students in life, they might think they want all their students to be self-reliant, responsible, socially skilled, caring people. Rewards and punishments produce only temporary compliance. They buy obedience (Kohn, 2006), but they do not help anybody develop an intrinsic sense of responsibility. In your own life, think of a task that you do not enjoy doing. For example, we personally dislike taking out the garbage. Now, think for a moment—what if every time we had to take out the garbage, someone said, "Good job taking out the garbage!" Would that be more motivating? It wouldn't be for us. Sometimes, things we might *assume* are rewarding, are actually not.

All Behavior Communicates Something

It is important to understand that all behavior communicates something. If a student is engaging in challenging behavior, ask yourself, "What might this student be communicating?" Once you have made your best guess as to what the student needs, try to meet that student's needs. I (Julie) watched a paraprofessional do this beautifully. A student, Hayden, was continually tapping a classmate, Sarah, on the back; the tapping seemed to bother Sarah. Instead of assuming that Hayden was trying to be obnoxious or to get attention, the paraprofessional interpreted Hayden's behavior as an attempt to interact with a friend. The paraprofessional whispered to Hayden, "Do you want to move closer and talk with Sarah? One way to start the conversation is to just say 'Hi.'" Hayden moved closer and said "Hi," and the conversation went on from there.

Some useful ways to interpret what a student is communicating include the following:

STRATEGIES

- *Ask them.* Say, "I see you are doing *X;* what do you want me to know?" or "It must mean something when you bang your head. What does it mean?"

- *Watch and learn.* Record everything the student does before and after a behavior. Meet with the team and try to determine what the student is attempting to gain from behaving this way.

- *Attribute positive motives.* One of the most important things is to consider what you believe about a particular child. Attribute the best possible motive consistent with the facts (Kohn, 2006). Assume that the student does not have malicious intent; the student is probably trying to get their needs met or to communicate something to you.

Another example involves a student who physically ran into a teacher in the hall, and the girl's backpack hit the teacher. The teacher bent down and began yelling at the student: "You gotta stop messing around! If you keep this up, you will hurt someone!" A paraprofessional who was walking with the class said, "I do not think she meant to run into you. I saw what happened; she was walking along and talking with her friend. She didn't see you stop, and she didn't mean to run into you."

This situation can be filtered through two different lenses. When you attribute the best possible motive consistent with the facts, you often see things in a positive and, possibly, more accurate light. This positive viewpoint opens the door for more humanistic approaches to behavior. On the other hand, when behavior is interpreted as malicious or mean spirited, it is all too easy to respond in a similar way.

Have you ever been out of control? What do you need when you are out of control? We personally need someone to listen, someone to talk to, someone to not give advice; sometimes, we need a nap or some time away. When students are in the heat of the moment, they often need compassion from a calm person. They need a paraprofessional who is safe, patient, and cool and who will gently provide support.

What students do not need in the heat of the moment—or ever, for that matter—is to be ignored; to be yelled at; to be treated with hostility, sarcasm, or public humiliation; or to be forcefully removed from the situation. Consider the following calm ways to approach students when they are experiencing big emotions that can help deescalate challenging behaviors.

Nine Calm Ways to Respond During Big Emotions

1. Remain calm and take a deep breath.
2. Tell the student, "I am here for you."
3. Ask the student, "What would help right now?"
4. Ask if a walk or a drink of water might help.

5. Ask the student to draw what is going on.

6. Draw together. Say, "This figure is you. Can you help me add details? What is in your head?" or "What are you thinking or feeling right now?"

7. Distract with humor.

8. Give the student a responsibility: "Would you take this book down to the library?"

9. Tell the student, "I am here to listen. You can tell me how you are feeling."

REFLECTIONS

What supports do you need for yourself to remain calm and collected during a potential crisis?

The Science of Stress

When students experience challenging behavior, they are often dealing with increased levels of stress due to academic, emotional, or social needs that are not being met. High levels of stress in anyone—child or adult—leads to a release of cortisol, which is the body's main stress hormone that works with the brain to control mood, motivation, and fear. We like to think about it as a built-in alarm system, best known for triggering what is known as a fight-or-flight response. When this physiological response occurs in students, we often see behavior outbursts and difficult-to-manage behaviors. These behaviors are not cognitive choices that our students are making in the moment; they are the result of a physiological reaction to environmental stressors.

Practice the Calm

It is important for educators to respond to students in calm, reassuring, and private ways when they are feeling high levels of stress, exhibiting challenging behaviors, or experiencing crisis.

Paula Kluth (2005), a friend and inclusive education expert, offers this advice:

When a student is kicking, biting, banging her head, or screaming, she is most likely miserable, confused, scared, or uncomfortable. The most effective and the most human response at this point is to offer support, to act in a comforting manner, and to help the person relax and feel safe. Teaching can come later. In a crisis, the educator must listen, support, and simply be there. (p. 2)

How Are the Other Students Behaving?

When students are supported by paraprofessionals, they invariably are under extra scrutiny. This sometimes leads to behavioral expectations that are more stringent for students with disabilities than for other students. We see this very frequently in classrooms. In one case, we heard a teacher tell a student to sit up tall while working, although two other students in the room were sleeping and one other student was crawling on the floor. Observe how the other students are expected to behave; the student being supported should not be expected to perform at a higher behavioral standard.

Hold Steady for Students

Josh Shipp (2015), author, speaker, and self-identified former troubled teen turned teen advocate, discusses the importance of holding steady for our students with challenging behavior when they act out. He uses a great roller-coaster analogy, explaining that when we get on a roller coaster, the first thing we do is test the safety lap or shoulder bar by shaking it, hard, before the roller-coaster begins. He says that we don't test the safety bar because we want it to fail. We test the safety bar because we want to ensure that it will keep us safe and secure. Shipp further explains that this confirmation test of safety and security is what students do when they challenge their educators.

The next time a student tests you with challenging behaviors, take a moment to think about the roller-coaster ride analogy. We then ask you to consider yourself as that student's safety bar. Help them know that you are there for them. Show them that you can hold steady when the ride gets rough.

Nothing Personal

As special educators ourselves, we dealt with our fair share of challenging behaviors. The hardest thing was not to take anything personally. I (Kate) had a student who was particularly good at figuring out my buttons and pushing them (or so I thought). But the best advice I ever heard was to remember that the challenging behavior was "nothing personal." The students I supported invariably had challenging behavior. Whether I was working with them or not, they all were learning how to manage their own behavior. Sometimes, I would tell myself, "It is not personal. Even though this student has just called me a b****, it is not about me right now." The challenging behaviors of some students are functions of their disabilities and they simply need to learn new skills, strategies, and coping mechanisms to help them reduce and replace challenging behaviors. Just as you would not get angry with a student who was having difficulty reading—because you would assume that this was a function of the student's disability—you should not get angry with students who are struggling to behave. The best, most humane way to respond in these situations is to be helpful, clear, and supportive.

Think Like a Parent

Remember that every student is someone's child. When faced with a student's challenging behavior, imagine that you are someone who deeply loves the student. Try to imagine what it would be like if you had watched the child grow and learn from infancy onward; how would you react from that perspective? How might you react if it were your son, daughter, niece, or nephew? If you react from a position of love and acceptance, you are much more likely to respond with kindness and humanity than with punishment and control.

Table 8.3. How to communicate with students after the behavior occurs

To communicate to a student . . .	You might respond with . . .
That the crisis is over . . .	"You are done with that now." "The problem is done." Have the student draw the problem, then have them cross it out to signify that the situation has ended.
That you validate this student's feelings . . .	"It's okay to feel that way." "I understand that was hard for you." "Now it's over." "I'm sorry that was so hard for you." "I can tell you were really frustrated, angry, or upset." Draw a picture of the student. Draw thought bubbles over the student's head. Ask the student to help you identify what they were thinking and feeling.
It is time to move on . . .	"What do you need now?" "What can I help you with to get you back to work?" "Do you want to take a rest and prepare to get yourself back together?" "Would you prefer to get right back to work?" "Draw for me what you need right now."

Helping Students to Move On

If a student has just had a significant behavioral outburst, they may be embarrassed, tired, or still holding on to negative feelings. It is important to help students move past these experiences. After an outburst, you should let the student know that the crisis is over, validate their feelings, and help the student to move on. The phrases listed in Table 8.3 are offered as a guide to help you think about how you can talk to students to get them beyond emotional crises, but the phrases should not be memorized and repeated. The most important thing is for you to have a calm, caring tone in your voice as you communicate with the student.

> You do not want to make the repair bigger than the problem.

Help the student repair any damage. When an adult makes a mistake or loses their temper, the adult first needs to repair the damage. Once, while giving a presentation, I (Kate) made the mistake of using someone in the audience as an example. I did not think it would embarrass that person, but I subsequently learned that it had. I felt awful; I had to repair the damage. I did so by writing a note of apology. Writing an apology note might not be the best way for a student to repair the damage after a behavioral outburst, but my point is that you should help the student identify what might help fix the situation and involve them in repairing it.

The solution should match the problem. For example, if a student knocks books off a shelf during a tantrum, the best solution is to have the student pick up the books. If a student rips up his artwork, the solution might be to have him either tape it together or create a new piece. If a student yells at a peer, a solution might be to have her write an apology note, draw an apology picture, or simply say, "I'm sorry." You do not want to make the repair bigger than the problem. The main goal should be to get students back to work in a timely manner.

Utilize Students as Problem Solvers

When a student becomes out of control, educators often try to implement a behavior management program that helps students comply with classroom rules in order to do something to rectify the situation. Instead of doing things *to* students, work *with* them. What follows is our favorite method for problem solving with students. It is important to note that you would not be expected to lead this but you might be expected to be an important member of the student's team when solving problems.

Problem Solve and Plan for Success

Educational scholar and author Alfie Kohn (2006) argued that "Our response to things we find disturbing, might be described as reflecting a philosophy of either doing things *to* students or working *with* them" (p. 23). By working *with* students, we can transform students into expert problem solvers. This process is not simple. To begin, if we are to problem-solve challenging behavior with a student, we must place compassion and care for the student at the very center of the process. To do so, we recommend assembling a team of educators, family members, and friends who support the student and care about their success. Once the team is assembled, the team should ask the student about their strengths, challenges, and what might be needed in order to be successful in certain situations. The problem solving should not try to fix the challenging behavior. Instead, it should focus on providing opportunities for the student to increase feelings of acceptance, belonging, empowerment, and success while simultaneously decreasing challenging behaviors.

REFLECTIONS

How might you support the student to become a problem solver and plan for their success? Which team members will you need to enroll?

Maintaining Consistency

When following a behavior plan for an individual student, it is important to be sure all members working directly with the student are following the plan in the same ways. As a paraprofessional, you will often be a consistent individual with the student, and this may mean you will be implementing parts or all of the behavior plan. It is critical that you have time to meet with the special educator, behavior specialist, or lead team member on the behavior plan so you know exactly how to implement the plan and from whom or where to seek support when needed. Several steps that you can use and/or suggest to the team to help support your consistent implementation of the behavior plan are as follows:

1. Create a checklist using all of the plan components for your student (you can volunteer to do this).

2. Ensure that there is a copy of the behavior plan for each adult who is supporting the student.

3. After taking data for a designated period of time, identify parts of the

STRATEGIES

Table 8.4. Maintain consistency

Support plan for student	Are you doing this consistently?	Notes
Use the daily visual schedule.		
Use mini schedules in each environment.		
Provide 2-minute transition warnings.		
Use timer for breaks.		
Have quick communication cards available at all times.		
Provide three movement breaks per day.		
Use transition item(s) (e.g., planner, hall pass).		

plan where you or others may not be following consistently. Determine the reason for the inconsistency.

4. If you find inconsistencies, determine steps to regain consistency.

Table 8.4 provides a sample plan for the team and a template for how each team member can double check to be sure things are consistent.

Commonly Asked Questions About Behavior Supports

FAQs

Q. If a student is not punished, won't they simply repeat the behavior?

A. We do not believe in adding on a punishment. In fact, much research has been done on the use of time-outs and punishments. This research suggests that punishments work in the short term but have long-term negative effects on students (Kohn, 2006).

Q. One of my students is not aggressive toward peers—only toward adults. What does that indicate?

A. This type of aggression usually indicates a problem with the type or intensity of support being provided. Students often lash out at paraprofessionals or teachers who make them feel different or uncomfortable because of the support being given. For example, I (Julie) observed a 12-year-old girl who was being aggressive toward the paraprofessional. I noticed that the paraprofessional was providing intensive support by sitting next to the girl. The paraprofessional was also using a technique called *spidering* (crawling your hand up the back of the student's hair), which was intended to lower the student's anxiety. However, the student seemed embarrassed and uncomfortable with that type and level of support. When the paraprofessional moved away from the student, the aggression stopped.

Q. I am being asked to provide extensive support and have been told never to leave the student's side. I know this is embarrassing to the student.

What should I do?

A.   You have to provide the type of support that the team deems appropriate. However, if you think it is not helpful to the student, work with your team and discuss when it might be appropriate to fade your support. Ask questions such as, "What would fading look like for this student?" or "What other types of support can be in place to allow for student success?"

Q.   **Should a student leave the room if they are distracting other students?**

A.   Leaving the room should be the last resort. Try many different stay-put supports. Help the student stay in the environment for all of the reasons mentioned in this chapter. If a student leaves every time they make a noise, that student learns that membership is contingent on being quiet or good. Of course, you want to think about other students, but when inclusion is done well, all students understand that a certain student may make noise and that the student is working on that, just as other students may be working on other skills. Most students are surprisingly patient when given the chance and some information.

Conclusion

The way educators and paraprofessionals plan for, support, and react to behavior is critical to student success. Remembering that all behavior communicates something and that all people need compassion and patience will help you be successful when supporting students. Supporting students who have challenging behavior is not easy; the final chapter of this book focuses on caring for yourself so that you can have the energy and ability to provide the best possible care for all students.

TO-DO LIST

To Do

After reading this chapter ...

- Complete the reflections in this chapter.
- Take 5 minutes and write a new story about a specific student.
  - What are this student's strengths, gifts, and talents?
  - What are some possible reasons for their behavior(s)?
- Write down one thing you can do today to build confidence in a student who is struggling and one thing you can do to lean in and provide the student with the certainty they are seeking. Implement those new actions as soon as you can.
- Create your own mantra like the one at the start of this chapter.

9

Respectful Support for Developing Student Independence

My freshman year, I felt like everyone in class had a teacher except for me: I had a helper. I wanted to be more independent, so my parents advocated for me. And things got better with my para. She helped me when I needed it, but it wasn't all the time. If I could give advice to paras, it would be that you should believe in your students. I think I just wish my teachers and paras would see me the way my parents see me—independent and strong. —Nicole (student)

In the last few chapters, we discussed strategies for supporting students academically, socially, and behaviorally. In this chapter, we build on all of these ideas in order to help paraprofessionals learn to fade support while increasing a student's confidence, resiliency, and independence. We provide strategies, digital resources, supports you can use on the fly, reproducible tools, and templates to use with your students and school team, and then we conclude with commonly asked questions and answers about this topic.

The Importance of Student Independence

When writing the current edition of this book, we realized that the topic of thoughtfully fading support and meaningfully developing student independence was significant enough for an entire chapter. In schools, we have observed many paraprofessionals who are extremely thoughtful in this regard. When student support is effective, research shows that teachers, students, parents, and administrators report that paraprofessionals positively support the inclusion of students with disabilities (Logan, 2006) and increase their participation and engagement in class activities, increase academic learning, increase

> **We do not need magic to change the world. We carry all the power we need inside ourselves already.**
>
> —J. K. Rowling

socialization with peers, and decrease challenging behaviors (Angelides, Constantinou, & Leigh, 2009; Chopra & Giangreco, 2019; Webster et al., 2010).

However, we also often observe and talk with paraprofessionals who do not have the tools to thoughtfully fade supports. Without these tools, the social, emotional, and academic impact that oversupport can have on a student is significant. The research in this regard is clear. Paraprofessional oversupport can hinder student inclusion in whole-class instruction and lead to fewer interactions between the student and their teachers and classmates (Cameron, 2014; Webster, Russell, & Blatchford, 2015). Students with disabilities who receive too much paraprofessional support are also less likely to be independent, support the learning of their classmates, and socialize with nondisabled peers (Symes & Humphrey, 2012).

We therefore want to make sure that we are giving you the tools and strategies to fade your support and provide opportunities for increased student success.

QUICK QUIZ

List three research-based reasons why paraprofessionals should work to build student independence.

Fade Adult Support

For every student, every day our goal as educators should be to help them to become as independent or as interdependent as possible. Oversupporting or providing supports that are unnecessarily intrusive has negative implications for students including social alienation and overdependence. Being mindful of fading your support can be the difference between a successful school day and a difficult one.

What to Do Even Before Prompting

Student independence and interdependence is so important that we are suggesting you do all of the following six steps before even offering a prompt—verbal, gestural, or otherwise—to a student:

- Make sure the entire class perceives that you are there to help all students.
- Watch before helping. Can the student figure out the task on their own?
- Give the student time. Does waiting help? Some students are simply processing.
- Can you set up the materials in a way that students will not need prompting? Color coding, numbering? Modifications? A list?
- Can you set up a self-monitoring system?
- Can you create a peer support for every student (e.g., "Every student work with your elbow partner to double check that you are on the right page")?

Provide Silent Supports

Receiving support is not always a comfortable thing. It can be stigmatizing and distracting to the student and classmates. Consider using silent supports, which allow support to be given without any auditory distraction. This might be as simple as writing a sentence on a note for your student. For example, you could write, "Come see me if you need help getting started," and then walk away and be seated in a place where students can easily seek you out. Or, you could make a larger announcement to the whole class: "Come see me if you need help on this task." Your student will then know that they can seek you out, and this strategy is now likely to benefit all students in class.

20 Ways to Provide Invisible or Silent Support

STRATEGIES

1. **Highlight the directions.** On a complex or dense worksheet or lab, use a highlighter to help the student easily identify key directions.

2. **Jot it down.** If the teacher gives directions verbally, write those directions down on a note and give it to the student (e.g., "Turn to page 421").

3. **Create a checklist.** Create a checklist of written directions for the student to follow (e.g., 1. read with a partner, 2. answer the question, 3. find another partner and compare).

4. **Provide a model.** For example, prior to an in-class task being assigned, model a similar math problem with the work shown and the correct answer on the top of the worksheet.

5. **Enlist a peer.** For example, say, "Claire, can you help Javier get his coat's zipper started if he needs help?"

6. **Create materials in advance.** For example, have key vocabulary from the lecture listed and defined on a piece of paper or pre-cut materials so that cutting is not required by the student.

7. **Reduce the work.** For example, if you know the student can complete three problems independently, expect only three answers rather than five.

8. **Use technology.** For example, provide ongoing feedback and support without peers or others knowing by typing comments on a Google Doc or using Google Chat with the student.

9. **Use Ask 3 Before Me.** Implement a classroom policy in which all students seek help from three peers before asking you or the teacher.

10. **Float.** Rather than sit next to the student, stand and move about the room to be available for everyone's support.

11. **Provide stop-by support.** This means that you only stop and check in on the student you support after you have checked in on at least six other students. Then, repeat the process.

12. **Use a sticky note or a bookmark.** Pre-mark pages in the text that the student needs to open.

13. **Prep for discussion.** For example, for students with complex support needs or who are building skills, write down several questions the students can ask or comments they can share during a class discussion.

14. **Provide a pointer.** Give students an object with which they can point to each word while they read independently or with the class.

15. **Transition wordlessly.** Use a timer on your phone or a stopwatch to let your student know it is time to transition to the next task or class.

16. **Engage partners.** Allow every student to have a designated walking buddy to get to the next class.

17. **Text support.** Use a student's phone to offer support via text or notes.

18. **Bookmark it.** Set up the students' laptops with bookmarked sites

so they can easily navigate to frequently used web sites (e.g., e-mail, Google Classroom, Khan Academy).

19. **Simplify.** If directions or language is complex, complicated, or provided too quickly, write it down in simplified language.

20. **Guide them.** Create a graphic organizer or other guided notes templates to help students organize key ideas from a lesson.

REFLECTIONS

Highlight the silent supports that you believe would benefit your student the most.
Which supports can you do on your own?
Which supports will you need to talk with teachers about?

Digital Supports to Build Independence

Digital supports are some of the most useful and relevant ways to build student independence. These tools are often commonly used by other students and therefore integrate into the classroom setup in natural and seamless ways.

Reading Pens

There are multiple brands of pens that students can use to read nondigital texts in an electronically generated, human-like voice. Many come with earbuds so the students can listen with privacy, and a built-in dictionary to display a word's definition and read it aloud.

Reader Pen—www.readerpen.com

Google Supports for Readers and Writers

Read&Write

This Chrome extension provides students with text-to-speech capabilities through synchronized highlighting, a talking dictionary, and a picture dictionary for use with web sites. *Read&Write* also opens PDF documents in new tabs that contain text-to-speech tools as well as annotation tools.

Google Docs

This free word processor provides students with word prediction, spelling and grammar support, verbal dictation, typing with voices, screen magnifiers, and the ability to share work with educators, other students, and families for feedback and support. It is also fully compatible with screen readers and braille displays.

Google Keep

This note-taking app provides different ways for students to take notes, such as with text, audio, images, and lists, and also allows students the option to color-code notes.

Organization Apps

Help students set up to-do lists, set reminders, and develop repeating tasks with apps such as iHomework, Todoist, or Priorities.

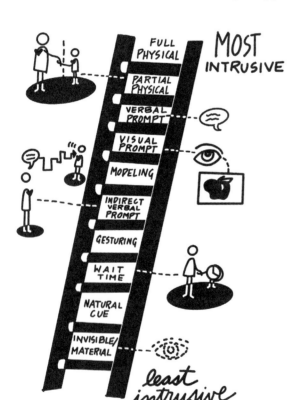

Figure 9.1. Prompting ladder.

The Prompting Ladder

Imagine you are very afraid of heights when looking at the prompting ladder in Figure 9.1. The key here is to start at the bottom rung (the least intrusive supports) move up only as far as necessary (toward more intrusive supports), and return back down as quickly as possible. For example, Rosa is a seventh-grade student who struggles to transition quickly between classes. The bottom two rungs of the ladder are the invisible/material cue (which in this example would be the bell ringing) and the natural cue (students getting up and moving). However, Rosa is not responding to these cues, and she is remaining in her seat. The paraprofessional tries wait time (the next step up the ladder), but Rosa still does not get up. The paraprofessional decides a gestural prompt (another rung up the ladder) will be the next support. When Rosa looks up, the paraprofessional smiles and points to the door. That doesn't work either. So, the paraprofessional next uses an indirect verbal prompt by asking, "Rosa, what are the other students doing?" Rosa looks around, gets up, and gathers her things for her next period. The paraprofessional notes that she had to go to an indirect verbal prompt. She will use the same prompting ladder tomorrow but will start again at the bottom rung with invisible/materials cues, go up only as far as necessary, and return to the bottom each day.

QUICK QUIZ

Fill in this blank ladder with each of the steps in order.

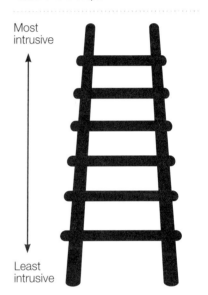

Most intrusive

Least intrusive

REFLECTIONS

REFLECTIONS

Think of a student you support. Now, think of only one skill the student struggles with (e.g., starting work promptly, lining up, sitting at the carpet for circle time). What types of cues do you use regularly? Imagine you recorded your own responses to the student and reviewed the video for the types and levels of support provided. What did you do yesterday? Tomorrow, can you return to the bottom of the ladder and keep going up slowly, only moving up to the next prompt when the student demonstrates that they need further support?

Developing Student Independence

An important part of schooling is preparing students to become more independent and to eventually take on more roles and responsibilities of adulthood. As students move from elementary to middle to high school, they are expected to take on greater responsibility for their own learning, become increasingly independent, and begin planning and making choices about their futures. There are many critical skills involved in developing independence, and the following section describes these skills, then outlines strategies for teaching them to your students.

Self-Determination

Self-determination can be defined as having the abilities and opportunities to make decisions about your own life. In education, it is considered best practice to prepare students to have the necessary abilities and opportunities to play a leading role in their learning and planning for the future. Research suggests that students with disabilities who have self-determination skills are more successful academically, contribute more actively to their school plans—such as IEP meetings, 504 plans, and transition meetings—and experience more successful postsecondary involvement in employment, education, and inde-

DEFINITIONS

pendent living (Test et al., 2009). In order to develop self-determination, students should begin learning these skills in elementary school and should have increasing opportunities for practice all the way until high school graduation.

Self-Awareness and Self-Knowledge

Students who are self-aware and self-knowledgeable can recognize and share their own preferences, strengths, skills, abilities, challenges, and needs. When students are self-aware and self-knowledgeable, they can use these understandings to improve on their schooling and life experiences. Students should therefore begin to learn about and share how they best learn and communicate, as well as what supports they will need to succeed.

DEFINITIONS

Self-Advocacy

Self-advocacy is defined as having the ability and confidence to stand up for yourself and ask for what you need in order to achieve a successful outcome. When students are able to effectively self-advocate for themselves with educators, peers, family, and community members, they are better understood, better supported, and have greater opportunities to achieve their goals.

Teaching Skills for Independence

Students do not learn the many independence skills discussed in this chapter all on their own. In fact, it takes many years for students to effectively develop and use these skills—and many adults still have difficulty with some of these skills. As a paraprofessional, you have a unique opportunity to implement strategies throughout the school day to help your students learn, practice, and receive feedback on these developing skills. All of the following strategies will help to increase a student's self-determination, independence, and confidence.

STRATEGIES

Strategies for Teaching Self-Determination Skills

- Talk with students about the choices they can make in their daily lives. Provide students with examples, such as choices for how they would like to complete a learning task or whom they want to eat with at lunch.

- Model the choice-making process for students. For example, you can model how you might choose a book you want to pick out in the library by talking through your process out loud.

- Help students set small goals that can be met over a short period of time. For example, an elementary student might set a goal of reading a children's book to their sister before bedtime. An older student might set a goal of texting a friend over the weekend or reading a certain number of pages in their novel for English class.

- Encourage students to set goals around areas of organization and work habits. For example, help your student set a goal to keep an organized locker or backpack. You could also help your student set a goal to ask you to review their homework or assignment planner at the end of every day with them so they know what they need to do for homework that night.

- Meet with your student to review goals that have been set by the student's IEP team. Have positive and regular discussions about the progress your student is making on various goals.

Strategies for Teaching Self-Awareness and Self-Knowledge Skills

- Talk regularly with the student about their strengths, skills, and needs.
- Check in with students about their preferences, interests, and skills as it connects to a particular activity or unit in class.
- Ask the teachers for an interests, skills, and preferences survey or a learning style survey to complete with your student.
- Guide students, or ask them to independently create a positive student profile about themselves in which they address their strengths, skills, preferences, and needs.

Strategies for Teaching Self-Advocacy Skills

- Encourage students to ask peers or teachers for help when needed.
- Encourage your student to use an "ask 3 before me" strategy in classes, in which they ask three peers before they ask their question to you or the teacher.
- Ask teachers for a self-advocacy survey to complete with the student and discuss those self-advocacy skills that the student wants to develop and/or improve on.
- Encourage students to advocate for their preferences, opinions, needs, and accommodations throughout the day. For example, if a teacher forgets to provide extended time on an assignment—and that is an accommodation your student receives—encourage your student to ask the teacher about extended time. Or during recess, help your student to share her opinion on the playground regarding what game they would like to play that day.

DIGITAL SUPPORTS FOR TEACHING INDEPENDENCE

The National Gateway to Self-Determination: www.ngsd.org
National Technical Assistance Center on Transition: https://transitionta.org
The IRIS Center at Vanderbilt: https://iris.peabody.vanderbilt.edu

The Value of Interdependence

We know we have provided many teaching strategies and rationales for helping students to build independence, but we want to also emphasize the interconnectedness of independence and *interdependence*. It is only through community and support that any of us can reach our goals. For example, we, the authors, depend on each other for writing support and we also look to our families for support when making big life decisions such as applying for new jobs, buying homes, or having children. We rely on others when it comes to automobile care, plumbing, taxes, and other services that it would be hard to exist without. And we certainly rely on assistive technologies such as cell phones, computers, and GPS to complete necessary work and day-to-day tasks. Then, of course, there is the flip side of the supports and people you depend on—all of the people who depend on you! Consider the family and friends who depend on you, as well as all of your students and colleagues.

We are all interdependent is an important concept to emphasize with your students. Research shows that when families, educators, and students expect and plan for interdependence for students with disabilities, those students have many more oppor-

It is only through community and support that any of us can reach our goals.

REFLECTIONS

What does *interdependence* look like for you? To whom and to what do you go for support in your own life? How much do you value that support?

tunities to partake in making decisions about their lives with support, which can lead to increased growth and maturity (MacLeod, 2017). In fact, a student in MacLeod's research study explained why he is proud of his interdependent skills in this way: "Well, I like the word *independent*, but I need to ask for help for [some] things. And I am able to do that" (p. 202). This demonstrates how effectively this student is using his self-determination and self-advocacy skills—two of the very important skills we have highlighted earlier in this chapter.

Some students will require more support than others. For example, some students will need support for their entire life with work, banking, food shopping, housing, and even personal relationships. However, it is important for us to know that achieving independence is not an individual act. For your students who require the most supports, it is important for us to help them feel empowered and have many opportunities to make choices and lead their own lives with the support of community. It is then that we can move away from the misconception that independence is the only goal for students. Instead, we can help many of our students achieve a more honest and realistic goal of interdependence.

> I think community is the foundation for self-advocacy.
> —*the father of a student with a disability*

Cultivating Resilience in Our Students

As paraprofessionals work to fade side-by-side support and build independence and interdependence, it often is necessary to teach students social and emotional skills that will assist in building resilience to help them through the most difficult challenges of life. Many education professionals believe that self-esteem is the answer to helping students build resiliency, but research shows that self-compassion is actually a more powerful tool (Neff, 2003). When students learn how to be more compassionate with themselves, they are better equipped to face failures and mistakes, and to deal with issues of confidence or discomfort.

STRATEGIES

Strategies for Teaching Resilience and Self-Compassion Skills

This section outlines three strategies for teaching students several important self-compassion and resilience skills that will help them to be more successful as they develop independence, including how to treat themselves kindly, an understanding that we are all in this together, and practices for mindfulness.

Treat Yourself Kindly

When a student is going through a difficult time or when you notice that their self-confidence is low, paraprofessionals can suggest they talk, write, or draw about what is going on and how exactly they're feeling. Be sure to offer the student language such as, "I feel frustrated…," "I feel disappointed because…," or "Things didn't go the way I wanted them to go…." You can also provide the student with a visual feelings chart to help them identify their emotions if words are too challenging. Then, once they have shared, ask the student to consider how they would help a best friend get through a challenging time. What would they say to that friend? What would they do for that friend? We recommend providing an example from your own life if this is a difficult concept for the student to understand. For example, share a time when you felt disappointed and how you would have liked a best friend to talk you through it. The more practice students have talking to themselves in kind ways, the more resilient they will become when facing difficult, disappointing, or painful experiences.

We're All in This Together

You can build on the strategy for teaching resilience and self-compassion by helping students understand that in life, we will all have many disappointments and struggles, both in ourselves and in our circumstances. Maybe they didn't pass the quiz, or they are having trouble making friends, or they are still struggling with reading—but they are not alone in those feelings or experiences.

Mindfulness

Mindfulness is the practice of becoming aware of our own emotions, thoughts, and surrounding environments. Teaching students how to practice mindfulness can help them face uncertainties, struggles, or challenges, and research has proven that the practice of mindfulness can improve attention, reduce stress, improve capacity for empathy and compassion, and help us to better regulate emotions and behaviors. Mindfulness can be formally introduced into classrooms and schools, but you can also teach your students simple and basic practices throughout the school day. For example, teach your students to practice breathing for 1 or 2 minutes. Ask them to focus or connect to their breath, and practice with them. When students focus on their breath, they can become more focused and attentive and learn to self-regulate negative emotions, anxiety, and stress. Another simple strategy is to have students touch their thumb slowly to each individual fingertip several times. With the rise in mindfulness practice and research, there are many great tools to use, such as mindfulness apps and breathing apps on your phone or tablet. You can also look for mindfulness practice videos online that have been specifically designed for the age of students with whom you work. With these simple practices, you can help your students recognize that their thoughts, feelings, stress, and anxieties do not determine who they are or who they can become.

Finally, take a moment and consider ways you might be an example and introduce self-compassion and resilience-building practices to your students. We know from emerging research that educators who practice self-compassion and mindfulness report lower levels of stress, more connection with students, and higher job satisfaction.

Supports on the Fly

Even the most well-planned and prepared silent and independence-building supports for our students can go awry, and you can find yourself scrambling to make something up in the moment. Imagine this scenario: To prep for the school day, you worked hard to create a modified math worksheet with model problems showing all the work; you pre-loaded the English e-text onto your student's tablet; and you created a simplified graphic organizer for the science lab. When the day begins, however, something unexpected happens and the schedule is altered due to an assembly. All of the teachers postpone their lessons for the next day, opting for quick filler lessons that can be done in less time—all of which you didn't know about. You find yourself scrambling to create all sorts of supports in the moment—both behavioral and academic! This is when you need a list of on-the-fly support ideas and go-to tools to use in a hurry. Remember that on-the-fly supports will not be perfect, but they will provide your student with much-needed access in a crunch. Several on-the-fly supports are provided in Table 9.1, complete with tools and tips to help with swift implementation.

ACTIVITY: Student Supports

ACTIVITIES

Observe the supports your student receives (from you, the teacher, students, other professionals, etc.) throughout the day. Use the reproducible data collection sheet (Figure 9.2) to take specific notes. In the "Class/subject and activity" column, describe the class, activity, and what the student is expected to do. In the "Type of support currently provided" column, include the type of support used and what it looked/sounded like. The example in the column "Ways to fade adult support" is included to provide inspiration on how to complete this data sheet.

After you have tracked support data throughout the student's day, we want you to notice how often the more intrusive supports—such as full or partial physical, modeling, and direct and indirect verbal supports—are provided to the student. Consider how you can begin to fade these intrusive supports and instead provide increased gestural supports, wait time, natural cues (e.g., peers, teachers), and invisible (e.g., material, environmental) supports. Perhaps you can reduce side-by-side support during math activities so that the student can

Table 9.1.   On-the-fly supports and implementation tips

Academic challenge	Academic support on the fly	Tips for implementation
Worksheet is too dense or crowded.	Cut the paper up and isolate sections to minimize an overly crowded page.	Use scissors on the teacher's desk.
The work cannot be done independently.	Provide support from a peer partner or small group.	Ask the teacher quietly if they would consider allowing students to partner or work in small groups for the activity because you didn't have time to prepare adapted text in advance.
Concepts are complex or complicated.	Provide visuals for a more concrete explanation.	Use a tablet, laptop, or smartphone to find images of objects or ideas that are depicted abstractly in a story. Share them with the student right on the device or print them out in the teacher's office (or wherever you have access to a printer).
Connections/relationships between concepts are unclear.	Draw arrows in the worksheet or text to show which ideas are connected/related. Write/draw the relationships on a separate piece of paper.	Find a pencil, pen, and paper. Check in with the teacher if you want to ensure that your connections are accurate.
Reading level is too advanced.	Use a laptop or tablet to find an adapted version of the history text on BookShare. Pull up the study guide (e.g., CliffsNotes) of the novel. Use the web site Newsela to find a similar article that addresses the same concepts at a more accessible reading level.	If you don't have a tablet or laptop with you or the student, see if you can borrow one from the general or special education teacher, librarian, or administrator.
Math problems are too complex.	Quickly rewrite problems or directions so the student can complete the math operations at their level (e.g., use a calculator to complete long division; multiply whole numbers rather than fractions; write out the operation needed to find volume).	Complete this while the teacher is giving directions if possible.
Complex or open-ended questions are not accessible.	Turn open-ended questions into multiple-choice or yes/no questions.	If the teacher asked the question verbally, write down the new question and possible multiple choice or yes/no answers for the student. If the question is on an assignment or worksheet, change it right on the paper, or overlay a strip of paper (or index card) with the new question.
Behavioral challenge	**Behavioral support on the fly**	**Tips for implementation**
Altered routine leaves the student anxious or upset.	Write out the new schedule and give it to the student to review. You can also use a visual schedule app on a phone or tablet to quickly create a new schedule for the student to follow.	Make sure the new schedule includes the time and the class/activity.
Student is up and out of their seat.	Quietly ask if the student would like to use flexible seating during this work time.	Get a music stand to create a standing desk or use a clipboard to create a movable writing option.
Student is shutting down and won't respond to your prompts to join in the activity.	First, ensure that the student has access to regularly used communication supports. Enlist a reliable and trusted peer to get the student involved. Write the student a note asking, "How can I help?"	If enlisting a peer, ask a peer, "Jeremy is needing some encouragement to get started. Could you go over and ask him to work with you on this assignment?"
Student is arguing with you.	Pause and breathe. Then: Can you distract with humor or another activity? If the student is very upset, say, "I see that you are frustrated. Can you tell me what you need?" If the student cannot verbalize, ask if the student can draw how they are feeling. If a school rule or class norm was broken, refer back to it and follow protocol with the student.	Many more strategies for dealing with challenging behaviors are offered in this chapter to support you.

Types of Support Data Collection Sheet

Class/subject and activity	Type of support currently provided	Ways to fade adult support
Example: English Teacher asks the students to take their homework out; teacher begins a homework review with the class.	Example: Indirect verbal Para asks, "Where do you keep your homework?" The student reaches into their backpack, pulls out a homework folder, and takes out English homework.	Para can use *wait time* and *natural cues*—students around focal student getting out homework and student follows their peers. If this is not successful, para can use *invisible support* and write a note to student to say, "English homework in BLUE folder."

Figure 9.2. Types of support data collection sheet.

access the math materials, peers, and teacher for support. Or, perhaps you can support the teachers by creating reading materials that are adapted at an appropriate reading level for the student; doing this will give the student a chance to learn independently so that you do not have to read to the student. The next steps for your student could also be as simple as fading from verbal to gestural prompts to help the student initiate a task. After all of these considerations, be sure to schedule a meeting with the student's team to discuss your ideas. We recommend using the following questions to guide a fading support conversation with the student's support team.

Fading Supports Team Discussion

1. During what activities, routines, or time periods is it absolutely necessary to be physically near this student?

2. How often (and during what activities) is the student provided with opportunities for choice in supports?

3. During those times in which adult support is needed, is it possible to fade to independence (done by the student) or interdependence (done with the support of a peer?)

4. What natural supports exist in this environment? Can anyone else in the environment provide more natural supports?

5. What changes to classroom structures, schedules, or content might help this student become more independent or interdependent?

6. How often (and during what activities) is the student expected to and provided opportunities to self-advocate (e.g., "I need support for . . .") regarding supports?

7. What are five steps that can be taken to reduce the level of adult support?

After this discussion, create a specific plan for using less intrusive supports across the day.

Commonly Asked Questions About Independence and Fading Support

FAQs

Q: What if my student needs intrusive supports due to physical disabilities?

A: This will certainly be the case for some students. However, we encourage you to use the data tracking and planning tools with your team to discover a variety of ways to use peers and invisible and material supports whenever possible. For some students, independence won't be the goal—interdependence with peers will be.

Q: I won't have very much to do if I'm encouraging only natural cues, peer supports, and material supports. What should I say to the team?

A: Work with the team to figure out what to do in order to help the student indirectly. For example, you might prepare materials for upcoming lessons. You might be directly supporting many students in the classroom.

You could station yourself at a table and students can come speak to you if they need something.

Q: **I worry that my principal will think I am not doing my job if I am not next to the student I am supporting. How do I deal with that issue?**

A: Make sure your principal sees and understands the fading plan you worked on with the whole team. It is important to communicate to administrators, faculty, and staff that fading support and building interdependence will be the goal for this student.

Q: **The teacher that works with me wants me to be sitting next to the student that I am supporting all the time. How do I communicate with the teacher that it might be intrusive?**

A: Share this chapter with your teacher and ask them to discuss it with you.

Q: **What if the student doesn't read on level and needs me to read the material for them?**

A: We recommend first trying the strategies we have listed in this chapter as well as in Chapter 6. Then, collect data about whether or not these less intrusive supports (e.g., materials, peers) are benefiting the student to access the content, discuss the data, and then make a plan with the team.

Conclusion

The ways in which paraprofessionals thoughtfully fade adult support, build resiliency, foster independence and interdependence, and prepare for inevitable disruptions are important for student success. Utilizing the least intrusive supports on the support ladder ensures that each student's needs for assistance are met without compromising that student's ability to participate as independently and authentically as possible. Communicating with your team will be essential when it comes to determining supports so that you can best understand the academic, behavioral, and long-term support goals for your students.

TO-DO LIST

To Do

After reading this chapter . . .

- Complete the activities and reflections in this chapter.
- Complete the data collection worksheet about the types of support the student receives throughout the day.
- Once complete, bring the data collection sheet to your team and plan ways to fade adult support.
- Have a conversation with a friend or colleague about your philosophy regarding support, independence, and interdependence.

Supporting Yourself

And be sure to keep your light bright and shining—you never know just how many people you may be a lighthouse for. You never know just how many people find their way home, in even the wildest storms, because you are there.

—Cleo Wade

Imagine the Feeling of a Full Cup

When our emotional, physical, cognitive, and spiritual cup is full, it is easier for us to share our time, knowledge, and compassion with others. When our cup is full, we have the presence of mind and energy to give to others, our patience levels are higher, and we can function better for both ourselves and our students. Alternatively, when we are depleted, exhausted, and running on empty—or solely on caffeine—we can be short-tempered, short on presence, and short on exactly what our students need from us: our positive attention, energy, and compassion.

It is our dream for all paraprofessionals to have full, overflowing cups. Those who are rested and in the right emotional and physical space can support all students with compassion and kindness. Supporting all students requires intense levels of energy, presence, and patience. One of the very best things you can do to be effective with students is to prioritize your own health, happiness and well-being. We believe that your success as a paraprofessional depends on your ability to make yourself a priority outside of the school day.

This chapter does not provide you with a recipe for how to care for yourself; we provide ways of thinking (i.e., habits of mind) and ways of being (i.e., specific practices and strategies) to improve your own mental health. Educators who are not rested, healthy, and reasonably content will have difficulty helping their students. Whether you deal with stress by running a marathon or by taking a bath, it is important to focus on what you enjoy and on what works to help you relieve stress and feel healthy and balanced.

The job of a paraprofessional is not easy. Then again, no job worth doing is really easy. You may find your job quite rewarding or quite stressful—or, like so many of us, it may vary from day to day. But one thing is certain: you need to take care of yourself to take care of others. You also need to set up your own support system. This chapter suggests habits of mind and habits of practice, and strategies for problem solving, networking, and self-care. We conclude with a paraprofessional-inspired mantra and encourage you to create a unique mantra for yourself.

Habits of Mind

This section focuses on two important habits of mind that you can begin to cultivate to help you interact more positively and effectively with yourself and others. We like to think about these habits of mind—be a light and examine your energetic contribution—as ways to emotionally and mentally set you, your colleagues, and your students up for connectivity and success.

Be a Light in Your School

As we walk through the schools in which we work, we often greet our colleagues by asking, "How are you doing?" In response, we hear phrases such as, "I'm busy," "I'm overwhelmed," "I'm under water," "I'm barely alive," or "surviving." It is not uncommon to hear many nonexamples of self-care in a school. For example, many of our colleagues may say things such as, "I was up grading until midnight," "I ate Cheetos for dinner," or "I didn't leave school until 6 p.m. last night." But this way of thinking often makes us feel more tired and depleted of mental and physical resources . . . and it will almost always affect your colleagues and students.

We ask you to consider how you might practice being a light in your school instead. The next time someone asks you how you are doing, consider ways you can answer honestly while still infusing energy and positivity. Maybe your response is as simple as "I'm happy to see you and the students."

ACTIVITIES

ACTIVITY: "How Are You Doing?"

Consider a few phrases that might come naturally to you when someone asks, "How are you doing?"

Examine Your Energetic Contribution to Your School

We are sure you can think of someone you have worked with who always manages to brighten the day with a positive attitude. These people see problems as challenges that can be solved. They see the good in every situation and can boost morale with their sunny dispositions. They are people we look forward to working with or just being near; they actually can influence our own moods because being positive is contagious.

Now, consider the energy you bring to work each day. For example, when you walk into a room, are you most often greeting everyone warmly? Making a light-hearted joke? Getting right down to business? Or are you likely to enter a conversation with a complaint or concern? The way you enter a room or begin a conversation matters.

Think about your last conversation with a colleague. What type of energetic contribution did you bring to the table? What did you say or not say? What was your body language like? Every single interaction we have at work—and everywhere—has a positive, negative, or neutral energetic contribution. How do you ensure that yours is positive more often than not?

One way is to think ahead to your next meeting or next interaction. How can you set the tone for a positive and productive conversation? Can you add humor and lightness? Can you practice truly listening? Can you start the conversation off on a positive note and remain so? Can you share a genuine compliment? This attitude and thinking will result not only in a healthier working atmosphere but also in a healthier outlook for you.

ACTIVITY: Cultivate Positivity

ACTIVITIES

Put 10 rubber bands around one wrist. Throughout the day, every time you say something positive, move a band from one wrist to the other. You can quickly see how measuring your positive statements can keep your attitude positive.

Habits of Practice

This section focuses on several important habits of practice you can use to help you feel more fulfilled and joyous, and begin cultivating a spirit of well-being in your life at home and at work. These habits of practice include daily gratitude practices, celebrating small things, laughter, and a focus on practicing fun.

Transform Your Life Using Gratitude

Gratitude can help us become more trusting, more social, and more appreciative of ourselves, surroundings, and relationships. This transformation can help us deepen our relationships, improve our mood, and become more productive and effective at work. If you have not tried a practice of gratitude in your own life, we encourage you to start. If you already have a practice, we hope you sustain the practice.

A simple but effective practice is to write down something you are grateful for every day, in whatever way feels best to you. Ask yourself, "What am I grateful for today?" Your gratitude writing can take many forms, such as the following:

- Writing in a gratitude journal
- Maintaining a gratitude file on your computer
- Sending a gratitude e-mail to yourself
- Sharing your gratitude via texts with family or friends
- Creating color-coded and formatted gratitude lists

ACTIVITY: Gratitude Practice

ACTIVITIES

Take a look at the gratitude writing ideas provided. Which form will your gratitude practice take? Will it be one of these or an even different idea?

Celebrate the Small Stuff

No matter how hard a particular day feels, try to stop and write for 5 minutes about *only* the delightful moments you shared with students and colleagues. For example, you might write about a student who so kindly helped another, or the student who was courageous and asked someone new to be their partner. You might also write about the kind note you wrote to a friend or the note you received from a teacher. Maybe it's the progress your student is making or how tasty your leftovers were for lunch.

Laughter Is the Best Medicine

One of the greatest joys of working in schools is how much fun you can have with the educators and students who are with you each day. Think back to a time you had a good belly laugh . . . you know, the kind where you were smiling for minutes afterward. Laughter produces physical and psychological benefits that have been documented for decades. These benefits include reducing stress, tension, and anxiety and increasing feelings of connectedness largely because endorphins are released in our brain when we laugh. You can use humor as a way to care for yourself inside school and outside of it. Inside of school, figure out ways to lighten the mood with professional and thoughtful humor. Enjoy a good laugh with your teammates. When at home, watch funny TV, listen to humorous podcasts or audiobooks, and laugh with your family. Incorporating humor and laughter into each day is an effective and fun self-care tool.

Bring the Fun

Brain research suggests that fun is beneficial to our experience at work and in our own learning because fun experiences increase dopamine, endorphins, and oxygen in our bodies, which encourages motivation for the task at hand. When we are in positive emotional or physical states, we trigger optimal brain activation. Although we encourage you to infuse more play and fun in your daily work, how you do so will depend on your personality. For example, some paraprofessionals might tell jokes to create a spirit of fun in the classroom or staff lounge. Others may crank up the tunes for an occasional dance party. Here are a few more fun ideas to borrow from others to share with students and colleagues.

- Joke of the day
- Dance party
- Funny video clips
- Dance meetings
- Scavenger hunts
- Dress in theme with colleagues
- Dress as twins with colleagues

Problem Solving

Although you have read this book and have several ideas and strategies to handle many different kinds of problems or situations, problems inevitably will

---

ONLINE RESOURCES FOR WELLNESS

- Shawn Achor is a happiness researcher who shares his thoughts about having a positive mindset in several TED talks.
- Gretchen Rubin has written several useful books on happiness and creating a happier and more well-rounded life. http://gretchenrubin.com
- Mindful Schools is a web site created to support the use of mindfulness and well-being for staff and students. www.mindfulschools.org

When we are in positive emotional or physical states, we trigger optimal brain activation.

arise that you may not feel prepared to handle. It is important to remember that you are not alone and that you have a network of support at the school. When you come across a problem that you are having difficulty solving, consider the following general ideas or suggestions:

- Talk with other teachers in the building.
- Talk to the student.
- Talk with the principal.
- Talk to a parent.
- Talk with other paraprofessionals.
- Bring the problem to the special education teacher.
- Talk to an OT.
- Write down the problem and brainstorm solutions.
- Go for a walk—think only of solutions during the walk.
- Draw the problem and the potential solutions.
- List all the potential solutions to the problem.
- Talk to your best friend or partner (keep all information about students confidential).
- Give it time.

If meeting with others or brainstorming solutions by yourself does not help you discover a new solution, you may need a step-by-step problem-solving process, such as creative problem solving (CPS).

The Creative Problem-Solving Process

The CPS process has a long history as a proven method for approaching and solving problems in innovative ways (Davis, 2004; Parnes, 1985, 1988, 1992, 1997). It is a tool that can help you redefine a problem, come up with creative ways to solve the problem, and then take action to solve it. We first learned this method and used it as teachers to solve problems with the students we supported. We continue to use this method to solve everyday personal and professional problems. Educational scholars, and creators and founders of the Creative Education Foundation and the Creative Problem Solving Institute, Alex Osborn and Sidney Parnes (Osborn, 1993), conducted extensive research on the steps involved when people solve problems. They determined that people typically use a five-step process, as described in the following sections.

Explore the Problem

1. *Fact finding*—Describe what you know or perceive to be true about the challenge. Who? What? When? Where? How? What is true and not true about this problem?

2. *Problem finding*—Clarify the issue. View it in a different way. Finish this sentence: In what ways might we . . .?

Generate Ideas

3. *Idea finding*—Generate as many ideas as possible; defer judgment and reinforcement (do not say things such as "good idea" or "that will not work," because then you would be passing judgment on the idea).

Prepare for Action

4. *Solution finding*—Compare the ideas against some criteria that you create. How will you know whether your solution will work?

5. *Acceptance finding*—Create a step-by-step plan of action.

The following examples describe how this process actually worked in solving a specific problem for a paraprofessional.

Case Example 1

Tom, a paraprofessional working with Trevor, a first grader, was having a difficult time getting Trevor off the playground at the end of recess. Trevor would run around and hide, and Tom could not reach him or get him to go inside. The end of recess time was becoming a bit like a game of tag, except that Tom definitely did not enjoy chasing Trevor around. Trevor would climb to the top of the slide, and if Tom started to come up after him, Trevor would slide down. If Tom slid down, Trevor would climb back up. This was almost humorous to watch unless you were Tom, who felt frustrated and embarrassed. Tom considered the communicative intent of the behavior and decided that Trevor was likely trying to communicate that he did not want to come in from recess. Knowing that information, however, did not help Tom identify what to do to get Trevor inside. He also knew that Trevor had a difficult time with transitions. Tom decided to talk to his team. They sat together and engaged in a CPS process, which is briefly outlined in Table 10.1.

Case Example 2

Felicia, a paraprofessional working with Becca, a 10th-grade student, was feeling defeated in her work because Becca would not engage with her. Anytime

QUICK QUIZ

What are the five steps in the CPS method?

Table 10.1.   The creative problem-solving (CPS) process in action

Stage of CPS process	Examples from Tom and Trevor
1. Fact finding	It doesn't work to wait him out. It takes easily 10 minutes to get him off the playground. He does not respond to everyone leaving the playground—he continues to play. He enjoys playing Tag with his friends. He has trouble with transitions. No one has ever asked him what he needs.
2. Problem finding	In what ways can we help Trevor return from recess promptly and happily?
3. Idea finding	Give him a time out. Have him lose minutes off his recess time. Give him a timer or watch. Have a peer help him in. See how long he will play outside before coming in. Don't allow him to go outside for recess at all. Make a sticker chart. Give him extra recess.
4. Solution finding	We want this solution to . . . (example criteria) 1. Enhance the image of the student among peers. 2. Promote independence or interdependence. 3. Appeal to the student. 4. Increase and promote belonging. 5. Increase interaction with peers. 6. Seem logistically feasible.
5. Acceptance finding	The team finally decided on a solution for this problem. What they did was to combine three ideas. They first met with Trevor to ask him what would help (they provided him a menu of ideas); he decided on a timer with peer support. They gave Trevor a watch timer and asked him to identify a peer whom he was to find when the timer went off. When the timer rang (with 2 minutes remaining in recess), the two boys found each other and went to line up together. Problem solved.

Sources: Giangreco, Cloninger, Dennis, and Edelman (2002); Osborn (1993).

Felicia came near to support her, Becca would close her eyes and rest her head on the desk. When Felicia prompted her kindly with questions like, "What's wrong?" or "Do you need help getting started with work?" Becca would make loud noises and keep her head down. Felicia felt like she wasn't able to do her job well and didn't know what to do, so she brought it up to Becca's IEP team. They sat together and engaged in a CPS process, which is briefly outlined in Table 10.2.

Building a Network of Support

If you were all alone in the universe with no one to talk to, no one with which to share the beauty of the stars, to laugh with, to touch, what would be your purpose in life? It is other life, it is love, which gives your life meaning. This is harmony. We must discover the joy of each other, the joy of challenge, the joy of growth. —Mitsugi Saotome (1986)

To sustain yourself as a paraprofessional, you need a network of caring support.

To sustain yourself as a paraprofessional, you need a network of caring support. Do you feel isolated in your workplace? Do you feel that you could use more support? Think now of all the people who love you and care about you. Then, consider others at work who also might feel isolated. In your school, classroom, or grade level, create a small team of support. There may also be problem-solving teams that already exist in the school; see if you could participate in one to create connections with like-minded colleagues.

Create a Team of Support

One fourth-grade team created a support team by taking turns bringing in breakfast on Friday mornings. They ate together and talked, with no agenda.

Table 10.2.   The creative problem-solving (CPS) process in action

Stage of CPS process	Examples from Becca and Felicia
1. Fact finding	Becca does not respond to verbal prompts from Felicia. She can easily miss an entire lesson and distract the class with noises during one of her shutdowns. She has difficulty asking for help from Felicia but in other situations has been known to ask for help from peers. She receives the majority of her support from Felicia, not from teachers or peers.
2. Problem finding	What are more effective ways to provide Becca with support?
3. Idea finding	Move her to the front of the class so she is close to the teacher to ask questions. Move Becca to a special education class where she has more one-to-one support. Fade Felicia's support so that she is providing gestural, material, and natural supports as often as possible rather than verbal prompts and supports. Have a peer check in on Becca. Create a behavior chart.
4. Solution finding	We want this solution to . . . (example criteria) 1. Enhance the image of the student among peers. 2. Promote independence or interdependence. 3. Appeal to the student. 4. Increase and promote belonging. 5. Increase interaction with peers. 6. Seem logistically feasible.
5. Acceptance finding	The team finally decided on a solution for this problem. They first met with Becca to ask her what would help during class and work with Ms. Felicia. They were prepared with a menu of ideas for her to choose from, and she decided she wanted to ask for help directly from the teacher or peers, and have Ms. Felicia set up her iPad, modify her materials in advance, and preview work with her during study hall so that she didn't need to sit side by side with her and provide verbal support during classes. Ms. Felicia was then free to circulate to support many students in class and would occasionally check in on Becca too. Problem solved.

Sources: Giangreco, Cloninger, Dennis, and Edelman (2002); Osborn (1993).

ONLINE NETWORKS FOR PARAPROFESSIONALS

- The National Resource Center for Paraeducators (NRCP) is a site dedicated to supporting a national community of paraprofessionals. There are discussion boards, resources, and even state by state supports. https://www.nrcpara.org

- We have an online community, Inspired Paraprofessional, on Facebook that includes more than a thousand individuals. Here, you can access paraprofessional resources and a larger community, and ask questions. https://www.facebook.com/inspireparaprofessional/

The conversations were fun and lighthearted, and the team members had time to simply connect with each other. They said that the Friday breakfast became a highlight of the week. Twice a year, they planned a Saturday morning breakfast to which they invited their families. As they ate together, they got to know more about each other and their loved ones. This helped to create a deeper sense of community for the professionals on the team.

If you are feeling alone or in need of support in your school, create your own team. Bring together like-minded people from your school community. Make sure the focus of the team is to lift one another up, and feel free to borrow the breakfast gatherings idea from the fourth-grade team. Then, rely on this team to support you when you need it and provide support to others when they are in need.

Build a Community With Other Paraprofessionals

A group of paraprofessionals at one school met after school every week and went walking together. Their contract time ended at 3:15 p.m., and they met outside promptly at 3:20 p.m., wearing sneakers. They walked a 2-mile path, sharing stories and problems and laughing together along the way. These walks helped them create a network of support, and they got exercise and fresh air while they talked.

Another group of paraprofessionals met in the library and formed a book group that alternated between reading work-related books and books selected simply for pleasure. At the beginning of the year, they set their reading list (which started with the book you are reading right now). They organized themselves in such a way that they ended up convincing the principal to purchase the books through their professional development funds.

When building your community, do not let your questions go unanswered. Figure out who can help you answer your burning questions. School is a busy place, and at times it may seem that no one has time to talk. If you have questions—and you undoubtedly will—write them down and find people who can help you answer them. Consider asking special education teachers, students, general education teachers, other paraprofessionals, principals, therapists, or any other knowledgeable staff in the school.

Care for Yourself

Have you ever been on an airplane and heard a flight attendant announce that if there is an emergency, you should place an oxygen mask on your own face before assisting your children? The idea behind that rule is that if the plane crashes, you want to make sure you are available to help the children. If you do not have oxygen, you will not be able to help them. In essence, that is what self-care involves: nurturing yourself outside of work so that you can be helpful and nurturing to the students you support.

Meet Your Own Basic Needs

Maslow (1999) has identified the basic physiological needs of every human; these include oxygen, food, water, and regulated body temperature (Figure 10.1). Like any other human being, you need to make sure your

Maslow's hierarchy of needs

morality, creativity, spontaneity, problem solving, lack of prejudice, acceptance of facts — 5

self-esteem, confidence, achievement, respect of others, respect by others — 4

friendship, family, sexual intimacy, sense of connection — 3

security of body, employment, resources, morality, family, health, property — 2

breathing, food, sex, sleep, homeostasis, excretion — 1

Self-actualization
Self-esteem
Love and belonging
Safety and security
Physiological needs

Figure 10.1.   Maslow's hierarchy of needs. (Source: Maslow, 1999.)

needs are being met before you can help meet the needs of others. You might have to bring healthy snacks to school to keep yourself fueled for a long day at work. You might bring a water bottle with you so that you can stay hydrated throughout the day. You also might want to have a sweater with you or dress in layers—in many schools, temperatures frequently shift. Maslow's next level of need is safety and love. Surround yourself with loving people so that you feel supported and cared for. Lastly, you need to get enough sleep every night. It is much more difficult to be prepared to support students if you are tired. These needs are at the very core of every person's physical and mental health.

Stop. Breathe. Meditate

Some people love to meditate. For others, the idea of meditation makes them break out in a nervous sweat. But meditation does not have to look like sitting still for an hour, thinking nothing but calm, present thoughts. Here, we provide several options for working mindful meditations into your busy schedule. The goal is to take a few minutes to return your thoughts to your body and your mind in order to reduce stress and increase mental wellness.

Walking Meditation

While walking your dog, taking a hike, walking to the copy machine, or walking around the track, focus your attention on one thing. It could be the sound of the birds, the feel of the ground beneath your feet, the artwork in the school hallway, or the sounds of students. When your mind wanders to tasks, to-dos, or negative thoughts, gently return to your original focus.

Task-Related Meditation

You can incorporate mindful meditation into daily activities. For example, washing your hands, folding laundry, commuting to work, washing dishes, or making lunches can become mini-meditation sessions. During these activities, focus on the experience and the sensations—the feel of the laundry, the warm water on your hands. If your mind wanders, bring yourself back to the task and experience.

Waiting Meditation

Anytime you are waiting in line—for example, in a waiting room, or waiting for students to finish lunch—observe your breath and surroundings. Use the time to do a whole-body scan. Are your muscles tense? Are you hot or cold? What sensations do you feel in your body? Take note of any sensations and turn calm energy toward those places. Relax your tense muscles. Unfurrow your brow. Breathe.

Mantra Meditation

Some people find that quieting their mind can be very difficult. If this is you, repeating a mantra aloud or silently for 5 or 10 minutes can be a useful tool for focusing your mind. In fact, the word *mantra* is derived from two Sanskrit words—*manas* (mind) and *tra* (tool). A simple Hindu mantra to try is *so hum;* say or think "so" as you breathe in and "hum" as you exhale. *So hum* is Sanskrit that translates to "I am he/that." You can also create unique mantras for various situations, for example, "I am calm" or "I am present."

ACTIVITIES

ACTIVITY: 10-Minute Meditation

Perhaps you are willing to embark on a seated meditation practice. If so, try this exercise:

1. Find a comfortable place where you will not be bothered.
2. Sit with your eyes comfortably closed and turn your attention inward. Empty your mind of chattering thoughts. Relax.
3. If your mind begins to drift, gently return your focus inward.
4. Sit for as long as you feel comfortable.
5. When you are finished, answer these questions: *How do you feel now? Are you energized, thoughtful, contemplative, relaxed, or anxious?* Gently acknowledge those feelings and consider trying meditation another time.

Find an Outlet

Caring for yourself is critical to staying on the job and feeling balanced while doing it. Find ways to sustain yourself while outside of work. Consider physical outlets such as yoga, running, walking, biking, hiking, or swimming. You can also consider spiritual outlets such as meditation, prayer, or yoga to keep yourself spiritually balanced.

Consider intellectual outlets such as playing games, reading, or writing. Or, try more creative outlets such as painting, sculpting, drawing, baking, cooking, scrapbooking, or generally creating something. Also consider self-pampering activities such as taking baths or getting massages. Employing these types of self-care strategies will help you feel balanced, healthy, and calm.

When working with students, you need to be constantly learning from them and for them. Our hope is that this book will be an impetus for your own learning. When reading this book, try out the strategies, and when you identify a strategy or idea that works, use it again. At the same time, remember that every context, every student, and every minute brings something new. It is important to reflect on when certain ideas or strategies work and how they work. The process is inevitably fluid.

Five More Practices to Support Your Well-Being

1. ***Be present.*** Practice staying in the moment when you are around students and colleagues. Don't space out or check your phone when someone is talking to you. Respond quickly and calmly to questions or concerns. Students will learn from your ability to be present with yourself, with colleagues, and with them.

STRATEGIES

2. ***Prepare for the day.*** At the beginning of each day, ask yourself the following questions:

   a. What is something I can get excited about today?

   b. What is something I want to achieve today?

   c. Who is someone I want to support today?

   d. Today will be a success if at the end of the day I feel...

3. ***Practice breathing.*** Throughout the day, pause to breathe. Breathe in deeply for 3 seconds. Hold for 3 seconds. Breathe out for 3 seconds. Repeat until you feel calm and centered.

4. ***Write your tomorrow.*** On a blank piece of paper, write your thoughts and intentions for the next day. Perhaps you write, "I will laugh with others. I will celebrate my students. I will feel refreshed and motivated."

5. ***Remember that you are not alone.*** Surround yourself with positive people who listen to you, support you, and celebrate you. Share your stories, share your positivity, and share your ideas. Build one another up. Educators who have a team are happier and more fulfilled, and we would love for you to join our large network of educators at Inclusive Schooling (www.inclusiveschooling.com).

REFLECTIONS

Create your own self-care plan. Which of the previously listed ideas do you already do? Which could you do more regularly? Which are you willing to try for the first time? Now, create a plan for yourself that could be used to nurture yourself every day in order to keep your cup full.

Commonly Asked Questions About Supporting Yourself

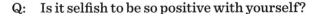

Q: Is it selfish to be so positive with yourself?

FAQs

A: Being positive with yourself is not selfish at all. In fact, the more positive you are with yourself, and the more you make time to fill your resources up and take care of your well-being, the more present you can be in all moments of your day and the more positive supports you can offer your students, colleagues, and others in your life.

Q: What if I don't have the time to practice self-care?

A: We understand, and we recommend looking for any small gap in your day where you might squeeze in the practice of gratitude, mindfulness, or any of the ideas provided in this chapter. Consider your morning commute, when you're in the car taking the kids to an after-school activity, or even when you're in the shower. Allow yourself permission to think creatively about your time.

Q: How do you initiate the "let's start a network" conversation with professionals who are like-minded?

A: We recommend starting the conversation by asking those individuals to lunch or coffee and being clear that you are interested in creating some form of professional support group—informal or formal, whatever makes sense. We think you'll be surprised by how many people say "yes" and how meaningful that first conversation can be.

Conclusion

© iStockphoto 1053304466.

We are so grateful for you. Thank you for reading this book. We hope these practices and ideas support you and deepen your love and excitement for working with students and working in the field of education. We conclude this book with a mantra for paraprofessionals—a call to center yourselves and be the educator you know you can be. We thank you for reading, and we wish you luck as you help all of the remarkable students who make us better, kinder, and more compassionate and creative humans.

The Paraprofessional's Mantra

- I support myself so I can support my students.
- I practice gratitude for myself and with my students.
- I am a light in my school and a light for my students.
- I value my students and tell them so regularly.
- I celebrate diversity with my words and actions.
- I am able to work with my team to figure out what students need.
- I set my students up for success.
- I respond with kindness.
- I begin with a positive perspective each day.

To Do

TO-DO LIST

After reading this chapter . . .

- Complete the activities and reflections in this chapter.
- Choose habits to develop . . .

- Your gratitude practice
- Your problem-solving practice
- Your meditation practice
- Create a support team.
- Connect with other paraprofessionals in person and/or virtually.

References

American Psychiatric Association. (2000). *Diagnostic and statistical manual of mental disorders, fourth edition, text revision (DSM-IV-TR)*. Washington, DC: Author.

Angelides, P., Constantinou, C., & Leigh, J. (2009). The role of paraprofessionals in developing inclusive education in Cyprus. *European Journal of Special Needs Education, 24*(1), 75–89.

Armstrong, T. (2000a). *In their own way: Discovering and encouraging your child's multiple intelligences.* New York, NY: Penguin Putnam.

Armstrong, T. (2000b). *Multiple intelligences in the classroom.* Alexandria, VA: Association for Supervision and Curriculum Development.

Ashby, C. E. (2008). *"Cast into a cold pool": Inclusion and access in middle school for students with labels of mental retardation and autism* (Unpublished doctoral dissertation). Syracuse University, Syracuse, NY.

Balfanz, R., & Letgers, N. (2004). *Locating the dropout crisis: Which high schools produce the nation's dropouts? Where are they located? Who attends them?* Baltimore, MD: Johns Hopkins University Center for Social Organization of Schools. Retrieved from https://files.eric.ed.gov/fulltext/ED484525.pdf

Bambara, L. M., Janney, R., & Snell, M. E. (2015). *Teachers' guides to inclusive practices* (3rd ed.). Baltimore, MD: Paul H. Brookes Publishing Co.

Biklen, D. (2005). *Autism and the myth of the person alone* (pp. 80–82). New York, NY: New York University Press.

Biklen, D., & Burke, J. (2006). Presuming competence. *Equity & Excellence in Education, 39,* 166–175.

Blatt, B. (1987). *The conquest of mental retardation.* Austin, TX: PRO-ED.

Bonner Foundation. (2008). Conflict resolution: Steps for handling interpersonal dynamics. In *Bonner civic engagement training modules.* Retrieved August 14, 2020 from http://bonnernetwork.pbworks.com/f/BonCurConflictResolution.pdf

Boston Public Schools. (2020). *Job listing: Paraprofessional [Sped Sub/Sep. Aide SPED inclusion Programs] [King K-8] (SY20-21).* Retrieved from https://bostonpublicschools.tedk12.com/hire/ViewJob.aspx?JobID=19664#

Brock, M. E., & Carter, E. W. (2016). Efficacy of teachers training paraprofessionals to implement peer support arrangements. *Exceptional Children, 82*(3), 354–371.

Broer, S. M., Doyle, M. B., & Giangreco, M. F. (2005). Perspectives of students with disabilities of their experiences with paraprofessional support. *Exceptional Children, 71*(4), 415–430.

Brown, L., Farrington, K., Knight, T., Ross, C., & Ziegler, M. (1999). Fewer paraprofessionals and more teachers and therapists in educational programs for students with significant disabilities. *The Journal of the Association for Persons with Severe Handicaps, 24*(4), 250–253.

Bui, X., Quirk, C., Almazan, S., & Valenti, M. (2010) Inclusive Education Research & Practice. Elkridge, MD: Maryland Coalition for Inclusive Education.

Callahan, C. (1997). *Advice About Being an LD Student.* Retrieved from http://www.ldonline.org/firstperson/Advice_About_Being_an_LD_Student

Cameron, D. L. (2014). An examination of teacher–student interactions in inclusive classrooms: Teacher interviews and classroom observations. *Journal of Research in Special Educational Needs, 14*(4), 264–273.

Carroll, K. (2014) Who Cares About Kelsey Screening Q&A discussion, Syracuse University. Retrieved from https://www.youtube.com/watch?v=iz1CHLayur0

Causton-Theoharis, J., Giangreco, M., Doyle, M. B., & Vadasy, P. (2007). Paraprofessionals: The sous chefs of literacy instruction. *TEACHING Exceptional Children, 40*(1), 56–63.

Causton-Theoharis, J., & Malmgren, K. (2005). Building bridges: Strategies to help paraprofessionals promote peer interactions. *TEACHING Exceptional Children, 37*(6), 18–24.

Causton-Theoharis, J., & Theoharis, G. (2008, September). Creating inclusive schools for all students. *The School Administrator, 65*(8), 24–30.

Choi, J. H., Meisenheimer, J. M., McCart, A. B., & Sailor, W. (2017). Improving learning for all students through equity-based inclusive reform practices: Effectiveness of a fully integrated schoolwide model on student reading and math achievement. *Remedial and Special Education, 38*(1). https://doi.org/10.1177/0741932516644054

Chopra, R. V., & Giangreco, M. F. (2019). Effective use of teacher assistants in inclusive classrooms. In M. J. Schuelka, C. J. Johnstone, G. Thomas, & A. J. Artiles (Eds.), *The SAGE handbook of inclusion and diversity in education* (pp. 193–207). Thousand Oaks, CA: SAGE.

Davis, G. (2004). *Creativity is forever* (5th ed.). Dubuque, IA: Kendall Hunt.

Donnellan, A. (1984). The criterion of the least dangerous assumption. *Behavioral Disorders, 9,* 141–150.

Doyle, M. B. (2008). *The paraprofessional's guide to the inclusive classroom: Working as a team* (3rd ed.). Baltimore, MD: Paul H. Brookes Publishing Co.

Education for All Handicapped Children Act of 1975, PL 94-142, 20 U.S.C. §§ 1400 *et seq.*

Endrew F. v. Douglas County School District, 137 S. Ct. 988 (2017).

Everyone Matters. (2013, August 14). *"DON'T LIMIT ME!" – Powerful message from Megan with Down Syndrome.* [Video file]. Retrieved from https://www.youtube.com/watch?v=YOwDfnoek6E.

FAS Community Resource Center. (2008). *Information about fetal alcohol syndrome (FAS) and fetal alcohol spectrum disorders (FASD).* Retrieved from http://www.come-over.to/FASCRC

Fay, L. (2019, August 7). 74 Interview: Researcher Gloria Ladson-Billings on Culturally Relevant Teaching, the Role of Teachers in Trump's America & Lessons From Her Two Decades in Education Research. The 74. Retrieved from https://www.the74million.org/article/74-interview-researcher-gloria-ladson-billings-on-culturally-relevant-teaching-the-role-of-teachers-in-trumps-america-lessons-from-her-two-decades-in-education-research/

French, N. K. (1998). Working together: Resource teachers and paraeducators. *Remedial and Special Education, 19*(6), 357–368.

Friend, M., & Bursuck, W. D. (2019). *Including students with special needs: A practical guide for classroom teachers* (8th ed.). Boston, MA: Pearson.

Gabel, A. (2006). Stop asking me if I need help. In E. B. Keefe, V. M. Moore, & F. R. Duff (Eds.), *Listening to the experts: Students with disabilities speak out* (pp. 35–40). Baltimore, MD: Paul H. Brookes Publishing Co.

Gardner, H. (1983). *Frames of mind: A theory of multiple intelligences.* New York, NY: Basic Books.

Giangreco, M. F., Broer, S. M., & Edelman, S. W. (2002). "That was then, this is now!" Paraprofessional supports for students with disabilities in general education classrooms. *Exceptionality, 10*(1), 47–64.

Giangreco, M. F., Cloninger, C. J., Dennis, R., & Edelman, S. W. (2002). Problem-solving methods to facilitate inclusive education. In J. S. Thousand, R. A. Villa, & A. I. Nevin (Eds.), *Creativity and collaborative learning: The practical guide to empowering students, teachers, and families* (2nd ed., pp. 111–134). Baltimore, MD: Paul H. Brookes Publishing Co.

Giangreco, M. F., Edelman, S. W., Luiselli, E. T., & MacFarland, S. Z. (1997). Helping or hovering: The effects of paraprofessional proximity on students with disabilities. *Exceptional Children, 64*(1), 7–18.

Girma, H. (2014, May 14). *Mainstreaming accessibility: Deafblindness, assistive technology and advocacy.* Retrieved from https://news.itu.int/mainstreaming-accessibility-deafblindness-assistive-technology-advocacy/

Golfus, B. (n.d.). The trouble with do-gooders. *Mouth Mag.* Retrieved from https://www.mouthmag.com/do_goodertrouble.htm

Gomez, L. E., & Bernet, P. (2019). Diversity improves performance and outcomes. *Journal of the National Medical Association, 111*(4), 383–392.

Gurin, P., Nagda, B. R. A., & Lopez, G. E. (2004) The Benefits of Diversity in Education for Democratic Citizenship. *Journal of Social Issues, 60*(1).

Hehir, T. (2002). Eliminating ableism in education. *Harvard Educational Review, 72*(1), 1–32. https://hepgjournals.org/doi/10.17763/haer.72.1.03866528702g2105

Hott, L. R., Garey, D., Chowder, K., Channing, S., Moore, A., Chin, M., McCarthy, S., . . . Copyright Collection (Library of Congress). (2007). *Through deaf eyes.* Washington, DC: WETA-TV.

Huefner, D. S. (2000). *Getting comfortable with special education law: A framework for working with children with disabilities.* Norwood, MA: Christopher-Gordon.

Individuals with Disabilities Education Improvement Act (IDEA) of 2004, PL 108-446, 20 U.S.C. § § 1400 *et seq.*

Institut Pasteur. (n.d.). *Louis Pasteur's biography.* Retrieved from https://www.pasteur.fr/en

Jones, R. C. (1998–2006). *Strategies for reading comprehension: Clock Buddies.* Retrieved from https://www.readingquest.org/clock_buddies.html

Kasa-Hendrickson, C., & Buswell, W. (2007). *Strategies for Presuming Competence.* Retrieved from https://tash.org/wpcontent/uploads/2019/03/Strategies-Presuming-Competence.pdf

Keller, H. (1903). *The story of my life.* New York, NY: Doubleday, Page, & Co.

Kliewer, C., & Biklen, D. (1996). Labeling: Who wants to be called retarded? In W. Stainback & S. Stainback (Eds.), *Controversial issues confronting special education: Divergent perspectives* (2nd ed., pp. 83–111). Boston, MA: Allyn & Bacon.

Kluth, P. (2003). *"You're going to love this kid!": Teaching students with autism in the inclusive classroom.* Baltimore, MD: Paul H. Brookes Publishing Co.

Kluth, P. (2005). Calm in crisis. Adapted from P. Kluth (2003), *"You're going to love this kid!": Teaching students with autism in the inclusive classroom.* Baltimore, MD: Paul H. Brookes Publishing Co. https://www.paulakluth.com/?s=calm+in+crisis

Kluth, P. (2010). *You're going to love this kid!": Teaching students with autism in the inclusive classroom, Second Edition.* Baltimore, MD: Paul H. Brookes Publishing Co.

Kluth, P., & Causton, J. (2016). *30 days to the co-taught classroom: How to create an amazing, nearly miraculous and frankly earthshattering partnership in one month or less.* Seattle, WA: Kindle Direct Publishing.

Knoster, T. P. (2008). *The teacher's pocket guide for effective classroom management.* Baltimore, MD: Paul H. Brookes Publishing Co.

Kohn, A. (2006). *Beyond discipline: From compliance to community* (10th anniv. ed.). Alexandria, VA: Association for Supervision and Curriculum Development.

Kornhaber, M., Fierros, E., & Veenema, S. (2004). *Multiple intelligences: Best ideas from research and practice.* Boston, MA: Pearson Education.

Kunc, N. (1992). The need to belong: Rediscovering Maslow's hierarchy of needs. In R. Villa, J. Thousand, W. Stainback, & S. Stainback (Eds.), *Restructuring for caring and effective education* (pp. 21–40). Baltimore, MD: Paul H. Brookes Publishing Co.

Latham, G. I. (1999). *Parenting with love: Making a difference in a day.* Logan, UT: P&T Ink.

Lavoie, R. (2005). *Social Skill Autopsies: A Strategy to Promote and Develop Social Competencies.* Retrieved from http://www.ldonline.org/lavoie/_Social_Skill_Autopsies%3A_A_Strategy_to_Promote_and_Develop_Social_Competencies

Learning Disabilities Online. (2020). *Kids' voices.* Retrieved from http://www.ldonline.org/kidzone

L.H. v. Hamilton County, Nos. 17-5989, 18-5086, 2018 WL 3966517 (E.D. Tenn., Aug. 20, 2018).

Logan, A. (2006). The role of the special needs assistant supporting pupils with special educational needs in Irish mainstream primary schools. *Support for Learning, 21*(2), 92–99. http://dx.doi.org/10.1111/j.1467-9604.2006.00410.x

Lorenzo, R., & Reeves, M. (2018, January 30). How and Where Diversity Drives Financial Performance. Retrieved from https://hbr.org/2018/01/how-and-where-diversity-drives-financial-performance

Lovett, H. (1996). *Learning to listen: Positive approaches and people with difficult behavior.* Baltimore, MD: Paul H. Brookes Publishing Co.

MacLeod, K. (2017). "I should have big dreams": A qualitative case study on alternatives to guardianship. *Education and Training in Autism and Developmental Disabilities, 52*(2), 194–207.

MacLeod, K., Causton, J., & Nunes, N. (2017). Sabrina's story: Collaboration for inclusion. *Rethinking Schools, 31*(2), 24–27.

Malmgren, K. W., & Causton-Theoharis, J. N. (2006). Boy in the bubble: Effects of paraprofessional proximity and other pedagogical decisions on the interactions of a student with behavioral disorders. *Journal of Research in Childhood Education, 20*(4), 301–312.

Maslow, A. H. (1999). *Toward a psychology of being.* New York, NY: John Wiley & Sons.

Mavis. (2007, October 7). *Living in the hearing and deaf worlds.* Retrieved from http://www.raisingdeafkids.org/meet/deaf/mavis/worlds.php

Minkel, J. (2015). *Why I prefer pre-teaching to remediation for struggling students.* Retrieved from https://www.edweek.org/tm/articles/2015/05/18/why-i-prefer-pre-teaching-to-remediation-for.html

Mooney, J. (2019). *Normal sucks: How to live, learn, and thrive outside the lines.* New York, NY: Henry Holt and Company.

Murawski, W. W., & Dieker, L. A. (2004). Tips and strategies for co-teaching at the secondary level. *TEACHING Exceptional Children, 36*(5), 52–58.

National Council on Disability (2018). IDEA Series: *The Segregation of Students with Disabilities.* Retrieved from https://ncd.gov/sites/default/files/NCD_Segregation-SWD_508.pdf

Neff, K. D. (2003). Self-Compassion: An Alternative Conceptualization of a Healthy Attitude Toward Oneself. *Self and Identity, 2*, 85–101.

No Child Left Behind Act of 2001, PL 107-110, 115 Stat. 1425, 20 U.S.C. § § 6301 *et seq.*

Orwell, G. (1981). Politics and the English language. In *A collection of essays* (10th ed., pp. 156–170). Orlando, FL: Harvest.

Osborn, A. F. (1993). *Applied imagination: Principles and procedures of creative problem-solving* (3rd rev. ed.). Buffalo, NY: Creative Education Foundation Press. (Original work published 1953.)

Page, S.E. (2008). *The difference: How the power of diversity creates better groups, firms, schools, and societies, Revised edition*. Princeton, NJ: Princeton University Press.

Palordy, G. J. (2013). High school socioeconomic segregation and student attainment. *American Educational Research Journal, 40* (4), 714–754.

Parker, K. (2008). *Meet RhapsodyBlue*. Retrieved from http://www.angelfire.com/country/rhapsodyblue22/page2.html

Parnes, S. J. (1985). *A facilitating style of leadership*. Buffalo, NY: Bearly.

Parnes, S. J. (1988). *Visionizing: State-of-the-art processes for encouraging innovative excellence*. East Aurora, NY: D.O.K. Publishing.

Parnes, S. J. (Ed.). (1992). *Source book for creative problem solving: A fifty-year digest of proven innovation processes*. Buffalo, NY: Creative Education Foundation Press.

Parnes, S. J. (1997). *Optimize the magic of your mind*. Buffalo, NY: Creative Education Foundation Press.

Patterson, K. B. (2006). Roles and responsibilities of paraprofessionals: In their own words. *TEACHING Exceptional Children Plus, 2*(5), Article 1. Retrieved from https://files.eric.ed.gov/fulltext/EJ967108.pdf

PEAK Parent Center. (n.d.). *Accommodations and modifications fact sheet*. Retrieved from http://www.peatc.org/peakaccom.htm

Peck, C., Staub, D., Gallucci, C., and Schwartz, I. (2004). Parent perception of the impacts of inclusion on their nondisabled child. *The Journal of The Association for Persons With Severe Handicaps. 29*, 135–143. DOI 10.2511/rpsd.29.2.135.

Pitonyak, D. (2007). *The importance of belonging*. Retrieved from http://dimagine.com/wp-content/uploads/2018/04/Belonging.pdf

Richardson, R. C. (1998). *Social skills instruction for culturally diverse adolescents with behavioral deficits*. Paper presented at the 18th Annual Super Conference on Special Education, Baton Rouge, LA.

Rosa's Law, PL 111-256, 124 Stat. 2643, 20 U.S.C. § 1400 *et seq.*

Rosenthal, L., Earnshaw, V. A., Carroll-Scott, A., Henderson, K. E., Peters, S. M., McCaslin, C., Ickovics, J. R. (2015). Weight- and race-based bullying: Health associations among urban adolescents. *Journal of Health Psychology, 20*(4), 401–412. DOI 10.1177/1359105313502567

Rubin, S. (2003, December). *Making dreams come true*. Paper presented at the annual conference of TASH, Chicago, IL.

Rubin, S. (2010, January). Living and thoroughly enjoying life in spite of autism. Paper presented at the Annandale Cooperative Preschool, Annandale, VA.

Ryndak, D. L., Taub, D., Jorgensen, C. M., Gonsier-Gerdin, J., Arndt, K., Sauer, J., Ruppar, A. L., Morningstar, M. E., Allcock, H. (2014). Policy and the impact on placement, involvement, and progress in general education: Critical issues that require rectification. *Research and Practice for Persons with Severe Disabilities, 39*, 65–74.

Saotome, M. (1986). The dojo: Spiritual oasis. In *Aikido and the harmony of nature* (pp. 246–248). Boulogne, France: SEDIREP.

Sapolsky, R. M. (2017). *Behave: The Biology of Humans at Our Best and Worst*. New York, NY: Penguin Random House.

Shipp, J. (May 27, 2015). Like the Lap Bar on a Roller Coaster, Teens Will Test You to See if You Will Hold [video]. Retrieved from https://www.youtube.com/watch?v=m51Qf8fc4UA

Snow, K. (2008). *To ensure inclusion, freedom, and respect for all, it's time to embrace people first language*. Retrieved from http://www.inclusioncollaborative.org/docs/Person-First-Language-Article_Kathie_Snow.pdf

Spectrum. (2020, March 11). *Do all autistic people think the same?* Retrieved from https://www.youtube.com/watch?v=SoWSuxBy6oo

State of Iowa Department of Education. (2019). *Special Education Eligibility and Evaluation Standards*. Retrieved from https://educateiowa.gov/sites/files/ed/documents/SpecialEducationEligibilityandEvaluationStandardsJuly2019.pdf

Strully, J. L., & Strully, C. (1996). Friendships as an educational goal: What we have learned and where we are headed. In S. Stainback & W. Stainback (Eds.), *Inclusion: A guide for educators* (pp. 141–154). Baltimore, MD: Paul H. Brookes Publishing Co.

Symes, W., & Humphrey, N. (2012). Including pupils with autistic spectrum disorders in the classroom: The role of teaching assistants. *European Journal of Special Needs Education, 27*(4), 517–532.

Tadmor, C., Satterstrom, P., Jang, S., and Polzer, J. (2012). Beyond individual creativity: The superadditive benefits of multicultural experience for collective creativity in culturally diverse teams. *Journal of Cross-Cultural Psychology 43*(3). 384–392. DOI 10.1177/0022022111435259.

Tashie, C., Shapiro-Barnard, S., & Rossetti, Z. (2006). *Seeing the charade: What people need to do and undo to make friendships happen*. Nottingham, UK: Inclusive Solutions.

Test, D. W., Mazzotti, V. L., Mustian, A. L., Fowler, C. H., Kortering, L., & Kohler, P. (2009). Evidence-based secondary transition predictors for improving postschool outcomes for students with disabilities. *Career Development for Exceptional Individuals, 32(3)*, 160–181. https://doi.org/10.1177/0885728809346960

Tomlinson, C. A. (2017). *How to differentiate instruction in academically diverse classrooms* (3rd ed.). Alexandria, VA: ASCD.

U.S. Bureau of Labor Statistics. (2019). Teacher assistants. In *Occupational outlook handbook*. Retrieved from https://www.bls.gov/ooh/education-training-and-library/teacher-assistants.htm

U.S. Department of Education. (2004). *Twenty-fourth annual report to Congress on the implementation of the Individuals with Disabilities Education Act*. Washington DC: Author.

U.S. Department of Education, National Center for Education Statistics. (2002). *The condition of education, students with disabilities*. Retrieved from https://nces.ed.gov/programs/coe/indicator_cgg.asp

U.S. Department of Education, Office of Special Education Programs, Individuals with Disabilities Education Act (IDEA) database https://www2.ed.gov/programs/osepidea/618-data/state-level-data-files/index.html#bcc; and National Center for Education Statistics, National Elementary and Secondary Enrollment Projection Model, 1972 through 2029.

U.S. Department of Education, National Center for Education Statistics. (2019). *Digest of Education Statistics, 2018* (NCES 2020-009), Chapter 2.

U.S. Department of Education Office of Civil Rights. (2016). Civil Rights Data Collection, 2015–16. Retrieved from https://www2.ed.gov/about/offices/list/ocr/docs/school-climate-and-safety.pdf

U.S. Department of Energy. (2012). *Department of energy diversity and inclusion strategic plan*. https://www.energy.gov/sites/prod/files/New%20DOE%202012-2015%20Diversityand%20inclusion%20Strategic%20Plan.pdf

Webster, R., Blatchford, P., Bassett, P., Brown, P., Martin, C., & Russell, A. (2010). Double standards and first principles: Framing teaching assistant support for pupils with special educational needs. *European Journal of Special Needs Education, 25*(4), 319–336. http://dx.doi.org/10.1080/08856257.2010.513533

Webster, R., Russell, A., & Blatchford, P. (2015). *Maximising the impact of teaching assistants: Guidance for school leaders and teachers.* London, England: Routledge.

Wheatley, M. J. (2002). *Turning to one another: Simple conversation to restore hope in the future.* San Francisco, CA: Berrett-Koehler Press.

Wilder, L. I. (1932–1943, 1971). The *Little House* books. New York, NY: Harper & Brothers (HarperCollins).

Will, M. (1986). *Educating students with learning problems: A shared responsibility.* Washington, DC: U.S. Department of Education, Office of Special Education and Rehabilitative Service.

Williams, R. (Presenter). (2008, August 24). Hearing impairment: A personal story [Radio broadcast]. In B. Seega (Producer), *Ockham's razor.* Retrieved from https://www.abc.net.au/radionational/programs/ockhamsrazor/hearing-impairment---a-personal-story/3201504

Wurzburg, G. (Director). (2011). *Wretches & Jabberers* [Film]. State of the Art, Inc.

Index

Page numbers followed by *f* indicate figures; those followed by *t* indicate tables.

Stress, science of, 127
Student descriptions, 64
    by parents, 64
    person-first language for, 74–75
    rethinking, 64–66, 65f
    by teachers, 64
    writing, 66–68
Students with disabilities
    aggression toward adults, 131
    anticipating needs of, 122–124, 123t
    autonomous, 121
    belonging and, 11–12, 12t
    dependent on supports, 92, 97
    descriptions of, see Student descriptions
    embarrassment in, 97, 131–132
    expectations for, 81
    getting to know, 41–42, 117
    inclusive education of, see Inclusive education
    increase in number of, 6
    independence in, see Independence in students
    individualized education programs for, see Individualized education programs
    interdependence in, 100, 121, 139–140
    labels/categories of, see Disability labels/categories
    laws on, 5–6, 13–14, 25
    loss of personal control in, 97
    mindfulness in, 141
    in non-inclusive classrooms, 8
    paraprofessional job description by, 5
    peers teasing, 24–25
    physical proximity to, 96–97, 99
    as problem solvers, 129–130
    questions about preferences of, 53
    rapport with, 117–118
    removing from classroom, 24, 99, 132
    resilience in, 140–141
    responsibilities of, 102
    rethinking, see Rethinking students
    right of, to communicate, 122
    universal desires of, 121
Supervision tasks, 4t
Supplementary aids and services, 14, 15f–16f, 17
Supports
    academic, see Academic supports
    asking students about, 81
    behavior, see Behavior supports
    dependence on, 92, 97
    for developing student independence, 133–146
    fading, 92, 100, 110–111, 134, 145
    offering, 82
    on-the-fly supports, 142, 143t
    from peers, 99

    silent, 134–136
    social, see Social supports
    tracking, 142–145, 144f
    types of, 101t

Task-related meditation, 155–156
Tasks, 4t, 81–82, 102
Teaching team, 45–61
    addressing conflict in, 55–56
    confidentiality issues in, 58–60
    co-supporting arrangements in, 54–55, 54t, 55t
    fading support discussion of, 145
    guiding questions for, 51–53
    making time for communication in, 56–58
    members of, 46–51
    overview of, 45–46
    positive behavior support by, 116
    problem-solving by, 130
    web diagram of, 51
Teasing, 24–25
Technology
    for building independence, 136, 139
    for deafblind students, 33
    in inclusive classrooms, 20
    for social supports, 106, 107–109
Time-outs, 121, 124, 125, 131
Timers, 83–84
Transitions, support for, 83–84, 116
Traumatic brain injury (TBI), 38–39
Trust, 117, 121–122

Universal design for learning (UDL), 19
Universal desires, 121
Unstructured time, 103–105

Velcro phenomenon, 97–98
Verbal support, 101t
Verbal/linguistic intelligence, 69t, 119t
Vision teachers, 50
Visual impairment (VI), 39, 40f
Visual schedules, 109, 109f
Visual timers, 83
Vocabulary Match-up, 105

Waiting meditation, 156
Walking meditation, 155
Web diagram, of teaching team, 51
Word window, 82
Working styles, 52

Get all 5 practical guidebooks—great for your whole school team!

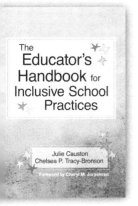

The Educator's Handbook for Inclusive School Practices

By Julie Causton, Ph.D., & Chelsea Tracy-Bronson, M.A.

As more K-12 schools move toward inclusion, how can general and special educators work together to create warm, welcoming classrooms where all students learn and belong? Discover practical answers in this friendly, down-to-earth teacher's guide. Filled with ready-to-use teaching tips, insights from inclusive educators, and examples that relate directly to everyday classroom experiences, this book will help general and special educators collaborate effectively and build a great "toolbox" of strategies to support all learners within inclusive classrooms. With this highly motivating guidebook close at hand, new and seasoned educators will create engaging, exciting, and joyful inclusive classrooms that support social and academic success for all.

Stock #: BA-79253 | 2015 | 232 pages | ISBN: 978-1-59857-925-3

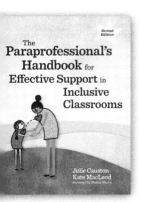

The Paraprofessional's Handbook for Effective Support in Inclusive Classrooms, Second Edition

By Julie Causton, Ph.D., & Kate MacLeod, Ph.D.

What does a great paraprofessional need to know and do? Find out in the new edition of this handy survival guide, equally useful for the brand-new paraprofessional or the 20-year classroom veteran.

Stock #: BA-54517 | 2021 | approx. 192 pages | ISBN: 978-1-68125-451-7

The Speech-Language Pathologist's Handbook for Inclusive School Practices

By Julie Causton, Ph.D., & Chelsea Tracy-Bronson, M.A.

This is the practical, friendly guide SLPs need to go beyond pull-out services and deliver successful communication and language supports as part of an inclusive school team.

Stock #: BA-73626 | 2014 | 184 pages | ISBN: 978-1-59857-362-6

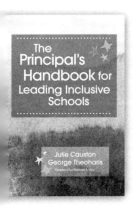

The Principal's Handbook for Leading Inclusive Schools

By Julie Causton, Ph.D., & George Theoharis, Ph.D.

Covering everything from the basics of special education to the everyday nuts and bolts of making inclusion work, this how-to book is the essential guide to bringing schoolwide inclusion from theory to practice.

Stock #: BA-72988 | 2014 | 184 pages | ISBN: 978-1-59857-298-8

The Occupational Therapist's Handbook for Inclusive School Practices

By Julie Causton, Ph.D., & Chelsea Tracy-Bronson, M.A.

This guidebook is packed with practical guidance and tips, examples that relate directly to an OT's daily practice, and first-person insights from seasoned OTs.

Stock #: BA-73619 | 2014 | 184 pages | ISBN: 978-1-59857-361-9